Parenting Children for a Life of Faith

Omnibus Edition

The Bible Reading Fellowship
15 The Chambers, Vineyard
Abingdon OX14 3FE
brf.org.uk

The Bible Reading Fellowship (BRF) is a Registered Charity (233280)

ISBN 978 0 85746 694 5
First published 2018
10 9 8 7 6 5 4 3 2 1 0
All rights reserved

Acknowledgements
Unless otherwise stated, scripture quotations are taken from The Holy Bible, New International
Version (Anglicised edition) copyright © 1979, 1984, 2011 by Biblica. Used by permission
of Hodder & Stoughton Publishers, an Hachette UK company. All rights reserved. 'NIV' is a
registered trademark of Biblica. UK trademark number 1448790.

Scripture quotations marked CEV are taken from the Contemporary English Version of the Bible
published by HarperCollins Publishers, copyright © 1991, 1992, 1995 American Bible Society.

Scripture quotations marked NCV are taken from the New Century Version, copyright © 2005 by
Thomas Nelson, Inc. Used by permission. All rights reserved.

Every effort has been made to trace and contact copyright owners for material used in
this resource. We apologise for any inadvertent omissions or errors, and would ask those
concerned to contact us so that full acknowledgement can be made in the future.

A catalogue record for this book is available from the British Library

Printed and bound by TJ International

Parenting Children for a Life of Faith

Helping children meet and know God

Omnibus Edition

Rachel Turner

Contents

Foreword 7

Introduction 9

PART I: PARENTING CHILDREN FOR A LIFE OF FAITH

1 Discipling proactively...12

2 Modelling the reality of relationship.....................................17

3 Making sense of life...25

4 Building a balanced view of God..33

5 Realigning wrong views of God 40

6 Chatting with God 48

7 Catching from God 57

8 Keeping it going 72

9 Surfing the waves...76

10 Praying with children..81

11 Helping children engage with church 91

12 Starting well with under-fives 97

PART II: PARENTING CHILDREN FOR A LIFE OF PURPOSE

13 Identity, relationship and purpose 106

14 Telling the whole story.. 111

15 Foundational purpose 119

16 Seeing power in the mirror... 122

17 Learning the way of love... 134

18 Finding our calling.. 145

19 Shaping our response 153

20 Poised to act... 163

21 Part of the body.. 172

PART III: PARENTING CHILDREN FOR A LIFE OF CONFIDENCE

22 Core of confidence 178

23 It's not about me 182

24 I'm not finished yet 190

25 Hearts and minds.. 196

26 Everyday applications 210

27 Who am I? 212

28 Encouraging for confidence... 220

29 Media and the world's messages 226

30 Comparison and contentment.. 237

31 Manliness and beauty... 245

32 Comparison and humility.. 251

33 Failure 263

34 Friendships and peer pressure 271

Conclusion.. 280

FAQs 281

Notes.. 287

Foreword

Rachel had me hooked by the third line of her book. Like many mums with sport-loving sons, I've experienced the longings she describes in her introduction. Most Christian parents long for their children to enjoy a deeper relationship with God – a relationship that is real and relevant to every aspect of their lives. We long to give our children strong spiritual foundations, which can equip them to become mature Christian adults. Sadly, we all know children who have grown up in loving families and great churches, but have never connected with God on a personal level.

Rachel's analysis of the problem is inspired: by highlighting the difference between 'God-smart' and 'God-connected' children, she points to the heart of the issue – and to some steps parents can take to make a difference. By using real stories, she helps bring theory to life, showing us how to help our children hold on to biblical truth, while experiencing a growing relationship with God.

Not all Christian parents will have the opportunity to put Rachel's suggestions into practice from the beginning of their parenting years. Not everyone will have the support of a like-minded husband or wife. Not all parents will have experienced God in the ways Rachel describes. Don't panic! As a result of reading Rachel's book, all Christian parents will be challenged and encouraged to develop a deeper relationship with God themselves, and to create windows into that experience, so that their children see how they, too, can live connected to God.

Catherine Butcher
Former Editor, *Families First* magazine

Introduction

'I just don't know what to do any more.' Sarah's face twisted in frustration and exhaustion as she shared her heart with me. Like many mums, she desperately longed for her son to enjoy church and have some sort of input about God. Lately, they had been heatedly clashing about Chris's desire to play football on a Sunday instead of attending church. 'He's eleven years old, and I still don't know if God is real to him at all.' She sighed deeply. 'I don't even know if he's really a Christian. What did I do wrong?'

Jemma had recently come into a relationship with God through an Alpha course and had been bringing her four-year-old daughter Jasmine to church ever since. She had seen that Jasmine didn't understand the changes that had been happening in their lives as a result of her decision, but she knew that her daughter had noticed a difference. Jemma was unsure how to talk about her faith with her child, much less how to help Jasmine have an experience with God herself. She longed for Jasmine to have a life with him in the way that she did, and was determined to give her daughter a childhood full of faith, but had no idea where to start, or how to include her unbelieving partner on the journey.

Richard and Jill have three children. Lily, their middle child, is an eight-year-old girl with big brown eyes, a cheeky, toothy grin, and floppy brown hair. She often had to arrive early to church as her parents helped out on the PA and coffee rotas and with the children's groups. Lily had been part of the church world since she was born. She knew the right answers to almost every question in Sunday school, which made her feel very clever indeed. Children at school bullied her a lot, and often her afternoons featured either a crying fit or an angry outburst at her sister, followed by extended time in her room, sulking and upset. Richard and Jill seemed at a loss as to how to stop this slow slide in their daughter's confidence. They knew that Lily was a 'Christian' but their hearts ached, wishing their daughter was able to find the peace, vibrancy and power that they found in their own faith.

From the moment our children enter our lives, our hearts begin to dream for them. We have hopes for their futures and a profound sense of wanting them to flourish in every area of their lives right now. As they grow, we agonise over their friendships, their character, their happiness, their self-confidence. We want the best for them. As Christian parents, our dreams for our children also include their spiritual lives. We want our children to find their own journey of faith and know the significant benefit it brings.

But parenting never really turns out the way we think it will. Parenting gets taken over by just being happy that we all survived the day, are relatively clean and generally were where we were supposed to be when we were supposed to be there. Family life can be chaotic and unexpected and delightfully ordinary. It can feel like we as parents will never quite get on top of it all.

Every once in a while a thought pops up in our minds. It stirs up our hearts as we watch our children at church, or as they head out to school. This is a sincere desire for our children to know God in a way that gives them life, makes them feel loved, helps them understand who they are, and gives them a purpose on this earth. And then a small person throws up, or we have to catch a toddler from running on to the road, or we need to answer our other child's question, and we are off again.

It doesn't seem to matter whether we are single, divorced or married; whether we are new to the faith or have been raised in it; whether we have newborns, toddlers, teenagers or grown-up children – we want more for our children spiritually than what they already have. We want all that God has for them, now and in the future, but it can often feel so hard.

It's not meant to be hard. Helping our children on their journey of faith is intended to be one of the most joyful, natural, significant parts of parenting. God designed it to be light, to be easy and to work in the chaos and beautiful mess of family life.

This book won't help you conquer the entirety of parenting. I'm sorry. It would be nice if it did, but I'm not that smart. It won't teach you how to discipline four children on the school run or how to create children who are brilliant cooks. This book is about one thing: equipping us, as we are right now, to confidently enable our children to have vibrant, two-way relationships with the God who loves them.

I believe that the more real stories we hear, the more encouraged we can become, so all the stories in this book are true. Only the names have been changed. My prayer is that this book helps you find your next steps in seeing your children grow in their connection with God. May God, our Father, give you sleep, stamina and the gift of time as you go on this brilliant adventure of parenting with him.

Part I

Parenting children for a life of faith

1

Discipling proactively

In my experience, there is a big difference between a God-smart child and a God-connected one. I'm sure you have met both kinds of children in your life.

A God-smart kid knows the right Christian answers off the top of their head. They can pop off a lovely little prayer out loud, they know their memory verses and they often know more Bible stories than we do. They know the rules for Christian living and can easily slot into the rituals at church. They are comfortable with how to do Christianity, but it all seems to stop at their head.

A God-connected child, on the other hand, seems to have something extra, something that goes beyond head knowledge. A God-connected child lives in a vibrant two-way relationship with God. They share life with him, play with him and interact with him throughout the day. They know they are loved and handle the world with the confidence that comes from having the peace and healing of the living God in their daily reality. Their head knowledge of God is just a part of discovering a lifelong heart connection with him.

Our hearts long to create God-connected kids, but we can often feel trapped into only growing God-smart ones. We pour our effort into taking our children to church and teaching them about God and the Bible, and thereby hope that one day they'll wake up and be magically God-connected. It can make us feel like powerless spectators cheering on our children in their faith journeys. But that's not God's plan for us.

God's plan

God has a plan for how to create God-connected children, and it may come as a bit of a surprise.

> Listen, Israel! The Lord our God is the only true God! So love the Lord your God with all your heart, soul, and strength. Memorize his laws and tell them to your

children over and over again. Talk about them all the time, whether you're at home or walking along the road or going to bed at night, or getting up in the morning. Write down copies and tie them to your wrists and foreheads to help you obey them. Write these laws on the door frames of your homes and on your town gates.

DEUTERONOMY 6:4–9 (CEV)

It appears that God's plan for children to learn how to connect with him happens during the most boring parts of life. Look at the passage again. The prime time for our children to learn about God is in the most ordinary moments we have together: when we are at home in our pyjamas staring off into space while eating bran flakes; while we are wrapped up with each other on the couch all looking at our phones and tablets; during the eye-pokingly boring bus trips, or while walking to school; during the third kiss goodnight or the half-asleep cuddles in the morning; while we are getting dressed in a panic for church, or decorating our homes.

God designed children to learn how to connect with God in the mundane parts of our days because that is where he is. He is with us in every moment, loving us as we think and laugh and sleep. He is guiding us as we ponder and remember our days and consider what to do next. He is powerfully present as we shop and encounter others. If we want our children to know how to access God in everyday life, then it has to happen in everyday life – with us.

Church leaders have no access to those ordinary places with our families. Our children's church leaders don't wake up in our houses or go on the school run with us. They don't stand bored in a queue with us or watch our oldest kid at his swimming lesson while listening to our other child read. The church, it seems, isn't in places that God has designed for children's discipleship to happen.

We as parents, carers and members of extended families are perfectly positioned to help our children meet and know God. We spend on average between 2,000 and 3,000 hours a year with our children, whereas church only has 100 hours of all-together event time a year. The church isn't meant to be the centre of children's discipleship. It could never be as effective as we can be in the spiritual life of our children.

But that doesn't mean we are alone. In biblical times, when God instructed Moses on how children could find connection with him, parents were part of close-knit extended families. Those extended families were part of a wider clan, and those clans were part of a tribe of people. No parent was on their own. In modern times, we can often feel the loss of that community. Not all of us have a Christian extended family or community that supports us.

It is important that you know that the church is behind you, is for you, is cheering you on and is the community you can rely on. Other Christian parents will have your back, and there are people of all ages in your church who are willing to surround you, love you and help you on this journey. They can't do the job for you, but they can make sure you aren't doing it alone. And they can be the extended family of love and encouragement for you and your children. We as parents were never designed to be parenting for faith alone, and if you don't have that community around you, please link yourself into a church and let some people know that you need it.

Trapped in waiting

If we are honest, the thought that we are the primary people responsible for helping our children connect with God is terrifying. It's such a precious part of our children's lives. We can feel hesitant. Some of us worry that we don't know how to do it well. Others of us worry about doing damage or pushing our children away from God accidentally if we are too proactive about it. We can end up feeling constrained, waiting for the right moment, waiting until our children open the spiritual door, waiting for the 'teachable moments' to arise.

It can feel a bit like skipping a rope.

Do you remember this game from the playground – two kids each holding the end of a skipping rope and a third kid ready to jump? Usually, there's a whole queue of children waiting for their turn, carefully observing the competition. The child at the front is in the hot seat, waiting for the rope of death to swing around until they can sense the rhythm. Once they sense the time is right, they leap in and jump as impressively as possible – up and down, with an added spin, or a double jump. Ideally, they eventually leap out of the swirling rope without ever blocking its path. In that case, they can triumphantly walk to the back of the queue while everyone gazes in admiration. More often though, the jumper inevitably messes up, and the rope hits them, ending their turn. The queue groans in sympathy (and sometimes judgement) as the jumper slumps back into the queue ready to wait for their next turn.

Sometimes we as parents feel trapped into that same skipping-rope way of spiritually influencing our children. We want to have a spiritual conversation, but it just never seems right. So we wait and wait, watching the spiralling rope of our children's spiritual interest until we sense a conversation may come. Nanny's health isn't improving, but we have been praying for her; finally the question arrives: 'Why hasn't God made Nanny better?' We leap in:

> Oh, yes! That is a very good question. God does heal people. I mean, he can, but it doesn't happen every time for lots of reasons that I don't fully understand, but God is real, and I know sometimes it doesn't feel like it but there are a lot of stories in scripture about that, and if you listen really carefully then God will speak to you, but you don't have to do it right now. Do you want to pray? Do you not want to pray? No, it's all right, we don't have to do it now unless you want to. Just know you can do it. And there are some Bible verses if you want – let me know.

And we leap out of the conversation. Phew! If we've managed to get out without our child hating us or hating God, we are triumphant. Behold – the spiritual parent! We managed to have one conversation with our child about God! Yes! Then begins the post-conversation doubt-everything-we-said debrief, as we try to remember what was said as we tried to shove every bit of spiritual information into the one opportunity that came up.

But that is not God's design. Look again.

> Listen, Israel! The Lord our God is the only true God! So love the Lord your God with all your heart, soul, and strength. Memorize his laws and tell them to your children over and over again. Talk about them all the time, whether you're at home or walking along the road or going to bed at night, or getting up in the morning. Write down copies and tie them to your wrists and foreheads to help you obey them. Write these laws on the door frames of your homes and on your town gates.
> DEUTERONOMY 6:4–9 (CEV)

God's plan isn't the desperate hope that your child will casually be interested once so you can throw as much stuff as possible in there. It's a proactive choice we make in the everyday. Not to add doing church at home, but to proactively do regular home life with God in it.

God has uniquely placed us parents in our child's life for a reason. The discipleship of children happens in the midst of the mundane, because God is a God of relationship in the everyday – even the boring – bits of life. And if God designed it that way, then it's also possible to see your child flourish in their faith, even when you are absolutely exhausted, feel like you only have half a brain, have not showered in three days and are fighting a cold.

The aim of this book is to give you, just as you are right now, the approaches, skills and confidence to help your children flourish spiritually. Your family is unique. It is different to everyone else's. You are the expert on your children and your family. You will be able to adapt everything to the way your family works best.

As a parent, you barely have time to go to the toilet by yourself, much less to sit around and think about the spiritual lives of your children in peace and quiet. So I want to leave you with a question to ponder: what are your hopes and dreams for your children's connection with God? You may want to jot them down on a piece of paper for each of your children, specifically thinking about the answer to this question: ten years from now, what do you hope each of your children's relationships with God will look like?

2

Modelling the reality of relationship

A long time ago, I was a lowly part-time youth secretary at a large church led by our senior pastor, Jim. He was a fantastic leader – incredibly kind, very humble, pastoral and wise; everything you could ever want in a church leader. He oozed Jesus. I loved being part of his crowd. I was one of 40 or so staff, and I felt so included as I watched him laugh with the senior team at the other end of the staff room. I got to shout, 'Hi!' with our group of administrators as he popped his head into our busy office each day. I loved hearing him preach and listening to all the stories about his family. He prayed for me once, with about 150 other people, at the end of a service. He was my leader, and I belonged to his crowd, and I loved it.

And then the incident happened.

It was at the annual staff retreat. After three days of visionary talks and enormous amounts of food, it was time to head home. Several of us from the admin team ran off for a last swim in the hotel pool. On the way back to our rooms to get changed to leave (there was no changing room at the pool), my friends thought it would be funny to leave me dripping in the hotel lobby while they ran ahead to take the lift without me.

As I waited for the lift to come back down, a puddle forming around me on the marble floor despite the four towels and robe I was wearing over my swimming costume, I saw them – the senior leadership team. They were walking out of the front door leaving our leader Jim behind in the lobby with just me and the hotel staff. He saw me and began to walk over, probably out of concern for me, as I looked like a drowned rat.

I panicked, because at that moment I realised something. I had comfortably been part of his crowd for five years, and yet I had never had a one-to-one conversation with him. I had no idea how to talk to this leader that I so respected.

My brain caught fire. 'What do I do? What do I do? Do I explain? Act casual? Ask a theological question? Tell him how much I want to be like him when I grow up? Would that be weird? Should I tell him my name? Wait, he should know my name. WHAT IF HE DOESN'T KNOW MY NAME? What if I tell him and he's insulted that I assumed he didn't know. Aargh!'

He was looking at me expectantly, and I realised that while I was screaming in my head, he had spoken to me.

'I've been swimming,' I blurted out.

'I can see that,' he said kindly as the lift doors opened and I dashed away. I was horrified and baffled. I felt like I had known my leader well, since I had been part of his crowd for so long. But when faced with a situation where I needed to talk with him, I froze. I realised how far apart we actually were and how little relationship really existed.

Many of our children feel the same way about God. We spend most of our time helping them feel comfortable in God's crowd by doing a lot of activities together. We meet together, sing and do church together; we even read Bibles together. We serve people together, pray together at mealtimes and bedtimes, and do outreach events at church side-by-side. Then we turn to our kids and say, 'You can have your own special one-to-one relationship with the God of the universe, who is powerful beyond all things. Good luck!' And we leave them alone to figure out how to embark on an individual journey with him. Most of the time, they have no idea how to make that leap.

If we want our children to learn how to have their own individual connection with God, then they need to see what it is like in the ups and downs of normal life. That's where we come in. God has positioned us perfectly so we can show our children an up-close view of what life with God looks like day to day, messy bits and all. When our children can see, hear and learn how our relationship with God affects our every day, then they can begin to explore what it looks like for them.

We do this naturally with other significant personal relationships. We don't fling open the doors and give our children all-access passes to view the intimate details of our marriage or friendships, but we do try to show them the 'tip of the iceberg' of what these healthy relationships are. As you know, only ten per cent of an iceberg is above water. We cannot see how big an iceberg is under the surface, but we can get an indication from how much we see above it. It is the same with our relationships.

Our children see how, when we are stressed, we turn to our friends for advice and connection. They hear us laughing together after they go to bed, and get a sense of the joy our friendships bring us. They know how we prioritise helping our friends, and the time we give to them. Through this experience of watching, listening and participating, they learn what to look for in a friend and how to be a friend to others. They are aware that our friendships go deeper than they can see, but they learn to watch and listen for the benefits of those friendships to us and the way we choose to commit our lives to them. Whether it's our friendships or relationships with our partners or work colleagues, our children are always learning from the little glimpses of these connections that we show them.

The problem is that we rarely allow our children similar access to our relationship with God. It can be utterly foreign to them. They often know what we believe, and they know that our beliefs steer our lives, but they don't often get to see how our relationship with God works and in what ways it affects who we are and how we live our lives. If we want our children to connect heart-to-heart with God and gain their identity and purpose from him in a living and active relationship, we need to show them the many tips of the icebergs that exist in our relationship with him. We need to learn how to do bits of our private relationship in a public sphere.

It's not about having the 'ideal' relationship with God

At this point, if you're like me, fear begins to creep in – my relationship with God isn't the ideal that I want my children to be looking at. We all know ourselves. We know our flaws, our sins, our imperfections, our laziness, our weaknesses and our strengths. The idea of using our internal relationship with God as a key influence in our children's lives can be scary and make us feel exposed.

I vividly remember a conference speaker once saying, as she leaned casually on her podium, 'Well, I just tell parents to be Jesus to your children, and as you are Jesus to your children they will see him and want to be with him.' The full force of that hit me in the chest. I thought, 'If my child's relationship with God is based on my ability to be Jesus and reflect him perfectly, then my child doesn't have a chance! I am not that good yet. I am trying, but if my child's future faith is dependent on my ability to reflect Jesus accurately at all times, then it will never happen.'

Luckily, that isn't the truth. That isn't why God put us in our children's lives. Jesus is the only perfect one we can model our lives on. What we offer our children is an invitation to journey through life with God alongside us.

We aren't trying to pass on our faith to our children. We want them to find their own way with God, however it looks for them, but we can be a slightly more experienced companion on the journey. We are co-travellers with our children on life's journey of faith. As our children journey through life in connection with God, they can look over at us to see how to negotiate the obstacles of life with God. They can see how we hold his hand during the joyful bits, and let him carry us during the hard bits. They can learn how to go on their own journey with him, by seeing the tip of the iceberg of how we do ours.

If we show them only that life is great, that we always pray and are always perfect, and that God wants us to be happy, then we're setting them up to be disappointed in themselves and the Christian walk. We're setting them up to feel like they're failing when they experience the downs within the many ups. I want my child to be able to handle anything in life, positive and negative, because they are walking with God. And at times we will look at the tip of our child's iceberg of their relationship with God and will learn some things too.

All we need to be is on the journey. When we're on the journey and they're on the journey, it's exciting because we get to walk together.

Create windows

Have you ever walked down a road of terraced houses? We used to live on such a street, and I loved looking into other people's windows. My husband said that doing so was rude – the net curtains hanging in the window meant, 'Don't look in my house.' I disagreed. What I found most fascinating was how, even though the houses all had same footprint as ours, the inside of each one looked vastly different. Some people had three sofas; others had only two armchairs. Some floors were carpeted; others were wooden. Some people had knocked out walls; others had extended to make space for a kitchen in the back. I loved walking along and exclaiming, 'Oh, look at that. What a good idea!'; 'Oh no, don't like that'; 'Hmm, we could try one of those bamboo screens. Very clever.'

People observe each other all the time. Most of the significant things I've learned about life with God, I've learned from watching other people and getting a window into their lives. Our children need us to open some windows into aspects of our relationship with God so they can see what life with God can look like.

To our children, our relationship with God may be shrouded in mystery. Perhaps we disappear into a room to 'spend some time with God', 'have our quiet time' or 'read our Bible notes'. Our children may hear music being played or total silence. Sometimes we come out different, sometimes not. For all they know, we are in there dancing naked while doing body art, or sleeping, or sitting quietly and staring mindlessly at the wall. On the other hand, God himself may have appeared in bodily form and be having tea and biscuits with us. Our children don't know.

Children may hear us say that we want to 'pray about' something and later see that we have made a decision about it, but what exactly happened and when? In their minds, praying consists of talking at God. So, did we simply process the issue out loud with God listening until we made up our mind? Or was it something more? If so, what? And how long did it take?

Do our children see those little tips of the icebergs – or is our relationship-with-God iceberg completely submerged? The key to creating windows is to allow little glimpses into the various aspects of our personal relationships with God so that our children and teenagers can see what it looks like to be involved in a two-way connection with an invisible person. Leave the door ajar when you have time with God, so they can see that you aren't floating four inches off the ground surrounded by white light. (If you are doing that, it will certainly function as a conversation starter later!) Seeing a person engage with God is fascinating, even more so if that person is your parent.

If you read your Bible, try doing it in a place where your children can see you. This gives you many opportunities to communicate to them about how you meet God through scripture. One dad noticed that he only read his Bible at bedtime or on his phone during church and that therefore his children would not know that the Bible featured at all in his life. So he decided to try to read a printed Bible (as opposed to on his phone) at some point during the day around his children. He put it on the kitchen table, and during the morning chaos of three children eating breakfast, he would read a bit to himself without feeling the need to make any comment about it to his children. He would leave it open as he moved on with his morning. After two weeks, one of his children brought their Bible to the table and did the same. After another week, another one of his children asked what he was reading about, and they had a fascinating conversation about the portion of scripture. Eventually, scripture became just a part of everyone's mornings, slowly and organically, because one parent created a window.

Creating windows isn't just about the distinctly spiritual things we do. Our children need windows into all areas of our lives with God. I knew one parent who was having a bad day, and her three-year-old was in the back of the car. Before they headed off to the park, she felt overwhelmed with all of life. Rather than just soldiering on, she put on music and told her child, 'I'm just going to have a little cry while Daddy God gives me a hug because I'm very tired, and then we will go to the park.' She leaned her head forward on the steering wheel while she prayed quickly. Her son chirped up from the back, 'Okay! Have good cuddles!' and sang away to the song until she was done. She then said, 'Phew, thank you for being patient. I really needed that time with God. I feel much better!' and off they went to the park. Her son eventually picked that up, and when he got upset in a children's group, I saw him say, 'I need cry cuddles!' and march himself to the corner to pray. He came back chirpy and happy.

From murmuring 'Thank you God!' when you find a car parking space close to the supermarket entrance when it's tipping it with rain, to sharing with your kid, 'I'm torn up inside about Grandma dying and when I feel that, I just talk and rant and cry and talk some more to God about everything I feel,' let your child see and hear the tips of the icebergs of your ups and downs with God.

When it's tough

Most of the time, children are completely unaware of how big a role our relationship with God plays in our daily lives, particularly in terms of how we overcome struggles, reach decisions and handle hurt. In part, this is because we rightly wish to protect our children. We are the parents, and we are not to burden them with our problems. But if we never model how to conquer those problems, then they won't have a framework to learn how to do the hard bits of life with God.

Debriefing is a helpful middle ground in this kind of situation because it means creating windows into the past. We don't have to walk our children through the full details of horrible circumstances, but we can share about how our relationship with God functioned in the midst of it.

Many times are ripe to share a personal story with your child – for example, when they are struggling with a particular situation. One dad told me how he was able to help his teenage son through a nasty break-up. He said to his son, 'I remember when my first girlfriend broke up with me. I thought she was the one. I just sat on my bed and cried – no, seriously, really cried hard. Best time I ever had with God, just me crying on a bed and knowing he was in the room with me. He didn't talk to me or show me anything, but it was so nice to feel him in the room while my heart was all torn up, and know he was there for me. I don't think I talked to anyone for a week. But I got through it, very slowly. I believe in you, son.'

Children also benefit from seeing how you make important decisions. You could, for example, recount situations from work. If you had a tricky moral decision to make, you could share about it over dinner, telling how God reminded you of a Bible verse that helped you make up your mind, or how scared or embarrassed you were and the way God helped you to overcome that feeling. Children need to hear how you think and make decisions with God alongside you.

Our mistakes become beautiful windows that our children can see into. Many parents have confided in me about their anger difficulties and how ashamed they sometimes feel after they yell at their children. I encourage them to help their children see how to work that out with God. Why not go to your child and say, 'I'm so sorry I yelled. That was wrong of me. I always want to have God's love and peace in my heart, but today I was tired and exhausted, and I let my frustration come out as anger at you. I'm sorry. Please forgive me. I'm not perfect yet; God is still working on me, and I'm still trying to be in charge of my heart. I will get better!'

Even our disappointments can be helpful for our kids. For example, you could say, 'I don't know how you feel, but I can sometimes feel disappointed when something I prayed for doesn't seem to have happened. I've been telling God all about it, because I wanted him to rescue my job, but I still got made redundant. You know how I've been dealing with it? I keep reminding myself that it says in the Bible that he works in all things for our good. So I keep telling him, "Okay, God, I'm looking for all the good stuff that you are going to do!"'

Remember, these windows exist not to show our children a perfect expression of Jesus but to allow them access to the way our lives entwine with our Father's, and to show them what it looks like when that happens. Jesus was a master at doing this. He taught his disciples not to publicise their giving to the temple, their prayers or their fasting. He taught them to keep these activities between them and God, not between them and the world's approval (Matthew 6:1–18). But this didn't mean that he hid everything from them. He built windows into his private life with his Father, so that his disciples had a front-row view whenever he chose to give them a glimpse. They knew his habits of fasting and prayer (Matthew 14:23), and his patterns of giving (Matthew 17:24–27), and they overheard his prayers well enough to write them down later (John 17). Jesus wasn't allowing them that access so that the disciples would huddle around saying, 'Wow! Jesus is amazing. He is the best pray-er I've ever heard. And isn't he holy? I mean, very impressive, really.' He gave them those tip-of-the-iceberg moments so that they could learn a new way of interacting with God their heavenly Father, in relationship, not just as part of the crowd.

What bits of your life with God could you easily create a window into so your child can see what life with him could look like?

3

Making sense of life

I remember the first day I arrived in Aberystwyth, Wales, to begin my master's programme. I got off the train and instantly got lost. Aberystwyth is not a big place, and yet as soon as I exited the station, I felt an intense sense of disorientation. I headed off in the wrong direction and it was ten minutes before I finally circled back to find the taxi rank in front of the station. As I collapsed into the taxi, I read out the name of the area I needed to get to. The driver didn't recognise it. 'L-Land-band-arn,' I said slowly again. After a long silence, his forehead scrumpled up as he uttered a word that sounded completely different to what I had said: 'Clanbathen?' I shook my head firmly and handed him the piece of paper with the name on it. He laughed at me and repeated the same word, reading it slowly to me. I realised very quickly that I had no idea how to read, speak or navigate in my new home. I needed help.

Have you ever been somewhere where you had no idea what was going on? A new school, a new workplace, a theme park, your in-laws' house? Do you remember that feeling of insecurity? It's one of the most common human experiences, and we naturally help each other out. We try to make sense of the world for each other, to enable people to understand their world and know how to engage with it. People take us on inductions at work, or a new friend explains how to get on the teacher's good side. We read our theme-park maps like they are scripture, and we get our partner to remind us who Aunt Jo is and what she did. It's as if we build a frame around situations and say, 'Look at this specifically. This is what you are looking at. This is how to respond. The zoo section of the theme park is always empty in the afternoon; let's do that last. Don't approach Michael on a Wednesday morning; if he worked last night, he'll bite your head off. Remember my parents insist on no shoes in the house; wear your good socks.'

When it comes to our parenting, we know this is one of the most foundational, enjoyable and downright annoying jobs we have as parents: to help our children understand the world, and learn how to engage with it. It's what we are here for! Our poor kids show up in this world knowing nothing, and we get to frame for them absolutely everything. If you ever had a small child in your life, framing the world for them was part of everyday life, involving walking down the road and talking, nonstop, about everything: 'Look, a tree! Trees have leaves on them. Whoop! Look at the leaves fall. Falling leaves. Mr Tree is changing his clothes for the season. No, no, no, don't lick the leaves. They could have poo on them. Dogs poo on trees. Not like you. You poo in your potty. Or try to. Not on leaves.'

Framing the world is a natural thing that we do, and our children seek it out – over and over: 'Why is the sky blue? Why can't I wear a swimming costume to church? Why does blood not explode out of my ears when I shake my head?' We respond to their questions, attempting to help them understand and learn how to engage with the world, and a significant amount of times eventually bailing out and saying, 'Because that's the way it is.'

We sometimes forget as our children get older that they still have questions. They still need us to help them understand the world of friendships, politics, perseverance, pain and healthy joy. They still have that internal 'why?' question. They still aren't sure what they are seeing or how to engage with it. And as parents, we step in and help. We give them a framework for life.

And they desperately need a spiritual one. We live in a hurt, broken and beautiful world in relationship with an entirely real and active God. Our children need help in understanding the world with God in it, and working out how to engage with him in response. It's as simple as doing what you are already doing, but making sure the reality of God is shared as well.

Whether it's while dropping off your child at school or dealing with a broken car, there are constant opportunities to frame for our children how to understand joy, friendships, purpose and, most of all, who God is in the swirl of life around them. Because God isn't a bolt-on to the side of life. God is a significant part of all of it.

If you are like me, a creeping worry begins to scream in the corner of your mind. I'm still learning how to live life with God. I'm not sure I know enough to build a framework for my child. If that's you, don't worry. Give your child as much as you have right now. And as you grow, you can share new insights with your child. You can discover new things together. As long as you are on the journey, you are on the right track, and you have a community around you to help encourage you.

So how do we make sense of the world for our children? There are three ways: explain everything; help them see relationship in the Bible; and get comfortable answering questions.

Explain everything

Parenting is a lot of explaining. It just is. It's a big privilege. We get to teach our kids how the world works. So, as you are explaining life, explain life with God. This becomes important because often faith and relationship with God get somehow isolated from real life. When we explain things well, it reconnects them.

Our children know that God is loving, but often struggle to figure out what that means when Grandma is dying from a stroke. Our children know about prayer, but they get confused about why God didn't do what they wanted him to. A lot of the spiritual problems children face are because they have been left to make those connections on their own.

If a child is being bullied, they can struggle to make spiritual sense of it. 'God loves me' is one of their few truths and they feel lost as to where he is. In the midst of getting involved with the teacher, giving your child practical coping skills and showing up at school with a placard against the other child, you can also help your child understand the spiritual part of this. You can explain how God is close to the broken-hearted, and how God gives courage. You can tell him how Jesus was spat on and punched for doing nothing wrong, so he understands. You can explain how you and God cope with the bullies in your life and what God has done. You can help your child understand the strength and the truth and the presence of God in their situation and help them connect with him in it. You can ask God what is going on inside the other child's heart and pray together for help and change.

When you are at church, whisper to your kid throughout the service and help them understand what is happening and how to engage. Instead of saying, 'Now we stand up and are quiet,' try sharing, 'Now we all stand up and, in the quiet, we connect with God. I'm going to think of one thing I am grateful that God has done for me this week, and say thank you to him while it is quiet. You can too if you want. Here we go!'

It even comes down to the regular bits of moving people between places. When you drop off your child at nursery, rather than the usual 'Daddy is going drop you off, but I will be back to pick you up soon. You will have lots of fun with your friends. I love you!' why not add a little bit of spiritual truth? 'Daddy is going to drop you off with God at your group, but I will be back to pick you up soon. You will have lots of fun with your friends. I love you!' The more we frame for our children God's place in the world, the more they will learn to engage with him in the everyday.

Share your stories

Your stories are critical in this, too, as you create windows into your life. You aren't just explaining how God works out there, but more importantly how God works within you. So much of our life with God happens in our heads, and our children never really get access to it. Part of the way children learn their way of viewing life is from us.

My dad was a police officer, and I would often wake up at 2.00 am, after he came home at the end of a shift, and see him reading his Bible at the kitchen table. (Unusually, my room was off the dining room.) I would watch him read, nod and write notes on a pad beside the Bible. Being a parent who naturally created windows into his life, he would leave his notes out, and in the morning I would often read his notes. My love of scripture started there.

But one day, when I was 14, as he was passing by he saw me reading the notes and told me, 'You know some days are really hard. I go to a call where I have to hold a dead baby or take a report from a raped teenager. And I come home and can feel overwhelmed.' He then reached forward and touched his Bible. 'Reading the Bible fills me up and nails it all down. Everything that I see, everything that I do, and everything that I feel just gets nailed down to the truth that never changes when I read it. I really need it.'

Whack! That moment seared into my brain. Anytime I read the Bible, anytime I see anyone read the Bible, that phrase comes back to me. This verbal framework all of a sudden slammed into place, and I understood what scripture was for and knew I wanted to engage with it.

When you talk about decisions, either you could say, 'We are going to sell the car', or you could show them the actual process of what happened, such as:

> I'm so sorry I've been stressed a lot. The car keeps having things wrong with it, and I've been so 'argh' about it all. I kept going on and on and on to God about how frustrated I was. But he soon told me that I was stressed because I didn't trust that he would help, even though he had so many times before. He's right. So I'm changing my brain. I'm grateful for this car and for how long we have had it. Now we'll see what God does next. He may provide a car, he may give us the means to pay for one, or we may be in a season of finding new ways to get to places, but I do trust that God will provide what we need. So we are going to sell the car.

When we do this, our children begin to see how God is a part of life, and how to engage with him in these normal situations.

Help them see relationship in the Bible

There are many different children's Bibles out there but most of them contain the same stories. We can get into the habit of reading Bible stories as stand-alone tales, rather than as part of the Bible's overall narrative. Also, unlike modern novels, scripture was written in a way that just gives the bare bones of the narrative, so the stories can seem to be just a series of things happening.

But scripture was not meant to be taken just a chapter at a time. The whole of the Bible helps us to understand each chapter. What gets missed out most often in our retelling of Bible stories is God's relationship with people within the story.

For example, look at the story of David and Goliath (1 Samuel 17). The story seems to be all about David; God does not appear at all, except when referred to by the other characters. I assume God did something fancy with David's stone, but it isn't made clear in the chapter. If we take the chapter in isolation, the story becomes all about what one brave human can do.

But when we take the surrounding chapters, and the whole of scripture, into account, the story of David and Goliath changes. The story isn't about brave David at all. It is all about David and God – about the times they spent on the hills tending sheep together, with David singing songs to God and God being with David as they fought off lions; about how God strengthened David, gave him songs and kept his right hand on his back. Fighting Goliath was just one thing God and David did together.

As we build frameworks for our children to understand the world and know how to engage with it, it is beneficial to keep calling attention to the relationship between God and the characters in the Bible. As you read the stories together, pause for a second and ask, 'What do you think God felt about that?' or 'Why was Paul so sure he wouldn't drown?' or 'Why didn't God magically appear and scare everybody, so they would listen to Peter?' Talk about the relationship between God and people in every story, so your children begin to expect it in their own life stories.

It also helps to build the framework before you need it. If you know you are going to have a significant change in your lives, read Bible stories and discuss them before making the big announcement. Then when your child hears you explain the news, they will already have had an understanding of what that looks like with God.

We at Parenting for Faith have done this in the book *Comfort in the Darkness*, retelling biblical stories of the night, sleep and dreams with the focus being on God's relationship with people.[1]

Explore questions together

Kids are full of questions, spiritual or otherwise. Over my 20 years of working with kids, I've had some baffling ones. I know many of us can be quite worried about answering questions. We can often feel as if we don't have enough theological knowledge or enough skill to explain complicated concepts.

Addressing children's questions goes beyond helping them find the biblical answer. It's about creating a culture where questions are okay. It's about exploring ideas together and sharing to the best of our ability the answer as we know it and what to do when we need more information. How we handle not knowing the answer can teach as much as answering the question. No matter what the question, we can usually answer it like this:

- What do you think? Many times children ask questions because they want to talk about something. Allowing them to answer first lets us access what is in their hearts and minds and hear what is worrying them.
- What do we know? There are things that we know. We may know a little, we may know a lot, but sharing the truth as we know it helps root our children.
- What do we not know? There will be many things that we don't know, but there are also many things that theologians and scientists don't know either. It can be useful to say, 'You know what? I'm not even sure people who study these topics know the answer to that one!'
- By how we personally handle it. In the end, how we as individuals work out this question in our own lives helps our children see the impact the answer has on one person's walk with God.

As an example, take the classic 'Will my pet gerbil go to heaven when he dies?' Given that a significant part of us is calculating what is for dinner and how we can get the kids to bed early enough to see the kick-off on *Match of the Day*, we could cut to the chase: 'No: gerbils don't have souls.' But that would be missing a great opportunity. We could instead answer it like this:

- (What do you think?) Hmm, interesting question. What do you think?
- (What do we know?) Well, I'm not 100% sure, but my memory is that the Bible doesn't say whether or not gerbils will be there. I think that the Bible says that there will be animals there.
- (What do we not know?) I don't know if that means Mr Meathead will be there or if those are new animals God has made. You know I'm not sure I know very much about this. Let's work together to find out some more information. We can ask Annie when she comes over tonight.
- (How I personally handle it.) I remember when I lost my dog, I wanted to cry and cry for a week. Being sad is okay. When I'm sad, I tell God all my thoughts, even the angry ones and the ones that don't have words, just feelings. When you think about it how do you feel?

This approach applies to all sorts of questions, from 'Why do bad things happen?' to 'Jesus says we are supposed to love our enemies. Satan is our enemy. Are we supposed to love Satan?' If we genuinely have no idea about the answer, then that is a great opportunity to say:

> What do you think? Very interesting. You know, I have never thought about this question before! What a great question. I'm going to do some research tonight about it and get back to you. Or we could call someone. Ooh, let's call Annie and see what she thinks! That's what I do when I don't have an answer to a question. I know that I can never know all the answers; that's why I'm glad I have wise friends who love God too and can help.

When we admit we don't know, but think it's important to find out, we are showing our children that a relationship with God isn't about always knowing the right answers or never doubting; it's about wondering and finding out and being okay with not knowing everything.

If you are like me, then you may also give answers that you later disagree with. I have done this many times. When we give answers that we wish we hadn't, we can always come back the next day and say, 'I was thinking. Remember yesterday when I said that the reason we can't see God was because of the amount of cake in the world? That was wrong – I looked it up. I'll tell you what I found out…' You will be surprised how quickly our children understand that we get things wrong sometimes and we are still learning, just like they are.

Be bold

Verbally framing for our children doesn't mean having to carve out special time to teach our kids. It's just doing what we are already doing but being bold to include the spiritual dynamic in the mix. It is easy; you already know how to do this. And it is vastly significant in the spiritual life of your child.

As you go through your weeks, try explaining more, sharing your stories, reading Bible stories with God's relationship with his people in them, and exploring questions together. You can do this because God picked you to be in the life of your kids. He is with you.

4

Building a balanced view of God

Working with children isn't usually glamourous, but once I was invited to work with some children at a camp in the Alps. As images of me spinning in ankle-deep grass singing 'The hills are alive' like Maria von Trapp flooded my mind, I quickly agreed. I pictured a group of children, all in matching outfits, laughing and obediently following me around while I helped them discover a deep connection to God rather than music. It was going to be perfect.

Unfortunately, rather than running into a replica of *The Sound of Music*, I discovered something quite surprising about how children react to God. As I started our sessions together, I noticed something odd. The children were all Christian, but they seemed utterly uninterested in connecting with God. No matter how much I taught them about how to connect with God in prayer and music, helping them learn conversational prayer and telling them personal stories, they still seemed resistant to try to connect.

My curiosity got the better of me, so I threw out the next session's teaching and went on an exploration. I asked the children to describe God to me, and they effortlessly began to rattle off a list of words: loving, kind, gracious, always there, knows everything. On and on they went until my flip-chart sheet was full. They knew all the right answers, they were all very God-smart, and yet the knowledge of who he was didn't make an ounce of difference to their connection to him.

I started a fresh sheet of paper. 'You have done a great job of telling me what the Bible says about God,' I said, 'but I would like for you to tell me what it genuinely feels like to have God in your life. Please describe to me your experience of who God is, to you. Describe to me the God you know.'

They looked at me nervously. No one spoke. 'You won't be in trouble. I honestly want to know,' I assured them. Slowly the flip chart filled up with a completely different list. To them, it felt like God was uninterested, powerless, changeable, uncaring, far away, grumpy. I realised that their problem with connecting with God wasn't because they didn't know how; it was because they didn't want to. We sometimes forget that for our children to connect with God, for children to build a relationship with him, they have to like him.

Many influences shape our children's view of God: the truth they know from scripture; their experiences of God in life and church; their friends' opinions; the world's picture of God from movies and social media; and what they see from extended family and us of what life with God can look like. It is a wealth of information for them to sort through, and how they put it all together in their heads creates a distinct view of God and, therefore, how they want to interact with him. Unfortunately, that can often become an inaccurate picture of who he is.

None of us would say that we have a 100% accurate view of God. We are all on the journey of figuring this out, of learning more and more about who God is, and our children are no different. We will only fully know God once we are standing before him in the life to come, and even then we won't be able to comprehend all of him. Often our kids opt out of a relationship with God because of the distorted view of him that has accidentally been shaped in their heads.

Shepherding their view

I live in Yorkshire and see a lot of sheep. I was once watching a farmer move his sheep from one field to another and was struck by how he did it. He didn't try to force the sheep to walk along a pathway. He instead, with the help of a few farmhands, waved the herd away from the spaces they weren't supposed to go into, and kept wide open for them the space to head in the right direction. Some sheep were running back and forth, but eventually, they were directed towards the right gate.

Children's views of God are constantly adjusting to every new bit of information and experience they have. Like the farmer, we don't need to try to hyper-control those views. Our role isn't to try to regulate them on a narrow path. Instead, we can stand back and give them a lot of freedom to discover God for themselves, while at the same time, when their understanding of God is heading too far in the wrong direction, redirecting them back to the truth. We can slowly and gently help shepherd our children to engage with a balanced and accurate view of God, because when they do, they will want to connect with him.

Helping our child build a healthy view of God is about rounding out their understanding of him, not pushing them in the opposite direction. Often children's 'wrong' ideas of God are narrow views of one or two aspects of his character, and therefore they see him only through a tiny lens. To help shepherd our children to see him accurately, we just give a fuller, broader view of God. God can be faithful and active at the same time. He can be loving and just. He can be strong and gentle. He can be all of those things. We can begin to create a fabric of understanding the fullness of God instead.

Finding your child's view of God

Each child will have their own personal view of God. It is helpful for us to take a good look at our children's current view of God, and how they are responding to him, so that we know how to help each one of them move forward. This isn't a spirituality test or a judgement of 'how good a Christian is my child'.

Parenting for faith is all about asking ourselves, 'What is the next step for my child spiritually and how can I help them take it?' Sometimes the first step is just getting to know where your child is at the moment.

Your observations

Most of us have been watching our children their whole lives. You already will know more than you think you do. If you were to jot down a few thoughts about each of your children's spiritual lives, what observations might you include? How do they respond at church or when you pray at home? What questions do they ask? How do they talk about God? What is your general sense of their connection with him? You will probably already have a sense of where they are.

Ask questions that don't have right answers

In trying to find out more about our children's view of God, we can often run into a problem. Christian children know the answers that they think we want to hear. They know the 'right' answers and are tempted to tell them to us when we try to delve into this area. So how can we genuinely find out what our children's honest views of God are when they don't tell us?

One of the most useful tools I have found is the ability to ask questions that don't have right answers. Ask questions that wonder about the things of God, such as, 'What do you think God is doing today? What is God's favourite Bible story? If Jesus was at your school as a kid, who would he most be like? Do you think Jesus fancied anyone in secondary school? You know how the Bible says that God rested after he created everything? Well I like to watch TV when I rest; what did God do?' We can ask questions that give our children the opportunity to say what they think rather than what the 'right' answer may be.

I would encourage you to try to hold off on correcting any wayward thinking at that moment, as the most powerful part of this exercise is in releasing your children to talk about their real feelings about God. You will be creating a family culture in which the sharing of genuine thoughts and wonderings is valued above the performance of 'right' answers. Open questions will help you form an insight into your children's views of God without needing them to express those views directly.

Use a visual image

Guided discussion is another, more direct, activity that will help you to see how your children view God and how they feel about their relationship with him. Create a casual time in which you suggest to your family that you each draw a picture of what God looks like, where you are in the picture with God and what your relationship with him feels like. Give some possible suggestions. For example, some people feel that God is a busy man and they are in a bubble and can't hear God; others feel that God is a really old man on a cloud far away. They can draw anything. Coach your children along if they need it, asking for more detail on their drawing of God or for more specifics about how they feel connected to God (perhaps by a string, separated by a wall and so on).

Don't let the children's drawings become pictures of the right answer. If you feel they need reminding, emphasise that you want to know what they honestly think and feel. If you notice them slipping into performing for you, there is always the option of saying, 'Really? Because I wondered if maybe sometimes you felt that [insert wise observation]. Many people feel that way sometimes. It's okay.' And don't forget to draw a picture yourself!

After the drawing time, share the pictures with each other and talk about them. Don't feel the need necessarily to solve any misconceptions at the time. Sometimes it is good to validate the sharing of our individual feelings about God, without needing immediately to correct or be corrected. This exercise is about taking a first step in helping children to own their relationship with God and in establishing the family as a great place to process your journeys with God. On the other hand, it might be a good time to discuss why we think in those ways about God and maybe start to realign some wrong ideas. Only you will know what is right at the time.

Beginning to build a healthy view of God

Farmers do two things when guiding sheep: prepare a way forward and redirect the sheep to get there. As we get to know how our children see God, we will be doing two things as well: building a strong, balanced foundation of who God is, and correcting any wrong views that they may be developing.

In the next chapter we will be looking at the five main skewed views of God that children have and how to realign those, but here I want to give you a few tools for how to proactively help your child know God well.

Broadening our children's understanding of God's character

My mum was an English teacher for most of my teenage years. In fact, she taught at my school. I found it strange to hear my friends and schoolmates talk about my mum, because they had a narrower view of her than I did. In class, they experienced mostly just her no-nonsense, creative, witty, serious side. From a lifetime of being her kid, I, on the other hand, also knew her to be kind, funny, caring and relaxed. As her child, I got to see many aspects of her personality, while her students only got to interact with a narrow part of her. I knew my mum better than they did because I had access to a greater part of her character.

With God, it is astonishing to think of all the different sides to his character. Scripture is full of descriptions of him. He is loving, gracious, all-powerful, all-knowing, just, wrathful, good, patient, generous, forgiving, holy, jealous, kind, generous, helpful, comforting, righteous, faithful, active, mysterious and truthful. On and on the list could go. But we often tend to cling to only two or three descriptors and try to communicate those to our children. Some of us want our children to know that God is good, gracious and loving, while others of us want to impress upon our children that God is holy, all-powerful and righteous. It is helpful for us to realise this tendency, so that we can be sure to mention the other aspects of God's character once in a while.

The way to help our children develop a healthy, balanced view of God is to ensure that they see the fullness of his character, not just a narrow part of it. Just like I knew my mother best because I was the one who saw the most aspects of her character, the more our children see of the width and breadth of who God is the more accurately they will understand him.

As we create windows into our lives and explain the world to our children, it is helpful to ask ourselves what aspect of God's character our children might need to understand better. If your child is struggling with people at school lying, you may want to create windows into your life of how God's unchanging truth roots you. You may also want to explain how God talks in scripture about liars and how David wrote a bunch of angry poems to God about a similar situation. Help your child learn how God's character is relevant to every experience of their lives.

Helping our children experience the character of God

To help our children grow into a relationship with God, we need to look at how good relationships develop. Among many other things, a relationship requires knowledge and experience. People who read my CV online may gain some information about me, but they can only really get to know me once they have met me and experienced my personality and friendship. Other people might meet me casually at a party or conference and experience something of my personality, but once we get into a conversation, one of the first things they will do is ask questions to get more information about me. This is how humans build and maintain relationships. We grow in our knowledge and experience of people, and thus grow closer and deeper in relationship. God meant our relationship with him to work in the same way – for knowledge about him and experience of him to go hand in hand.

Until our children experience God for themselves, he won't truly make sense to them. As we help our children understand more of the fullness of God's character, it is useful to be thinking, 'How can I help my child experience this aspect of God's character?' We may tell them God is loving, but until they experience his love through prayer or action, it's just a God-smart fact. We can help our children meet with God through prayer in a way that connects them to the actual love of God (chapters 6 and 7 will help with that). We may tell them God is just, but until they experience partnering with God to bring justice to those who are struggling, they may not fully understand that part of God's character. We can help our children feel God's heart for justice and find their next steps in participating in God's heart for those who need justice through action (chapters 15 and 16 will help with that).

Whatever it is, helping our children experience God's character for themselves helps them get to know God broadly and fully.

As we try to build healthy, balanced views of God, our children are being exposed to a myriad of other influences as well: media, friends, their own experiences of God and of the church. All of that influences their view of God. Occasionally that means they end up with an unbalanced or unhelpful view of God. At those times, we, like that farmer, are called to be there to help redirect them back. The process of building healthy views of God and refocussing warped views will begin to release your child to see God for who he is, and will empower him or her to crave a relationship with God. In the next chapter we will look at common ways children's views can become skewed, and how we can realign those views.

5

Realigning wrong views of God

Sometimes, our children's view of God gets skewed. When we can recognise this and redirect our children back to a healthy, balanced view of God, we can empower them to continue to connect with him. In this chapter, we will explore five of the most common skewed views of God that people have. These views aren't outright lies about God (for example, that he is a genocidal psychopath); they just overemphasise a few of God's many attributes in a way that pushes children away from God.

Distant God

The first wrong view, which most of us have experienced, is the idea of a distant, busy God. God is far away on a cloud somewhere, working hard. He's got the world to run, people to save, babies to make, decisions to make about where people go after they die, missionaries to call, famines to sort out. He exists far away in heaven, removed from our ordinary lives here on earth.

Faced with this view of God, children are hesitant. They can feel their insignificance in the face of all God is doing, and how far away he is. For instance, at bedtime they'll want you to pray instead of them. They may get nervous, or stop after half a sentence and say, 'No, you do it.' You may notice them feeling stressed or at a loss about what to pray about, appearing to have no idea what to say to God.

Often this is because it takes a lot of courage to interrupt a busy God. They don't want to mess up and get him annoyed with their little prayers. They may not believe that he will care about the small stuff they want to say. They'll want to save up their prayers for the big ask. When something terrible is happening, then they can say, 'God, God, can you pay attention to little me for a very brief amount of time, because I have something really big to ask you?' It can be hard to get a child who has a distant view of God to casually pray or to do something fun with God because they view him as too busy and too important. They don't want to frustrate him.

Realigning the 'distant God' view

Where is God?

The view of the 'distant God' is widespread among children, as many books and songs unwittingly contribute to an image of God as being far removed from us. In both classic artworks and popular culture, God is depicted as being in the clouds above us, wrapped up in his heavenly home, busy doing things. We often look up or point up when referring to God, and many songs refer to God 'looking down on us' from above. It is not hard, therefore, to see where the 'distant God' view originates.

If our children view God as distant, we can proactively bring to our children's attention God's promise that he is with us always, and we can explore with them what that promise means about God and our relationship with him. Tell stories about how we know God is close to us and what average life with God looks like for us in the everyday. We can talk about pictures or songs that contribute to the view that God is far away and ask them why they think people portray God like that. Moving to the next step, we can redraw the picture, or discuss how the song could be changed to make it more like the truth.

Pray slowly

One small way we may have accidentally helped build this view in our children is by how fast our words come out when we pray. To children, it can sound as if we are talking faster than they can, which implies to them that prayer time needs to hurry up a bit or that God doesn't want to be kept waiting. They can hear in contrast how slowly they pray and become self-conscious that the busy God will get bored. In our effort to help them, we may jump in during prayer time to complete their thought or finish sooner. All of this can leave our children thinking that prayer time needs to get done quickly and efficiently because of God's personality, rather than because we as parents have other things we need to get done downstairs.

We can reshape this for our children by slowing our speech to the pace of our child's and aiming for prayer times to be casual. We don't need to be afraid of long pauses, or accidentally saying the wrong thing. If children are struggling, a simple 'Take your time; God isn't in a rush! He really wants to hear what you want to say, and he loves waiting to hear all of it!' may help to relax them.

Don't prepare them

Another accidental way we may contribute to the 'distant God' view is by prepping our children on prayer. When we are faced with children who don't know what to pray, we naturally want to help. So we ask what they want to pray about and help shape what they want to bring to God before we get down to prayer. Sometimes we feel the need to censor our children's plans for what they want to pray about, like their desire for a trip to Disneyland or for their favourite football team to win.

There are very few relationships in our children's lives where they have to rehearse what they want to say before they say it. When we help our children think through what they want to say to God before they do it, it creates in their minds a God who is easily offended and cares more about performance than authenticity.

The next two chapters address how to help our kids find their heart-to-heart connection with God in prayer, but for this specific instance, one way to refocus this view is to say, 'You know, God loves hearing everything that you want to tell him. There is no way to mess up talking with God.'

Happy God

Super-nice, super-jolly, super-passive: this version of God smiles through whatever happens. He sits back and enjoys the worship we send him and has a clichéd response to everything. He's happy, and he wants you to be happy, no matter what. On the surface, this view of God doesn't seem too harmful, but children react to it in two different ways.

On the one hand, some children forge a pleasing 'performance' attitude towards God and major heavily on asking for things in prayer. They attempt to charm God by their goodness, so that he will favour them with good things. They can be very competitive with other children, trying to be the 'best', seeking God's approval as their glittering personalities earn them currency to spend.

On the other hand, some children can be dismissive of and disconnected in their response to this type of God. They can see him as being petty and playing 'favourites'. If they have low self-esteem, they feel as if they could never compete with the 'good' children for his affection and favour. His perceived jolliness means that they often feel he doesn't care about the realities of their lives and the difficulties they experience. He holds no answers for their deep questions, and he doesn't tolerate sadness, anger or pain for very long. His goal is to make us jolly, like he is, and many children can't connect with that idea.

Realigning the 'happy God' view

When I feel… God is…

Often, especially with younger children, we focus on the nice things about God (God is loving; God is caring; God is good) and on what God wants us to do (God wants us to obey, be kind, share, etc.). Children at this age are learning about cause and effect. Sometimes these two ideas get paired together: God loves us because we obey, are kind and share; therefore, if we don't do those things, then God will stop loving, caring and being happy with us.

We can begin realigning the 'happy God' view by adding some helpful relational truth to our times together. Read the parable of the prodigal son together and explain that, just like the father in the story, God loves us no matter what we do. Even if we have done something wrong, God wants to run to us and hug us, so that we can live close together again. We can also ensure that we focus less on what God wants us to do and more on how to do relationship with him. Try using 'when' statements: 'When I feel lonely, God is with me'; 'When I feel scared, God protects me.' This builds an understanding of God and relationship, and it still works with the cause-and-effect awareness that the child's brain is processing.

It's okay for things not to be okay

Another thing we sometimes do that endorses the 'happy, optimistic' view of God is to answer children's questions or respond to their difficulties with glib answers, excuses or clichés, such as 'I know he's annoying you, but God loves him too, so you need to be nice to him,' or 'You just need to have faith.' These statements tend to invalidate our children's emotional experiences and imply that God wants, first and foremost, for them to get over their pain quickly and return to a happy-go-lucky emotional state.

Children need to know that God walks with them in their pain and sees the reality of their situations. Sometimes life is great, and sometimes it's not, and God sticks with us in the middle of it all. They need to know the scripture that says, 'The Lord is close to the broken-hearted and saves those who are crushed in spirit' (Psalm 34:18). It doesn't say, 'God's annoyed at the broken-hearted and wants them to get over it and be happy.' Kids need to be reminded that when they are sad, God isn't saying, 'Come on! Cheer up and get over it!' He comes and sits next to us when we're broken-hearted and listens to us when we talk.

We can help our children by giving them options when they are upset, for example, saying, 'It sounds as if you are getting really angry and stressed. When I feel like that, I like to take a short loo break[2] and talk to God about it all. He helps me calm down and work out what to do. Do you want to take a break?' We can take the opportunity later to talk about the situation and how God loves us even in difficult circumstances.

We can also help our children by sharing with them how God ministers to us during those confusing, angry or sad times in our lives, as they may not yet know that aspect of his work. Correcting this wrong view may be as simple as beginning to model how God partners with you in your life and encouraging your child to trust him to do the same.

Angry God

He sits in the sky on his throne of judgement, critically watching every moment of our day to spot our sins. When he sees one, his anger flashes and punishment pours out. He is easily offended and requires everyone around him to be as perfect as possible. This view of God produces fear in children and a desperate need to perform. He is impossible to please, so the stress for them is on doing what God says to avoid his displeasure. Love rarely enters into it. Children don't seek a relationship with this God, as the whole goal is to keep their head down and avoid being seen.

Realigning the 'angry God' view

None of us ever wants to communicate this view of God to our children. Many of us have been raised with this view, and so are acutely aware of the damage it can cause.

Changing how we describe sin

Often this comes down to how we handle the concept of sin. We often simplify our description of sin to mean 'something we do wrong that hurts God', after which we must apologise so that God can forgive us. This description of sin, however, sounds like we are kicking God in the shins. We sin, and God says, 'Ow!' We then have to say sorry, and God rolls his eyes and says, 'Well, because Jesus died on the cross I have to forgive you. Fine.' And then we go back to everyday life, except now warier of God. Children can grow to expect that God is always feeling a bit hurt or resentful towards them unless they can stay on top of apologising or not sinning. So how do we realign this view of God? The main way is by changing our view of sin and the way we communicate it to children.

Sin robs us. It steals our peace, our joy, our connection to love, our purpose on this earth, and the feeling of being free. Sin hurts us and others. It makes a mess and puts a wall between God and us. It was never God's plan for us. When we steal, it makes people distrust us. When we lie, it breaks our connection with others. When we think angry thoughts about people, it takes away our ability to love God and others. And the world hurts because of it. God doesn't want that for us; he loves us too much. And he sent Jesus to take all that off us.

When we describe sin like that, it becomes something that we can drop at any moment before running to God instead of running away from him. Getting rid of sin is about connection with the God who seeks to be close to us.[3]

Presenting a rounded view of scripture

Check what Bible stories you are emphasising. Sometimes we may focus on the stories of war, battles and large miracles because they seem exciting, but between the pictures and the stories our children may get the impression that God is violent and vengeful, rather than getting the full view of his character that comes from reading other scripture. If you feel your child sees God as angry, it may be helpful to switch to a children's Bible that does a good job of presenting a broader picture of God's character, such as *The Jesus Storybook Bible*.[4]

Unpredictable God

He is mysterious and changeable. We never know how he is going to react, and we can't guess his plan. At first, children angrily struggle with this God but eventually respond with defeat and dismissal. In their view, God will do what he wants when he wants, so there isn't much point in trying to persuade him or even being around him. Most circumstances they see, good or bad, happen because of God, so they don't know how to feel about him. They can feel like victims to God's whims, and feel under pressure from adults to accept their fate with contentment. They rarely want to invest in a relationship with this God because they know they want people they can count on, and this God isn't one of them.

Realigning the 'unpredictable God' view

Staying rooted in what we know

Sometimes when we are faced with the mysteries of God, we feel the pressure to come up with a reason for situations that we don't understand. We sometimes tell children, 'God works in mysterious ways,' 'God has a bigger plan,' or 'One day we will know why God did this.' Other times, we guess. We'll say, 'I don't know; maybe God was trying to teach someone a lesson, or maybe God was punishing them, or maybe we don't know why it happened, but God had a purpose. All things have a purpose.' When we guess, we aren't helping our children find peace and comfort in the mystery of God. Instead, we can simply answer to be best of our ability.

One boy I worked with had a mum with cancer, and his father was desperate to know how to help him connect with God about it. The child's grandparents and family friends were giving him all the above 'assurances', which were making him wobble enormously in his view of God. Instead, I encouraged the father to chat honestly with his son and model for him how he was processing the experience. He ended up having an in-depth conversation with his son, saying:

> I don't know why Mum has cancer. I don't think God gave it to her, because that doesn't fit with the loving Father God that I know in the Bible and my life. I'm not sure there is a reason. I think we live in a world that got broken by sin and evil, and it's not yet fixed and perfect in the way that it will be in heaven. Your mum has cancer, and we are all scared and upset about it. What I do know is that God loves me and you and your mum and has promised in the Bible that he will walk with us through everything in our lives. He has promised that he will take away our fear and will fill us with his love. With every tear we cry, he is right there, catching them and storing them up; he is right here, comforting us and helping us. I know that, and I believe that. It helps me to chat with him about how I feel and to listen to what he says back to me about it. I don't feel alone when I'm with God. In the meantime, the Bible says to keep praying, so we're going to keep doing that too!

This helped the boy enormously in his faith because, instead of being put in a helpless position under an unpredictable God, he was rooted in the truth of who God is, what the Bible says about God and how relationship with God works in a situation like this.

Explaining everything

As we talked about in the previous chapter, sometimes God looks mysterious because we haven't explained enough, particularly in church. Church is where children learn to see what God's family is like. If we don't explain it to them, it can look mysterious and weird. Whether you attend a church that values ritual and liturgy, a wildly charismatic 'free church', or a place that worships in silence, it all needs explaining. Take the time to explain why you and your church worship the way you do, what God is doing in the midst of it all, and how it affects you in your journey.

Buddy God

The last distorted view is that of the 'buddy God'. It's all about me. I am special, wonderful and loved. God likes to be my buddy and follow me around; he does everything with me. I am at the centre of my relationship with God. God is essentially my sidekick, helping me do everything I want to accomplish.

Initially, kids respond well to this view. Then they get bored. This view results in God eventually being the annoying friend who has no personality and who follows you around wanting to do whatever you do. If you find your children are bored with God, it usually is because they have this view. Sometimes we want our children to feel so loved by God that we forget to say, 'God is mighty, and he is doing things in the world. He is healing, rescuing, weaving together, changing nations, calling the lost to himself. And he invites us to join him in his work.' When we make faith too child-centred, we rob God of his power, majesty and purpose and reduce him to being a sidekick.

Realigning the 'buddy God' view

Watch the news with your kid; ask, 'What do you think God is doing here? Where is God? What does scripture say God is going to do in this situation? What do you think God is gonna do next?' Explore with your child what they feel God is asking them to do with him, and help them take a step out in their purpose. We explore this more in Part II.

6

Chatting with God

I looked out over 200 bored faces. I was teaching 'prayer' to eight- and nine-year-old children at a summer conference, and it did not look as if it would go well. They were bored as soon as they knew the topic – but I knew that wouldn't last long. I began to ask them to explore with me what prayer is and how we do it. With rolled eyes, answers started to come in. We gathered a very extensive list. According to the children, the general guidelines of prayer are as follows:

- Prayer is talking to God about specific things you want to bring to his attention.
- Primarily included in each prayer should be a 'sorry', a 'thank you' and a 'please' section, unless it is a grace prayer for mealtimes or an absolute emergency – when 'please help' becomes enough and you are off the hook for the 'sorry' and 'thank you'.
- In general, you need to sit still and be quiet, close your eyes, fold your hands, start with 'Dear God' and end with 'Amen'.
- God is always available to hear you, and you can do this type of prayer any time, but you have to wait for a while to see the results if there are any.

I asked if they had any questions about prayer, and not a hand was raised. Nope, it seemed they had it all sorted.

With a smile, I asked them what they would think if I told them that they didn't have to do any of the things they'd listed. What if I told them that they could tell jokes to God, cry in front of him, watch TV with him, ask him questions and hear his answers? What would happen if they didn't sit still, or close their eyes, or say 'Dear God' and 'Amen' when they prayed?

There was a considerable pause, and the little heads started shaking a universal 'no'. They smiled uncomfortably and visually checked with the other leaders to see if anyone was going to stone me for my obvious heresy. One boy piped up, 'If you don't do those things that we put on the board, then it's not prayer! It won't work!' The group erupted in agreement: hand after hand shot up in the air. After several minutes of listening to the general discussion on why it wouldn't work, one brave girl raised her hand. 'I'm not sure if it would be okay to do what you say, but if it was... I'd really, really like it and would maybe like to do it more. Praying would be totally different, like having a friend instead of talking to God.'

Have you ever noticed how hard it can be to get children to pray out loud? Children who we cannot get to stop talking in daily life miraculously freeze when it comes to prayer. I began to realise that in our effort to help children pray to God, in trying to create a formula that would help them, we have ended up slamming down restrictions on them that are limiting their connection to him. Our children have been trying to figure out how to 'do prayer' instead of relaxing into enjoying a relationship with the God who loves them.

In my relationship with my husband, saying 'thank you', 'sorry' and 'please' is important, but it is not what the relationship is built on. If I came home and said, 'Dear husband, thank you for taking the bin bags out of the bins. I'm sorry for accidentally turning off the computer when you were in the middle of your game. Please take the bin bags all the way outside, to the wheelie bin. The end,' and walked away, we wouldn't have a relationship! My connection with my husband is made through sharing stupid stories and heart-to-heart talk, and through laughing and having adventures together. Amid those things, I also say 'sorry', 'please' and 'thank you', but those expressions are not central.

Neither should they be the centre of our kids' relationships with God.

Prayer is supposed to be an uncensored heart-to-heart flow of life together with him. The psalms are full of this heart-flow of words – emotional, raw, off-the-top-of-your-head outpouring. This is what is on offer to our children: an authentic connection with God through prayer that enables every part of their hearts to be open to him. I call it 'chatting'.

I use the word 'chatting' with children because they instinctively know what it means: an informal, relational communication that can be about anything. It's also, to be honest, much more reflective of how we pray as adults. Our prayers in our heads are full of half-sentences, memories and partially finished thoughts. Life with God is messy, informal and often grasped in the in-between times.

Chatting is vital, because for children to trust God with the big stuff in their life, they have to trust him with the small. If they can talk to God about how they feel about the texture of their socks and their favourite toy, then they will feel confident to talk to him about how they feel when their parents fight or when they are scared at school. Relationships are born and grown in the everyday sharing of small things as well as big things, and God longs to hear about all of it. Most children have been given a clear sense of what is 'proper' to talk to God about, but we can lift that lid off for them so that they feel the freedom of having a 'friend and family' connection with him. Everything is on the table: TV programmes; funny stories; how they feel about the colour of their underwear today; bodily functions; sports; anything and everything. Most children giggle and feel a bit shocked that God would care, but this way of praying brings them such freedom. I tell children, 'If it's in your head or heart, he wants to know!'

Avoid the high-priest role

Before Jesus came to earth, Israel encountered God through a mediator, a high priest. This priest was super-impressive, super-holy and super-clean. He had the authority, power and awesome responsibility to speak to God for the people of Israel, bring God their sacrifices and make sure God was happy with all of them. He was also responsible for passing on God's words to the people so that they could know his commands and encouragements – a bit like an ancient note-passer. The high priest was a fortunate man, because he was the only person in the entire nation who was allowed to come directly into God's presence, in a room of the temple that no one else could enter and in which he only could once a year. The Israelites had to experience God through him: their way of knowing God was through the words of the high priest. He mediated between them and God (see Exodus 28:1—30:10; Leviticus 9:15–24; Leviticus 16; Hebrews 5:1; 9:7).

When Jesus died on the cross, a significant thing happened in the temple in Jerusalem. The veil separating the Most Holy Place, the room that was only for the high priest and God, from the rest of the temple was torn apart (Matthew 27:51). Jesus' death and resurrection changed forever how people could encounter the living God. No longer were we reliant on someone to stand between God and us. Jesus made it possible for us to encounter him daily, moment by moment (Hebrews 6:19; 10:19–22).

The trap we fall into is that we still feel a need to stand between our children and God. We are clinging to the role of high priest as if they still need someone to interpret God for them. See if any of the following statements ring true with you.

- My children won't be able to understand prayer. I need to help them do it in manageable chunks.
- My child doesn't know what to say, so I will do it for her until she becomes more confident.
- I don't want them to lose their reverence for God. Aren't we called to fear the Lord?
- I don't want my child to be disappointed with God. What if she prays and nothing happens? What if the thing she doesn't want to happen does?
- I don't want my child to be hurt. What if all the other children hear God's voice and my child doesn't? I don't want my child to think God doesn't love him.

I'm not sure that this is a conscious decision, but the desire to act like a high priest comes out clearly in our actions and words. I find that this approach comes mostly out of fear and distrust of God. On some level, perhaps a part of us believes that if God and our children interact unsupervised, the risk is high that they will be bewildered, hurt or somehow let down by who he is and what the reality of life with him is like.

It scared me so much when I saw that mindset in myself. In my passion for children to be close to God, I fell into the trap of fearing and distrusting God's very nature. I think we all need to face this question when we look at our role in parenting our children for relationship with him. Do I trust God? Do I know him well enough to be sure that he is a gentle God who reveals himself with faithfulness, patience and love? Do I trust that he knows my children better than I do, loves them more than I do and longs for a relationship with them more than I do? Do I trust that he created my children's minds and that he can create two-way communication with my children on their levels in a way that is relevant to them?

It is right to want children to have a safe place to encounter God. My initial solution to that desire, though, was to put myself between God and children. I was the safety gate. Since seeing this tendency in myself, I've changed the boundaries. I don't want to be the safety gate between God and children. I want to be the usher – the one who guides a child into the presence of God and stands guard to protect their time and space as they interact. I want to be the one who walks with the child away from that encounter and helps him to process the way it changes his situation and life.

As we help our children to build that two-way connection with God, we need to ask ourselves periodically, 'Am I putting myself in the middle of this relationship, or am I functioning as a guide?' Chatting is a handy tool, because it releases us from being in the centre of our child's communication with God.

Empowering chat

Create windows

There are two ways we can help our children pray.

The first is to start creating windows into how we chat with God. If you usually pray silently, then the only way you can do that is to start chatting to God out loud. I know, I know, this will be awkward, but the only way your children are going to see that you are chatting to God in your head is if you let it come out of your mouth occasionally. You don't need to start praying aloud all the time, but once in a while, when your child might overhear, vocalise your chatting. While you are cooking or doing DIY, start chatting aloud about how you feel about something or about your kids. Pray for whatever you want; just let it come out of your mouth so that your kids can overhear you connecting with God and learn how to do it and how normal and natural it is. If you're in the car and happen to pass an accident, let that knee-jerk prayer – 'Oh God, keep us safe and heal those people' – slip out of your mouth rather than stay in your thoughts. Create windows into how your informal chatting with God works.

The second way is to be as informal in your prayer times together as you are in your own private chats with God. During her bedtime prayers, a friend's five-year-old daughter said:

> Hi, Father God! I had so much fun today, especially when I got to do girly stuff with Mummy when the boys were playing football. I don't know why you made football, anyway. It's silly. I had a bad part of the day when Tommy pushed me, and I got cross and smacked him. He makes me sad when he pushes me all the time. Can you make him stop being mean to me? I don't want to be mean either, but it's hard when he makes me cross. I'm going to sleep now. Will you please be in the room with me, 'cos I get scared sometimes. Oh, and please take care of Uncle David and Auntie Sue and Mummy and Daddy. I like them a lot. Love you!

She felt free to use this sort of informal chat with God because that is how her parents prayed with her.

The main thing to remember is that we want to train our children to communicate what is on their minds in the way they want to, instead of trying to translate it into a language that they feel is more acceptable to God. Share with your children how and when you chat with God. Most children are shocked to discover that we chat to God while driving, in the shower and on the loo. I take God out to dinner and a movie sometimes and chat with him through the whole thing. Share with your children when you chat with God. It will free them to find their own times with him too.

Introducing chatting to your children

You can also actively disciple your children in how to chat with God. Often, children need us to guide them through the process a couple of times before they get the hang of it. Remember, we are trying to empower their relationship with God and not put ourselves in the middle of it. So we can help to set up a situation for our children to try this way of sharing with God.

First, you may want to tell them about how the disciples spent time with Jesus. When Jesus was on earth, he lived side-by-side with his disciples. They were pioneers in a new way of interacting with God, a new way of praying. When Jesus and the disciples woke up in the morning, I doubt that Peter wandered in for breakfast, noticed Jesus in the corner reading the morning news and said, 'Dear Jesus, please do not make us walk today. It is really hot. Amen,' and continued on his way. That would be rude. These men got to live with Jesus, who was fully God and fully man at the same time. They slept in the same house, ate food, laughed, debated and enjoyed themselves together. I can't say for sure, as the Bible isn't clear on this point, but I'm almost certain that they must have played some ancient version of 'I spy with my little eye' while on those long walking trips. In any case, they must have been bored together at some points, as well as being busy and serving alongside each other. These people did real life with Jesus and talked about everything. God cares about everything that is in our hearts. He wants to hear our ups and downs, our anger and our silliness. He wants to laugh at our jokes and chat throughout the day with us. There is nothing we cannot say to God.

After you have talked to your children about chatting with God and how he loves to hear about the little things in life, wait a short while and then have a go. Tell them that you are going to suggest something for them to tell God silently, and they can nod at you when they have finished. Once they nod, you can give another suggestion. This prayer is just between them and God, so make sure they know that you don't want to hear the answer: they can tell God in their heads. (Children under six struggle with praying in their heads, so often I invite them to whisper their prayer into their hand or their pillow, so that it's clearly between them and God, not them and me.) I structure the topics to interweave big and little issues, so they can experience a range of emotional sharing.

Some suggestions for what to pray about include the following. Say to your children, 'Tell or show God...'

- Your favourite colour
- What you hope you are having for pudding tomorrow
- A joke
- The name of a person who hurts your feelings sometimes
- Which you would rather have for a pet: an elephant or a bear
- One thing you have to do every day that you wish you didn't have to do
- The best movie you have ever seen, and why you liked it so much
- One thing that you wish was different about your family
- Your favourite place in the whole world
- One thing you like about yourself
- One thing that makes you super-scared
- How you feel about God: you can say anything!
- The person you are most glad that God created
- A time when you felt so lonely you wanted to cry
- One memory or picture in your head that you wish you didn't have
- The stinkiest smell you ever smelt

This list could go on. Tailor the questions to the age of your children, your family circumstances and the range of fun or serious things that you would like them to be sharing with God. This is a way of giving your children permission to talk to God about things at both ends of the scale: silly experiences, family situations, school bullying and so on. There is something compelling about watching your child tell God a joke, with a giggle on their face, and then be given permission to tell God how they feel when Mummy and Daddy fight. A key to helping children to build a relationship with God is to show them that the connection with him is about everything, all the time.

Keep them focused on sharing emotions and thoughts

To simplify prayer, we often reduce it to an exercise in sharing information. If we want God-connected children, however, we need to help them create a pattern for sharing their thoughts and feelings. This is the essence of relationship – the ability to share our feelings with others.

As children grow in their ability to recognise their emotions, they will develop in their ability to share them, and it is important that we make God a pivotal person to share those emotions with.

You can model this for your children by doing it in your own prayers. For example:

> God, thank you so much for giving us another day together. I'm feeling really tired and a bit sad because I'm missing my husband Joe while he's on his trip. You have been helping me a lot every day, and I love feeling close to you. Thank you, too, for my son and daughter. They make my heart so happy, and I love being their mum.

Learning to share feelings is a great way to become proactive in discipling children in their relationship with God.

Often, we train our children to pray at the end of the day as a catch up, but chatting with God is a wonderful way of processing emotions while they are happening. God can handle being around us when we are angry, sad or irrational, so why not encourage your children to go for a walk in the garden and tell God how they feel when they are so annoyed that they want to scream? Or you might encourage them to find a secret place where they can share their hurt and sad feelings with God.

When working with older children, I often show them some key psalms. They are usually shocked by the emotions that the psalmists were 'allowed' to express to God. Take some time to find the right psalms to echo your children's emotions and experiences, and then encourage them to vent their frustration at God any time they want. If they like, they could also write their own psalms to God, expressing the way they feel.

Using non-verbal expression

Some children connect better with non-verbal ways of expressing themselves and sharing their thoughts and feelings with God. Some love drawing pictures of their feelings and experiences; others love journalling; others love choosing pop or worship songs that express how they feel and playing them for God. Some children need permission to share how they feel with a big growl or yell (somewhere that it is okay to make noise). Some children need reminding that just inviting God to sit in a room with them while they are crying can be a way of sharing their feelings with God. You know your child best. Perhaps you could enable your children to try some of these different ways of expressing themselves to God.

Chatting is releasing

Chatting with God can release something wonderful in children because it frees them to be themselves and to share their lives with God. This allows their spiritual lives to pervade their everyday experience. Whenever a family or community begins to explore this idea of chatting with God, I often hear stories of the impact it is having on children's lives. For example:

- A three-year-old's favourite thing to do is to play and chat with God in her room.
- Stewards at a summer conference reported that the loo and shower queues were longer than usual because the cubicles were taken up by children: their little voices could be heard taking a 'private' opportunity to chatter away to God.
- A girl from a broken home who would rage at her parents found that the best way to cope was to pour out her feelings to God instead of kicking and screaming.
- An older boy felt that all his feelings would get stored up inside him when he was bullied at school, and his hurt and shame and embarrassment would be like 'acid in my heart'. He found that chatting with God allowed all those emotions to drain away.
- A 16-year-old girl felt far from God, but within a week of her dad telling her about chatting to God she began to spend school lunchtimes with him, sitting in the middle of the playing field just talking about everything. It completely changed her life, because she was given permission to chat about everything with no effort.

Chatting with God is a key step for children in sharing their lives with God instead of performing for him. It is something that all of us long for in our lives, and we can help equip our children for the reality of this kind of relationship with God. Every child communicates differently. I suggest you start with chatting, but don't be surprised if it turns into something bigger. The goal is for chatting to become an integral part of your child's daily life. They will begin to find their favourite ways of chatting with God. Some may want to write God letters or go riding their bike with God. It will naturally become something reflective of your child, and when it does you will begin to see the fruit.

As you go on with chatting, you will notice that your child needs you less and less. The goal is for us to back out of it so that we no longer need to suggest things for them to chat about but end up saying, 'I love you. I'm leaving you with God tonight. You and God have a good chat, and I'll talk to you in the morning.' And you can go, knowing that your child knows how to access God.

7

Catching from God

When I met Colin, he had been in two foster homes since being taken away from his family situation almost three years before. Eleven years old and recently adopted, he felt as if he had a 'volcano' of hurt and anger inside him. The smallest spark could set him off and, when it did, he lashed out at anyone around – screaming, kicking, punching and throwing things. After he'd exploded, he often crawled into his wardrobe and closed the door in an attempt to hide and feel safe. When the volcano erupted, he felt as if he couldn't stop it, and it often scared him to see 'who I really am inside'.

Veena and Ron, Colin's adoptive parents, had been actively modelling the reality of relationship with God at home and decided that they needed to be more proactive in creating opportunities for Colin to connect with God. I worked with them on how to help Colin hear God's voice, and they began to look for a chance to introduce the ideas to their son. One night, Colin talked about how his biological father had always called him 'useless', and Ron felt that this might be a good opportunity to help Colin connect with God. He told Colin how God was good at taking away bad things that people have said to us and replacing them with the truth. He offered to help Colin hear what God had to say about it. Colin hesitantly agreed, and Ron briefly outlined for Colin how to 'catch' God's voice. After a lightning-quick prayer from Ron inviting God to meet with him, Colin sat in silence, waiting, as Ron had told him to, for God to do something. 'Okay, God,' thought Colin, 'if I'm not useless, then what am I?'

Instantly, like writing on the inside of his mind, the word 'wonderful' appeared with little stars and fireworks exploding around it. Colin's eyes flashed open, and he whispered, 'He said something!' Ron asked about it excitedly while a smile lit Colin's face and warmth spread through his chest. 'Wonderful,' he said, out loud. 'Wonderful with fireworks.' Something broke in Colin and tears began to pour down his face. Quickly he shoved his face into his hands to hide it, and Ron gently asked if he could let God keep on talking to him. Colin nodded and, over the next couple of minutes, God and Colin met heart to heart – Colin chatting to God and God chatting back.

To be in a relationship, communication must flow both ways. Not many of us would stay in a relationship where we were the only one communicating, and we had to guess how the other person was feeling and thinking. It's no fun chatting unless the other person chats back! God is faithful to communicate with us in a variety of ways, and we can train and equip our children to seek, expect and know his voice in their daily lives. It is an essential part of helping our children to have a relationship with him, because when they can access his voice, they have access to the heart of him: his truth, love, healing, encouragement, holiness, challenges, peace and so much more.

The Bible is full of God's promises that we will hear and know his voice. There are promises that he will speak to us when we call, and even when we don't. He speaks in different ways and gives us new and delightful revelations. For example, he says, 'Call to me and I will answer you and tell you great and unsearchable things you do not know' (Jeremiah 33:3); 'For God does speak – now one way, now another – though no one perceives it' (Job 33:14).

God promises that we will grow to recognise his voice so well that we will run away from any other. For example:

> The one who enters by the gate is the shepherd of the sheep. The gatekeeper opens the gate for him, and the sheep listen to his voice. He calls his own sheep by name and leads them out. When he has brought out all his own, he goes on ahead of them, and his sheep follow him because they know his voice. But they will never follow a stranger; in fact, they will run away from him because they do not recognise a stranger's voice.
> JOHN 10:2–5

God even promises that he will send his Holy Spirit to help us hear him clearly, and that the Holy Spirit will help us and guide us in this journey of understanding. For example:

> I have much more to say to you, but right now it would be more than you could understand. The Spirit shows what is true and will come and guide you into the full truth. The Spirit doesn't speak on his own. He will tell you only what he has heard from me, and he will let you know what is going to happen. The Spirit will bring glory to me by taking my message and telling it to you. Everything that the Father has is mine. That is why I have said that the Spirit takes my message and tells it to you.
> JOHN 16:12–15 (CEV)

Our lives can be full of God's voice and his communication. Many of us continually long for more of it in our lives, and we want our children to have a lifetime full of connection to God. So what is our role in connecting children to God's heart and voice?

The Eli calling

When Jesus lived on earth, some people brought their children to see him. When the disciples tried to turn them away, Jesus insisted, 'Let the children come to me, and don't try to stop them!' (Matthew 19:14, CEV). He didn't say, 'It is important for children to learn about me. Create some fab church programmes and a ten-step guide to teach children how to treat me correctly, and hopefully some will love me eventually.' He said, 'Let the children come to me, and don't try to stop them.' Children, like all people, have a natural ability to encounter God and an innate desire to be with him.

I think that the real honour and privilege we have in our parenting of children might be described as an 'Eli calling'. Samuel was an Old Testament prophet who guided Saul as the king of Israel and found and anointed King David. He was given to the temple of the Lord as a small child and was raised by a priest named Eli. Take a minute to read this story, paying particular attention to how Eli reacts to Samuel's experience with God. The story is from 1 Samuel 3:1–10 and 15–20 (CEV).

> Samuel served the Lord by helping Eli the priest, who was by that time almost blind. In those days, the Lord hardly ever spoke directly to people, and he did not appear to them in dreams very often. But one night, Eli was asleep in his room, and Samuel was sleeping on a mat near the sacred chest in the Lord's house.

Everyone is in bed. Samuel is sleeping as close to God as he can get, right next to the high-priest-and-God-only room, the Most Holy Place. Eli is evidently in some other place, bedded down for the night.

> They had not been asleep very long when the Lord called out Samuel's name. 'Here I am!' Samuel answered. Then he ran to Eli and said, 'Here I am. What do you want?' 'I didn't call you,' Eli answered. 'Go back to bed.' Samuel went back.

My, what an obedient child! Or just one with a history of getting out of bed a lot! I love Eli's response. Since ancient times, the response to a child out of bed has always been the same.

Again the Lord called out Samuel's name. Samuel got up and went to Eli. 'Here I am,' he said. 'What do you want?' Eli told him, 'Son, I didn't call you. Go back to sleep.'

Notice the very good parenting style here: the firmer tone and the 'return' technique.

The Lord had not spoken to Samuel before, and Samuel did not recognise the voice. When the Lord called out his name for the third time, Samuel went to Eli again and said, 'Here I am. What do you want?' Eli finally realised that it was the Lord who was speaking to Samuel. So he said, 'Go back and lie down! If someone speaks to you again, answer, 'I'm listening, Lord. What do you want me to do?'' Once again Samuel went back and lay down. The Lord then stood beside Samuel and called out as he had done before, 'Samuel! Samuel!' 'I'm listening,' Samuel answered. 'What do you want me to do?'

God told Samuel an important message: we are skipping ahead in the story a bit.

The next morning, Samuel got up and opened the doors to the Lord's house. He was afraid to tell Eli what the Lord had said.

It wasn't good news for Eli.

But Eli told him, 'Samuel, my boy, come here!' 'Here I am,' Samuel answered. Eli said, 'What did God say to you? Tell me everything. I pray that God will punish you terribly if you don't tell me every word he said!' Samuel told Eli everything. Then Eli said, 'He is the Lord, and he will do what's right.' As Samuel grew up, the Lord helped him and made everything Samuel said come true. From the town of Dan in the north to the town of Beersheba in the south, everyone in the country knew that Samuel was truly the Lord's prophet.

I find it very powerful that God chose to speak to Samuel without being asked to. It was Eli's role to point to God's already-existing voice in Samuel's life. It was Eli's job to say, 'That is God speaking,' and to guide Samuel in what to do when he heard God's voice. Eli trusted God enough and respected the child Samuel enough to let them interact with each other without feeling the need to control the conversation. (Remember that this was a time when it was rare to hear the Lord speaking.) Eli then debriefed Samuel after his experience (although I don't recommend threatening the Lord's wrath if you can't get your child to talk!) and modelled how to submit to the word of the Lord with grace and humility.

This was a good spiritual parenting experience, but it could so easily have been missed. With a child out of bed three times in quick succession, Eli could have hit the roof, dragged Samuel back to bed and yelled, 'I *told* you to stay in bed. I am *not* calling you. *No*, you can't have any water, and I *don't want* to see you up again!' Eli was tuned in enough to notice in the middle of the night that God was speaking to this child; to guide Samuel in how to respond; to keep himself out of the middle of the interaction; and to debrief Samuel in the morning to talk about what had happened. Look at the fruit of this encounter in Samuel's life. God's call was established, a lifetime of blessing was begun, and his vocation was planted within him throughout the coming years, from one encounter with the Lord that Eli stewarded well.

God is calling each of us to a similar role. To help our children to connect with God and grow in relationship with him, we need to take Eli's lead and:

- Prepare our children for the ways God speaks.
- Identify in their lives the places where God is moving, and validate their experience with him by guiding them forward in response.
- Debrief them on their experiences, helping them to learn to discern what is and isn't God's voice.
- Proactively show them how we respond to what God is communicating to us and create new situations for them to continue to encounter God.

Preparing children for the ways God speaks

A big question that often pops up from people I work with is 'What if God doesn't say anything to my child?' But we have seen in the Bible that God is talking – first one way, then another – and his plan is for us to know his voice. It isn't a question of trying to get God to speak. God is already speaking to our children; he is already blessing them, touching them, loving them. He is already giving them gifts, whispering in their ears, comforting them and forming them. Our children might just not be aware of it. Samuel didn't even know the Lord when God spoke to him: he couldn't recognise God's voice (1 Samuel 3:7). But God was persistent, and, with God's faithfulness and Eli's partnership in the intended encounter, Samuel's life changed forever.

Catching God's voice

So how do we help children learn to recognise and know God's voice? In talking with children, I use the word 'catching' to mean perceiving God's voice, as it helps children to picture the approach we need. 'Prayer' brings with it all the connotations of restriction and one-way communication. 'Listening' implies that the process is ears-based only so that children can become fixated on 'hearing'. I use the word 'catching' because it implies a readiness and awareness to receive what God wants to communicate with all the tools we have at our disposal.

I explain it to children like this: when God made us, he made us for the whole purpose of hanging out with him, chatting with him, talking back and forth, and being in a relationship with him. So that's how he made our bodies. He made our bodies to catch everything he wants to say to us and, because he is pretty clever, he doesn't talk in words. He talks in a whole bunch of ways that our whole body can catch. When we catch, we need to be ready. It's really hard to catch when we're not looking. God's messages can pass by us unnoticed if we're not aware that he may be trying to communicate to us. Other times, we can forget to keep all our ways of catching ready. We can be so focused on one way that we miss how God is speaking to us. There are several main ways that we can catch what God is saying to us.

With our brains (Acts 2:17–18; 9:10; Joel 2:28)

Pictures or movies in our minds – Take a second to close your eyes and picture your family. When we do this, we are not seeing people with our eyes; we are picturing them in our mind. That same place of picturing is a prime communicating area for God. We can use it to show God pictures of how we feel, our memories or hopes, or what has been happening in our day. He also loves dropping into that place pictures of his own that he wants to show us, movies of how he sees things, and his hopes and dreams and suggestions for us. Children can be very visual and creative, and God often meets with them in this way. Have some pens, colour pencils and paper available for them to draw what God shows to them, so that they don't forget it and so that you can discuss it with them.

Words in our minds – If we can sing in our heads or read a book quietly, we can identify that place in our heads where we can put words and 'hear' things without using our ears. We often chat to God by speaking only inside our heads, and he can chat back to that same place. Some children have full conversations with God, while others 'hear' only words or phrases. God can remind children of Bible verses they may have learnt, and he often gives them a Bible verse reference to look up, which they have never read before, so that he can continue to speak to them through his word. Again, having some paper and writing materials available helps children to solidify their experience in this area.

Guided thoughts – Sometimes, when we are thinking a lot about things, solutions pop into our minds. Other times in our ponderings, we arrive at a place where we feel good about what we have decided. God loves helping us to think about big questions and can participate in that process. This experience is slightly harder for children to identify, but, by their pre-teenage years, they can have begun to hear God's voice in their thinking and decision-making. For example, I was doing some work with pre-teenagers and teenagers in Switzerland, and we were outside spending some free time with God. The children were all over the side of a hill, writing, drawing, swinging, reading and doing whatever enabled them best to connect with God. I noticed that one girl kept staring at the facing hill with fierce determination. God pointed out to me two trees on the hill, isolated in the middle of a huge field, that I felt he wanted to speak to her about. I wandered over and casually said, 'Hey, have you noticed those two trees over there?' I got an excited smile. 'Yeah! God's been showing me them and telling me all about how we are like them.' God was not just dropping words in but guiding her thoughts and speaking to her about trees that had been planted many years ago.

With our ears and eyes (2 Kings 6:10–17; Acts 7:54–56)
Some children hear God's voice audibly sometimes or see things that aren't there for everyone's eyes to see. I have never experienced this kind of communication, but I have worked with adults and children who have. It can be one more normal way of perceiving God.

With our skin (1 Kings 8:10–11)
The skin is the biggest organ of our body, so it makes sense that we can catch a lot from God with it. Common experiences when catching with skin are feelings of warmth or tingles, a heavy head, or sometimes the feeling of a hand on the back. It's important for children to understand that this is just one of the ways we can catch from God. Some people experience it often, and some people rarely do, just like all the other ways. I tend to avoid describing it in detail to children, as I never want to suggest to them what 'should' happen or encourage them to perform. I just let them know that they may catch in that way and watch what happens. When they describe to me their experience of catching with their skin, if it sounds right, then I validate it.

One child new to catching from God complained that a big hand kept resting on his back while he lay on the ground and listened to God, but when we watched, we could confirm that no one was around him. Another four-year-old described to her mother that, when she prayed before going to sleep, she felt God putting things into her hands. These are normal experiences that aren't to be overpraised or unacknowledged. It is just another way that we can catch from God.

With our feelings or emotions (John 14:27; Philippians 4:7; 1 Peter 1:8–9)

God created emotions, and we can catch these from him if we are willing. Often, children who are ready to catch with their emotions can receive his peace, excitement, joy and sense of justice in wonderful ways.

With our guts (1 Corinthians 12:8; John 4:1–9)

This is the feeling that you know that you know! Anyone who is open to catching from God can get a feeling of what God wants them to do or a sense of the rightness or wrongness of a situation. If children are playing a game that is a little dodgy, a child who is open to God can often feel a strong sense that it is 'wrong' and decide not to participate. Other times, children may feel strongly that they need to pray for someone or ask someone a question. They can't necessarily tell you why, but they sense that God is nudging them in a certain direction.

In dreams (Genesis 20:3; Matthew 2:13; Job 33:14–18)

God speaks in dreams, and our children can catch some great stuff from God while they sleep. Not every dream is from God, but, every once in a while, they will get a sense that maybe God was trying to tell them something in a dream. A notebook next to the bed can enable children to write their dreams down if they want to so that you can discuss them together.

* * *

God speaks in various ways and, as individuals, we are all unique, catching better in some ways than in others. Eventually, we all develop our own patterns of how and when we catch God best. It is wonderful to see children develop in different ways: some connect with God best outside in nature, as God guides their thoughts of him; others love quiet, and solitude inside as God shows them Bible verses; while others paint conversations with him in pictures. While it is good to encourage children to develop their preferences, it is also important that we keep presenting them with new options and new experiences, training them to stay open to every way of perceiving God, so they don't miss anything that God has for them.

'What happens if children don't catch? I don't want my child to feel left out or ignored by God. I don't want him to feel hurt and then walk away from his faith.' This is a question that I get asked whenever I speak at an event. It is an understandable question. Each one of us has had a specific, unique journey and relationship with God. We have experiences that we cherish in our lives with him, and we all have questions, doubts and struggles. Somewhere along the road, some of us have been wounded or felt that God has let us down, specifically when it comes to hearing God speak. Many of us have felt the sting of longing to hear God's voice at a particular moment in time and finding that it didn't happen. This experience may have significantly shaken our faith, or it may not even have surprised us.

The problem is that sometimes we pass on those questions, doubts and struggles to our children as truth, in our words, advice and guidance. We let them attach to our children and then feel hurt for them as they struggle under the weight of our difficulties. My view is that learning how to live in relationship with God is not as easy as we would like to make it for children. We are all on a journey of relationship, learning to hear and access God's voice in our lives. We are on the journey, and our children are on the journey. To say that we want our child's journey of connection to God to be always uncomplicated and successful is unrealistic, and doesn't serve them well. Our privilege is to help them learn how to walk this relational path with God, not hide it from them. We get to walk with them through joy and success and struggle. We get to shape their experiences for them so that they can view their 'disappointments' from a more positive and proactive perspective.

Will there be times when your child doesn't catch God? Yes; absolutely. That is the reality of living as imperfect people in a broken world. But the goal isn't to have a successful moment of catching from God; the goal is to develop a consistent connection with him, and we can teach children how to handle all aspects of that connection. When a child is struggling to catch, I validate that experience as well. I say, 'That's okay; I sometimes find it hard, too. Sometimes my brain is too busy, or my heart is too loud, or sometimes I just can't connect. But we do know that God loves us, is talking to us and wants us to know his voice. So we'll keep being open to him. Why don't you tell God how you feel about it? Sometimes I feel cross, or sad, or both. Why don't you tell him?' If your child is continually struggling, have a look in the FAQs where there is more help for what to do if your child seems to be perpetually stuck.

Helping our children on the journey

I firmly believe that God is already talking to our children, and it is our job to help them identify this. We have been given the opportunity to direct their attention to their lives and say, 'Look! That's God!' Sometimes God speaks clearly to them without their being briefed on the experience at all. Once children open up to the possibility that God may speak to them, and they begin to understand and experience his doing so, it can happen anywhere at any time – in the back of the car, at school, at bedtime or while they sleep.

At some moments, as he did with Samuel, God speaks to our children, and they come to us in the middle of an exchange with him. Often, this happens when children unexpectedly become aware that God may have spoken to them out of the blue or in response to their questions. Children can be so shocked to catch God speaking that they completely disengage from the experience to come to tell us. These are the times when children need us to help them identify God's voice, validate their experience and guide them to know what to do next. It is important that we celebrate with them when this happens, but the goal for their lives isn't to manage to hear God's voice but to engage in a relationship with him.

We can be overjoyed for our children that they and God are meeting up, and we can give them suggestions for what to do next. Most of the time, we may simply need to guide them to reconnect with God, so they can finish the encounter that they or he started. Sometimes, children need validation to feel encouraged to go back to their encounter. Sometimes, like Samuel, they need more directions for how to respond.

A good approach is to ask your child a natural follow-up question. One mum in my church told me a story of her nine-year-old daughter, Natalie. She was sitting in the back seat of the car while her mum drove. All of a sudden, she gasped and said, 'I was thinking about school and my friends, and God showed me a picture of a dolphin jumping and diving in the sea!' 'That's great, sweetie! Why do you think he showed you that picture?' asked her mum. 'I don't know!' Natalie replied, picking up her book to start reading. 'Well, why don't you ask him?' her mum suggested. 'Um, okay!' Natalie put the book down and looked out of the window, reconnecting with God. After a few seconds, she piped up: 'He said that my heart was the sea and he was the dolphin, and he was going to dive in and play with me in my heart. Close and fun-like.' Natalie smiled broadly. Natalie's mum had been able very gently to turn her child back to God to complete the conversation that God had started, just by asking a question and nudging her back to the place of receiving.

One four-year-old boy, Jonathan, told his mother about two dreams he'd had on two successive days, which he thought were from God. The first day, he said, he and Jesus were on a donkey going to Jerusalem. They were having a great time, singing songs and laughing. Then they came to a river and Jonathan said, 'Jesus, what is that?' Jesus said, 'It's me! Any time you are sad or lonely, you can drink it, and I'll be with you!' His mother's jaw dropped, and everything in her wanted to launch into a three-point explanation of the significance of the symbolism of water and Jesus, but one look at his face stopped her. Jesus had revealed a part of himself to Jonathan, and it was perfect for him. She just said, 'Yep, that sounds like a dream from God to me.' His little face scrunched up as he nodded and said, 'I think so, too.'

She nodded with him and replied, 'Sounds like you are catching some good things from God in your dreams. I'm looking forward to hearing about any more you think God has given you.'

The next day, Jonathan came back to her. He suffered quite badly from nightmares and had recently been up for significant portions of the night, several nights a week. Jonathan said that he'd had another dream in which he and Jesus were back on the donkey, heading for Jerusalem. A lot of scary black monsters ran towards them, trying to attack and pull Jonathan off the donkey. Jonathan was very scared but Jesus said, 'Don't be scared. I have given you some of my power. Tell them to go away because I said so.' Jonathan said, 'Okay,' squinted his eyes, put his hand out in a stop sign and said very loudly, 'You guys go away because of Jesus.' Instantly, the black scary monsters screamed and went away. His mother confirmed to him that it seemed that God had given him a great dream with some good advice, and that if he ever had another nightmare, he should do what Jesus told him to do.

Jonathan's mum reported to me weeks later that, occasionally, she still heard her son squeak out in the middle of the night, 'Go away because of Jesus' power inside me.' When she checked on him, he was snuggled in bed with a smile on his face. He slept through the rest of the night, undisturbed. She could see the fruit of her 'Eli calling' night after night in her son's sleep.

Debrief and discern

The morning after God had spoken to Samuel, Eli made sure he asked what God had said. We are the mature and wise people whom God has placed in our children's lives to help them process their encounters with him. We are also the people whose job it is to help them learn to recognise God's voice. It is so amazing to hear our children tell us of their encounters with God and how they are doing in their relationship with him. We can help to guide their thinking and ask crucial questions that make them think hard about how those conversations with God affect the choices in their lives.

It is also our job, though, to make sure our children have the skills to recognise when the voice they hear is not from God and to know what to do about it. This responsibility terrifies many people, and I understand their concern. We don't want our children running around thinking every thought that pops into their head is from God. But, for many of us, this means that we have shied away from wanting our children to connect with God, for fear of opening the 'floodgates of ambiguity', as one parent put it.

I am not scared by this, as I see part of my job as helping my child learn to distinguish God's voice from other voices. Remember the passage in John that talks about the shepherd leading his sheep? 'His sheep follow him because they know his voice. But they will never follow a stranger; in fact, they will run away from him because they do not recognise a stranger's voice' (John 10:4–5). Connecting to God involves a process of learning to recognise God's voice so that eventually we know it so well that we can boldly reject any other voice that tries to pass as his. If I called to your children, they would probably ignore me or stay away from me, even if I used their names. When you call your children, though, they recognise your voice because, over the years of their lives, they have become attuned to it (even if they pretend not to hear!). They will learn to recognise God's voice only by perceiving it over and over again, with you helping them to identify and affirm it accurately. The more they experience it, the more they will know it and begin to recognise it on their own. Children need to learn how to take what they catch and make sure that it is from God.

Three measures of discernment

Does it sound like God?
When our children begin to catch from God, one of the first things to teach them is assessing whether what they are perceiving matches what we know about God from the Bible. Does what they are catching align with the God that we know?

Children do this kind of thing all the time in their everyday lives. For example, let's assume you have always told your children that they can never drink blackcurrant squash in the living room. Their world will end if they drink blackcurrant squash in the living room; all their privileges will grind to a halt if they drink blackcurrant squash in the living room. It has been like this for their whole lives. What would happen if I came over to your house and said to your children, 'Hey, let's take this blackcurrant squash into the living room and drink it on your parents' white sofa? Your parents said it would be all right'? There is no way they would believe me. It has nothing to do with me: they know you, and there is no way you would say that. Anything that they perceive in their encounter with God must be held up to the same sort of standard.

This is one of the times when it helps to be both God-smart and God-connected! If your six-year-old child is chatting to God after putting in a terrible performance at a flute recital, and if she feels rubbish and thinks that God thinks she should give up the flute because she will never be any good, you can help her hold that experience up to God's character and his word, saying, 'Hmm, I'm not sure that sounds like something God would say. Let's see. We know that God loves us and loves to be involved with us. We also know that his voice brings us encouragement and joy. It sounds as if you feel hurt and put down by those words. I don't think that was God at all. I think we can throw those words away. They don't get to stay in your head.'

It's vital that we don't only help children to discern God's voice, but also teach them what to do, when they are tuning in to God, with thoughts that aren't from him. Any thoughts that are potentially damaging to themselves or other people don't get to stay in their heads. I explain to children that they can put those negative words or pictures in a box in their head and shrink it until the box disappears, because God doesn't want us to let those thoughts hang around. God only wants us to have positive ideas in our minds (Philippians 4:8).

What is the fruit?
God wants to draw us close to him, to encourage us, to give us hope, to take us on the journey of becoming more like him. If what we perceive from him makes us want to distance ourselves from him, then it probably isn't from God. Even when God convicts us of sin, it is to show us his grace and to invite us to put aside what is holding us back. I tell children that if they feel afraid or as if they want to run away from God, then this probably isn't from God and we can put that out of our heads. God's communication will always draw us in.

What do wise people think?
God has put us in a community of people who also are connected to God, so if we aren't sure what God is communicating to us, we can write it down and talk about it with others. It is still up to us to decide for ourselves what God is saying, but other people can help. Sometimes other people can be wrong, but getting their input can be helpful if we aren't sure.

* * *

Discernment is a journey that we all are on, but you are a gift to your kids as you walk alongside them while they find their own path.

Proactively model and create new situations

Modelling

We are perfectly positioned to model to our children how to catch God's voice. God has placed our children in our homes so that we can walk with them as we go on our faith journeys. They are like sponges, soaking up what they see as we pioneer the journey ahead of them, so we need to provide a framework from which they can deal with any spiritual issue that heads their way.

Children need to see us engaging in this aspect of our relationship with God. They need to see how we catch his voice and what impact it has on us. We need to remember to create windows into our experiences of catching from God. If you keep a journal, you could occasionally show your children some pages that you feel are appropriate to share. Talk about how God's voice has influenced the way you feel about current situations, or helped to shape your decisions. Take Bible verses that God has used to encourage you and stick them on your mirror so that your children can see how to use God's words to remind them of his truth. Invite them to catch what God has to say to you. In my prayer journal, I have several handwritten notes and drawings that children in my church have received from God to pass to me. I cherish them very much, and so do the children.

Creating new opportunities to connect with God

At the end of the story of Eli and Samuel, we see the fruit of their encounter with God. The Lord is with Samuel as he grows up and eventually becomes universally hailed as a mighty prophet of God. To me, this implies that there were many more encounters as Samuel grew in his relationship with God and his ability to identify and discern God's voice. We, too, need to be continually looking at how to encourage our children to step into these encounters again and again. Remember, these are individual times of building a relationship with God that you can help your children to identify – a bit like setting times for friends to come home to play or scheduling visits. Eventually, the goal is for your children to handle all of that themselves, but, until they do, you can help.

Journal – Many children love the tangibility of a journal. In it, they can record conversations they have with God (a common practice); pictures from God or to God; things God says; memories that God reminds them of; letters to God; and so on. It also gives children a record of God's encounters with them for those wobbly days that all of us have, when we are convinced that God never speaks to us. They will have a whole book to prove otherwise.

Bedtime – This is a great time to create space for your children to hear from God. You can build into the bedtime routine a two- to ten-minute span when you play worship music, and your children chat and catch with God, or write in their journals.

Family times or family decisions – If a family decision is coming up, you could try asking the whole family to spend some time catching from God about it. Then everyone can come together as a family and discuss what God is saying to you all.

Reading a story – This is a fantastic way of helping children engage with God. Take a quality children's book and, when you have finished reading it to your children, suggest a question to ask God and catch his answer. For example, Max Lucado's book *You are Special* is about a wooden man named Punchinello who lives in a town where the inhabitants give shiny stars and black dots to praise and tear down each other.[5] Punchinello eventually learns that it doesn't matter what the other people say; it is what his master thinks about him that counts. The more he cares about his master's view of him, the less those stars and dots stick to him. After reading, it would be very easy to say, 'Sometimes we all feel worried about what other people say about us, but it is more important to know what God thinks about us. Why don't we ask him?' Take some space for you both to catch from God what he says, and discuss it.

Asking questions – Sometimes children need to be helped to see when a question would be a good one to take to God. The Bible says that the Holy Spirit will 'guide you into all the truth' (John 16:13), so we should encourage our children to feel free to ask God anything they want. 'Sounds like a good thing to ask God' can become a standard phrase in your house.

These opportunities to connect with God will be original and personal to each of your children. Every child is different, and you will be able to create what each of your children needs, based on how well you know them.

8

Keeping it going

Parenting children for faith is a grand adventure. It is always changing, always shifting, always new. In the previous two chapters we looked at the foundational approaches of chatting and catching in helping our kids connect directly to God in prayer. But after we get them going in it, then what?

We keep discipling them in their connection with God, wherever that leads next. Often we as parents get stuck here. How do we proactively build into our children the values, habits and character that God is looking for? How do we keep proactively helping our kids connect with God past teaching them to chat and catch? It can feel overwhelming to look at everything that we could be doing spiritually with our kids and try to figure out what is the right thing to do.

Parenting for faith is simply a process of asking ourselves and God, 'What is the next step for my child spiritually, and how can I help them take it?' We don't need to get overwhelmed by everything that we might do. We can do what is in front of us and take the next step.

You may not know it, but you already have great skills in proactively discipling your kid using what I call 'the six-stage circle'. As I have parented and worked in churches as a children's minister or youth worker, I have noticed that the most effective way of discipling a child is to take them on a journey, gently but deliberately. I find it useful to see this discipleship as a circle, one stage leading to another, as shown in the diagram opposite.

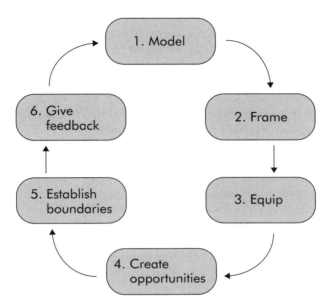

Here's an example of how the six-stage circle works. I have a friend who loves Leeds United. His children love Leeds United. My friend didn't have to convince his children about the merits of the football club or worry that they wouldn't like Leeds United when they grew up. He didn't restrain himself from trying to influence his children's choice of football team until they were 'old enough to choose for themselves'. Completely unconsciously, he discipled his children into a love of Leeds United, using this circle.

- He *modelled* what living a life loving this football club meant. He couldn't not do so! He watched the matches on television, wore the T-shirts, defended his team vigorously to others in front of his children, cheered when they won, was gutted when they lost, and knew all the details of all the players and told his children all about them.
- He sat his children down and *framed* for them how the game was played, how the coach was strategising, and why he loved this club so much. He framed for them why he attended the matches, who he went with, and where they sat and why.
- From the time his children were tiny, he was *equipping* them to love the team. He covered them in Leeds United kit: onesies, hats, scarves and pennants. He played football with them outside and chose to 'be' a certain player when playing. He bought them posters and taught them all they needed to know to be able to talk about player transfers and offside injustices.

- He *created opportunities* for his children to experience the team, watching matches on television with them, and even letting them stay up late to watch the big matches. The momentous day arrived when he took his children to see the team play live in the stadium. Eventually, as they grew, these outings became a key part of their father–child bonding times.
- This father light-heartedly *established boundaries*, swearing off the flying of any other colours in the house and jokingly ribbing his friends who supported another team. His children knew who he wanted them to support.
- He gave his children fantastic *feedback* by roaring with laughter when they voiced an opinion in line with his own. He swept them up in a hug when they were indignant about a referee call. He listened to their questions carefully and answered with focus and passion.

Whether it's passing on our love of a football team or showing our kids how to clean the house, this circle is often present in our parenting. When we harness this natural process deliberately to disciple our children spiritually, it can be a powerful tool.

You see, we were placed in our children's lives to do this easily. Each of these stages is a natural part of our lives with our children. We naturally live life in front of our children, talk to them about what is happening, equip them to do things for themselves, create opportunities for them to try things out, establish boundaries for them to live within, and chat to them about how their behaviour impacts others.

Any value we want to instil in our children can be worked around this basic progress circle. Whether it's a love of musicals or *Star Trek*, or how to eat healthily or use power tools, we naturally utilise these stages. Anything we want them to begin to own as a core value or belief, we can simply choose to 'take around the circle'. It doesn't require a lot of time or effort, just a choice.

The problem is that with faith we often miss out on doing the complete circle. We default to using just two stages: modelling ('See what I do? Okay, now you do it!') and creating boundaries ('In this family, we go to church!') Discipleship is coaching our children in their relationship with God, not enforcing religious activity. If we want to truly disciple our children in their relationship with God, then we need to start including all the stages of the circle.

For instance, with chatting and catching:

- *Model* – Are we creating windows into our chat-and-catch life? Do our kids hear us chatting and see you catching?

- *Frame* – Do we talk to our kids about how we catch from God? Have we framed for them how it can look different in various people?
- *Equip* – We all need equipping in chatting and catching. Sometimes our children need longer for us to lead them in it. But if we find them getting reliant on us, then train them how to do it themselves. Have them tell stories to God, or suggest different things for you to chat to God about collectively. Go on adventures or challenges, where they learn new ways of chatting with God: while riding a bike or at the beach. Try new ways of catching. Talk about how to handle it if they are struggling to catch and give them ways out of it. Equip them for their next steps.
- *Create opportunities* – Just because our children know how to chat and catch, doesn't mean they don't need us to show them where all the opportunities are. Chat in the shop; whisper, 'Let's ask God for one thing he wants us to do while we walk to school'; pause when you are stressed and ask them to pray for you to catch peace. Create opportunities that give them a chance to try, and that expand their idea of where and how they can connect with God.
- *Establish boundaries* – If we are having a time of chatting and catching, it's okay to give boundaries. We can tell our children, 'This is our time to connect with God, and you can do that any way you want. You can lie there with God, chat to him, catch from him, draw a picture, sing a song, or even sit and be bored. But you can't distract other people or interrupt their connection with God. Okay?'
- *Give feedback* – When your children pray for you, tell them afterwards what God did. When you hear them chatting, tell them how excited you are that they and God have a good connection. Show them the fruit of their connection with God in their lives, such as: 'Since you've been connecting with God, I feel like you've been more peaceful or less worried. Is that true?'

This six-stage circle is key for us as spiritual parents. From Bible-reading, to loving people well, to cultivating a heart of joy, to serving with humility – whatever you want to train in your kids – have a think through the six-stage circle and consider how you want to begin to disciple your children in it.

9

Surfing the waves

One thing you will notice about your child's connection with God is that it seems to come in waves. They are really into watching *Friends and Heroes*, and then they go off it. They are having a great time during bedtime prayer, and then suddenly it's like wrestling an antelope to get them to focus. They like reading the Bible, and then they hate it. They don't believe in God, and then spend 15 minutes singing along to a worship CD. Wave after wave, things come up; interest arises and then it disappears. Our lives with them also go in waves. We move to a new house, and it seems all of life is about this seasonal wave; someone gets sick, and it knocks us all sideways. It can make us feel unsure about what is happening.

This is one of the main reasons why we can't rely on our children's interest or experience to establish in them a deep connection to God. Our children need a proactive parent, one who talks about God and grows their children's faith. But that doesn't mean that these waves aren't useful. When used alongside the tools we have already learned, the waves of our children's interest can create great opportunities to do spiritual parenting well.

All we need to do is learn how to surf.

Lessons from surfing 1: not every wave is your wave

When you sit on a beach, you notice that the waves are never-ending. They come large and small, but they keep coming. Some are better for surfing than others. I love watching surfers dodge waves, judging them to be not quite right. Other waves are perfect for surfing, but the surfers aren't in the right position to catch them. Surfers don't feel under pressure to catch every wave. They jump on the ones they can and let the others pass by.

Our children's spiritual lives are like the ocean. Their circumstances, brain development, personality and interests – the things God is growing in them – generate waves. Don't feel bad if you miss out on a spiritual wave that is happening in your kid's life.

Your child asks an excellent question about God, but you are busy telling off your other kid and you just snap at them to ask it later. Your son is reading a book, and you come up to tell him to go to bed, but only after you turn off the light do you realise you have just interrupted your kid reading the Bible. Don't worry. Waves aren't limited. You catch the ones you can. Don't stress about the ones you can't.

Lessons from surfing 2: see the waves in your child's life

A novice surfer can see only that there is a wave coming. An experienced surfer can see from afar what waves are worth catching and why, based on size, colour, shape, speed and so on. You will learn to see the waves in your child's life. One of the most significant skills we can learn is how to spot a wave of our children's spiritual life coming. Identifying these waves takes experience with our children and knowledge of what the pattern of waves looks like in their lives. At first we won't see much, but we will get better. Too often we think that the only things to be seen are obvious questions that our children ask, such as 'Why does God let bad things happen?' But there is so much more to look for.

- *Interests* – What is your child interested in at the moment? It might be books, bands, sport, anything. Sometimes your kid becomes obsessed with something. Notice it.
- *Curiosity* – Often your child will get curious about what you are doing, hover around the worship team after church, or watch an old person carefully walking. They may sneak on to the stairs to listen to your midweek group meet in your house, or protest at having to go to bed when a church meeting is happening in your living room. Something is happening in your child that you can capture.
- *Anger* – Bill Hybels calls this 'holy discontent'. What gets them angry? What do they talk the most about? In church what is the thing that annoys them most? Often you will find that if they vigorously dislike something, that can be a wave that is useful to surf as well. It may be showing you where their passions are and where they want to be purposeful.
- *Stories they act out* – You may find your child obsessed with being the rescuer, being the protector, bringing justice or caring for those stuffed animals that need healing. There is a wave of something rising inside them that you can notice.
- *Spontaneous ideas* – Sometimes your kid will come up with a weird and fun idea: church at home; sleeping with their Bible strapped to their head or under their pillow; raising money for twinned toilets; or listening to the same Bible story a thousand times.

The waves come big and small. They happen daily, and they are well worth watching for. Some we may recognise but need to let go past for many reasons – we may not be in the right position, we may have recognised it too late, or it may be too small to bother with. The more we learn to recognise the waves, the more we can choose which we want to surf.

Lessons from surfing 3: paddle at the right speed

To catch a wave, a surfer has to paddle at the same speed as the wave. Too slow and they will miss it; too fast and they aren't surfing. Once we see a wave rising in our child's spiritual lives, our job is to paddle – to come alongside our children at the same pace as their wave. We can often get excited and try to jump ahead and lead them in it, but that will result in us not surfing the wave well.

Have you ever discovered a new song or band you like? You are grooving along, then the song ends and you think, 'That was amazing!' A wave of interest has arisen. It is wonderful when your friend replies, 'You like that? Have you heard their other song? You are going to love this!' and plays you a brilliant second track. You are hooked! You end up binge-buying music tracks. But what would have happened if your friend either completely blanked you and never helped you find the next track, or grabbed your phone and made you a five-hour playlist with all the 'must listen to' tracks in order of their inspiration so you could understand the history of the song's development? It would kill your interest.

But when someone comes alongside you just at your pace and facilitates your next step, it's genius. Our children's waves are the same. To catch a wave, we need the right pace. Our child asks a question about the Bible and either we overreact ('Oh, you are interested in the Bible – let's do a family devotional every day and memorise scripture and have a one-year reading plan!') or we decide just to sit back and see what happens; both times, the wave passes. To catch the wave, all we need to do is come alongside them, at the pace the child is moving. If they ask a question, answer it and ask another. If the conversation wanders, follow them. Look at the six-stage circle and see what stage would be helpful for their next step.

Lessons from surfing 4: the wave lasts as long as it lasts

Surfers can ride a wave for five seconds, 15 seconds or for what seems like forever. Sometimes the wave looks like it will last a long time, but then it suddenly breaks on top of the surfer. Waves can be unpredictable in their length and strength. Surfers simply try to ride a wave as long as they can and then swim back out for the next one.

The waves of our children's lives are similar. Some spiritual waves may look great, and then collapse quickly. Our child may be passionate about mission, but by the time we have bought a biography of a famous missionary in the country she is interested in, she has decided she isn't interested at all. Other waves may last longer than you think – a thousand questions at bedtime, wanting to hear the same CD over and over, or listening again and again to the same worship song. It's worth staying with it, even if you are getting impatient. The moment is now, so ride it and follow their lead. It may take sacrifice – longer at bedtime or that extra conversation or time during the school run.

All waves break eventually. Be prepared to let them go gracefully. We've all had the experience of trying to continue with something that our kid doesn't want to do. This isn't homework; it's their wave. When you see the wave begin to peter out, bail out before it breaks. It's okay. Don't be disappointed or worry that they are backsliding. There will be another wave.

Stories of surfing

One mum brought her one-year-old to a conference I was speaking at. We were talking about how to surf the waves of our children's spiritual lives when, during the closing worship, this tiny child crawled down the centre aisle to the base of the stage and stared at the band playing. The parent came to pick up the child, to carry her to the back, but paused and decided to see where this baby's curiosity would lead. It seems so simple to ride the wave of a child's interest in worship, but it took a choice from this mum to sit on the floor in the front of the room and allow her child's wave to continue. Her child sat on her lap as she whispered that God was here and music helps us connect with him. We all watched as the one-year-old sat transfixed for the next 30 minutes, well past the end of the session, as the band continued to play. She was unusually peaceful. Later the mum told me that she had never seen her child sit still for that long, and she felt that God was doing something significant. The mum asked for the recording of the session and told me later that every night that week, the child listened to that recording over and over again with the same sense of peace.

One six-year-old I know suddenly decided that she wanted to take notes on a flip chart as the preacher was talking, in order to make it easier for people to remember the sermon. Her parents thought they would surf the random idea wave that was rising in their child to see where it would go. They decided to create an opportunity for their child to try it. They got a piece of flip chart paper, asked the leader if it would be all right, and made space for their daughter to take notes. They allowed their daughter to not go out to the children's group, but stay in the sermon and take notes at the side of the church, so as not to distract from the sermon, but still be visible if anyone wanted to look. They laid down the boundary that as soon as their child got distracted or bored, she should stop and go to the children's group. This child had previously had no interest in listening to a sermon. For the entire 45-minute talk, this six-year-old took copious notes summarising each point. She left the service feeling incredibly empowered and useful to people in the room. She never did it again, but it did shift how she felt about church. She began to feel needed.

Whether it's a love of stickers, their interest in the book you are reading, a new passion for art, or a desire to become an entrepreneur, our children's lives are full of waves. These waves are opportunities to disciple our children. Enjoy it. It can be a grand adventure.

10

Praying with children

We had just finished the funeral in the back garden. Her older brothers had quickly run off to continue playing, but Alice was still beside herself with grief. At eight years old, it was her first experience of death, and she was taking it quite hard, especially as it was such a close friend who had died – her pet gerbil, Wonder. I saw her run up the stairs to her room. Her father, Kevin, followed her up and sat down next to her as she curled up on her bed, looking woefully at the empty cage on the desk opposite. They had had many discussions over the past day about death and sadness, but Alice still seemed to be experiencing a lot of conflict.

Kevin decided that Alice needed some help processing her grief, and he thought that connecting with God about it might enable her to begin to move on. Kevin gently suggested to Alice that he would like to help her have a chat with God about what had happened and how she was feeling. 'Oh yes, Daddy, please,' she replied. 'Could you ask God to help Wonder have a good time in heaven?' Tears welled up in her eyes. Kevin thought, 'Help a dead gerbil have a good time in heaven? This is going to be interesting.' Kevin smiled at his daughter. 'Okay, darling, I'm going to chat to God a little bit, and then I'm going to stop, and we are going to be quiet for a while. While we are quiet, you can chat to God about how you feel, and I want you to wait and catch with your whole body what God wants to give you. After a while, I'll check on you to see how it's going, okay?' Alice sniffled. 'Okay, Daddy,' she replied.

Kevin put his big hand lightly on her back while Alice closed her eyes, as she liked to do whenever she caught from God. Kevin began: 'Father God, you love us so much. God, Alice is feeling very sad, and her heart hurts very much because Wonder died. He was such a fantastic friend to Alice, and she is feeling scared about what life will be like without him. Please come and speak to her.' He paused. 'Now let's wait,' he said. Seconds ticked by while he watched his daughter's face as she connected with God, and he saw her body relax. He could sense that she was chatting with God and that he was connecting back.

After about two minutes, Kevin felt it was right to check on how she was doing, so he asked gently, 'How's it going? What has God been doing?' Alice opened her eyes and smiled a little. 'He feels sad for me', she explained. 'He said that Wonder was a gift he gave me and that he will give me more gifts like that – friends and things that help me feel safe inside and happy inside. He showed me a picture of him sitting in my room with me when I get lonely and think of how much I miss Wonder. I feel quieter. It's nice.' Kevin smiled. 'Good, I'm glad,' he responded. 'Do you want to spend more time with God, or have you finished?' Alice shrugged and said, 'I've finished.' 'Do you want to write down what God said or draw the picture in your journal?' asked Kevin. 'Yes, but not right now. I'm going to go and play with James and Pete,' she concluded. As Alice ran down the stairs, Kevin breathed a sigh of relief and thanked God for his faithfulness to minister to the broken-hearted.

For the most part, when we train and empower children to build a relationship with God by catching his voice in their daily lives, it requires little involvement on our part in the actual encounters. Sometimes, though, our involvement is very helpful. There are times in all of our lives when situations are overwhelming or it is difficult to see a way out of them. We may feel trapped in our feelings, locked into a corner or just pushed down by others. Often, in specific times of grief, hurt, bullying, difficult family situations or intense social conflicts, our children need our proactive intervention to help them connect with God, just to get the ball rolling and to reopen that area for them in their lives. If you see your children looking lost, struggling to connect with God or lacking confidence in themselves, it might help to offer to pray with them.

Here our approach to praying with our children will be slightly different from that in the situation we discussed in Chapter 7: this time, we are playing an active role in the encounter with God, while still ensuring that we are not in the middle of it. Our main role in these situations is to connect our children to God in a way that empowers their relationship with him and doesn't make them dependent on us to continue the connection.

It is a very simple model that ensures consistency with all we have been teaching them about the connection to God but still places us in a position of influence and assistance. I will explain the model and then include a few stories so that you can see how it works out in different situations.

Understand

As always, it helps if we can get a handle on what the issue is. I have made so many mistakes by assuming that I know what the problem is or by minimising the issue, instead of taking an extra ten seconds to make sure I clearly hear what is being said.

Explain

Take a couple of seconds to explain what is going to happen. Adults may have people praying with them regularly, but for children, it can be a new experience. For the first few times, it helps to let the child know how it is going to go. Children find safety in knowing what you are going to do, what God is going to do, and what you expect them to do. They especially need to be told how they will know when it's over. I often ask children to close their eyes and hold their hands out loosely in front of them as if they were ready to receive a gift from someone. For many children, this helps them to be aware of and open to what God is doing.

Touch

Touching our children while we pray together is natural and biblical. It helps them know that you are there and not going away, and it empowers them to feel braver in opening themselves up to what God wants to do with them. I find that a simple light hand on the shoulder does the trick. If the hand is too heavy or moves around, it can distract the other person from their connection with God, so make sure your child is comfortable.

Pray

The purpose of the prayer isn't mainly to pray for our child but to guide them to God so that they can meet with him. This can be hard to do because we love praying for our children and we love talking a lot when we pray. Our children don't need us to speak to God for them, though; they need us to help bring them to God so that they can talk to him themselves. If we fall into the trap of praying in long and complicated sentences, we can communicate to our children that the way we pray is important, and that we are much better at it than they are. They may begin to become dependent on our prayers, instead of feeling empowered in their own connection. We will be most effective if we focus on a few guidelines.

- Instead of repeating the facts of the situation, communicate to God the heart of the matter. In the case of the dead gerbil, Alice mainly wanted God to help her gerbil have a good time in heaven. The heart of the matter was that Alice was hurting and scared, so that is what her father brought to God.
- Keep your prayer to three or four simple sentences. This helps the child to stay engaged and focused on the upcoming encounter instead of being bored and

disengaged because you are doing the praying for them. Even if the child's house blew down, his cat is missing, his school hours have extended until eight in the evening, and all of his friends have decided they won't play with him anymore, we can still reduce our prayer to three sentences. (I would suggest, 'Father God, Joey's life is going crazy right now, and he is feeling all sorts of feelings. He feels lost and angry and sad, and he needs your help. Please come now and calm the storm in his heart and mind so that he and you can meet, and you can give him what he needs to make it through.') It is worth practising this in advance: when issues arise in your child's life, think, 'How would I pray about this in three sentences?' so that you are ready with the skills when you need them.

- Try to keep the invitation vague at the end. When I ask God to minister to children, I try to stay as open as possible to what God wants to do. It would have been very easy for Kevin to ask God to bring peace and comfort to his daughter Alice, but this would have influenced Alice to be expecting only those gifts from God. Instead, Alice got something very different. There are definitely circumstances where specific requests are helpful, and we should feel free to ask for specific things from God, but, as a general principle, I try to stay open. God knows what my child needs much better than I do.

- Don't say, 'Amen.' Often, children hear 'Amen' as 'The end' and disengage. Instead say to the child, 'Now let's wait while you and God chat and catch with each other. I'll check on you in a bit.'

Wait

Waiting can be the hardest part of the prayer for us, as we have no control over anything but ourselves in the deafening silence. This is when our faith truly goes on the line because we tell our children, 'Now you and God get to meet,' and we have to trust that God is faithful to be there. Everything in us is screaming, 'God, you'd better be here speaking to my child and giving her what she needs because this child is precious to me and I want her to know you, so don't disappoint her. Now, God, speak now!' while we keep calm and confident smiles on our faces, waiting and watching.

Knowing our tendency to rush this part of prayer, I would encourage you to wait for an average of 30 seconds before moving on. That's 30 real-life seconds, not counting to 30 as fast as you can! Another good measure is to wait as long as you can bear, then wait ten seconds more. At first, we think, 'My child will never sit still that long,' but that is only because we have never seen them wait in prayer, or because we haven't trained them to do so. If a child's eyes pop open before the minimum time is up, I often say, 'Not yet; let's wait a bit more so that you can catch from God.' My minimum waiting times tend to be ten seconds for children up to five years old, 30 seconds for five to sevens, and between 30 seconds and one minute for children over eight. Having said that, I've seen under-fives waiting for ten minutes, five to sevens having a blast with God for 15 minutes, and nine-year-olds out for 45 minutes to an hour, so there is no hard-and-fast rule. My 30-second guideline is meant more for those of us who tend to rush than for the children who are meeting with God.

It is important that we keep our eyes open and watch our child to see how they are doing, but try not to read too much into what we see. Adults become adept at showing other people how they feel when they pray, but children are often without that device. 'Bored' often looks the same as 'having an amazing encounter with God', so trust that God is speaking. Feel free to pray silently for your child while he or she is meeting with God, while also keeping track of time.

Check

When you feel it is right, quietly ask your child an open-ended question such as 'How is it going?', 'How are you feeling?' or 'What has God been doing?' Checking in this way is often harder than we think, as our brains may freeze and we end up asking, 'Did God say anything?' or 'What did you catch?' These sorts of questions may imply that either God or our children might fail. Open-ended questions allow our children to process their experience, no matter what it was.

It's possible that we may interrupt a good conversation or experience that the child hasn't finished yet and may want to get back to. (I have been told by numerous children when I checked in on them, 'Shhh, you're interrupting God,' or 'We're busy!') If in response to your question, you get 'Good' or 'He's helping me,' I would suggest you say, 'Great! You keep going with God as long as you want!' Then wait for a significant time longer – until you are pretty sure they have finished. Children need to know that we want them to spend as much time as they like with God; they should feel no time pressure from us at all.

If a child seems eager to talk, this would be a good time to debrief. It is also the time to affirm them and help them with discernment if they are struggling. Sometimes a child will answer, 'I don't know,' or 'Fine.' That's not a negative answer; nor is it a cop-out. It usually means that they haven't fully worked out what has just happened. Ask some follow-up questions to allow them to process their experience out loud: 'Tell me more about it'; 'What happened when we went quiet and waited?'; 'What did you feel like?' These questions may help them to replay the experience in their head.

Offer

After we have finished checking in and debriefing, it is important that we invite the child to go back and spend more time with God. Often, a response to being with God is to want to spend more time with him or to connect with him about more specific issues. Be willing to stay and help the child reconnect, or leave them to sit and catch more from God. Suggest things that you feel are appropriate for them to do as a follow-on from their experience – for instance, writing in a journal or drawing what God showed them; chatting and catching with God later on their own; or coming to you for help to connect with God again.

As I have said, this is a simple model that will become more streamlined; the more you do it, and the more your children become familiar with the process. Eventually, it will equip them to seek God for the deeper, more complicated issues that arise in their lives.

Examples

Let's look at some more real-life examples of parents who have prayed with their children, to see the model in action.

Charlie shifted uncomfortably in his seat, his feet tapping nervously on the floor. Charlie's dad, Jon, leaned over to check on how his seven-year-old son was doing. Charlie had two more performances to watch before his turn, and he was desperately uneasy. 'You okay?' Jon whispered into his son's ear. Charlie kept looking at the floor as he nodded. 'You want me to pray with you?' Jon asked. Charlie's eyes stayed on the floor as he emphatically nodded. 'Okay. I'll pray, and then we'll be quiet for a bit so that God can meet with you, and then I'll check and see how you're doing. I promise that you'll have plenty of time to get ready for your turn, okay? I'll watch the performances, trust me. Just you-and-God time now. Okay?'

Charlie sighed and nodded slowly. Jon lightly put his hand on his son's tiny shoulders as Charlie tilted his hands up and closed his eyes. Jon prayed, 'Father God, thank you for all the gifts and character you have given to my son. He is nervous and wants to do well today in his performance. Please come and meet with him right now and pour into him all he needs to be himself and do well.' Charlie's feet stopped tapping, and his head dropped a little as Jon watched God pour peace and confidence into his son. A performance piece ended, and Charlie's head began to come up, but Jon quickly whispered, 'Plenty of time,' and Charlie settled back into catching from God.

When it was time, Jon squeezed his son. 'How are you feeling now?' he asked. Charlie's eyes met his dad's with a relieved smile. 'Good,' he replied. 'What was God doing?' Jon enquired. Charlie explained: 'Made me stop feeling jittery in my hands and my insides and told me that he is excited to hear me play. He knows how much I like it, and he likes it, too.' Jon smiled. 'He certainly gave you a gift for it!' he said.

* * *

A scream punctured the air, and Helen ran into her three-year-old daughter's room. She found Amelia on the floor, clutching a bleeding knee that had just taken the brunt of an awkward fall on to a sharp toy. Slightly relieved at the small size of the cut, Helen compassionately swept her daughter into the bathroom to wash and cleanse it. Clearly shaken up, Amelia was still crying and shivering, and Helen realised that the actual fall must have been scarier than its consequences. Helen offered to pray with Amelia and cuddled her close as she accepted.

Helen explained quickly that she was going to chat with God and then they were both going to wait to catch what God wanted to say or give to Amelia. Then Helen would check to see what God had been doing. Amelia's little head nodded against her mother's chest as Helen got comfortable, before praying, 'Father God, Amelia got very scared by her fall. Her body is all shaky and hurt. Please come and chat to Amelia and give her everything she needs to feel better.' Helen dropped her voice to a whisper: 'Let's wait and see what God does! Don't forget to catch with your whole body!' Amelia's shaking stopped, and her breathing slowed as they waited in silence on the floor of the bathroom. After 30 seconds or so, Helen asked, 'What is God doing?' Amelia smiled and replied, 'I'm catching on my skin! He's putting water on me to cool me down!' Helen smiled back and exclaimed, 'Oh, good. I'm glad you are all cooled down and feeling better! Thank you, God! Do you want to spend more time with God?' Amelia jumped up. 'Yes!' she cried. 'A God story!'

* * *

Yvonne's eleven-year-old son, Thomas, trudged into the house and threw his school bag on to the floor. When she inquired about Thomas' day, Yvonne got the usual shrug but felt in her spirit that something was worse than usual. She came into the living room and sat next to her son on the sofa. Seconds passed in silence, and then Thomas began to pour out a story of a teacher who had embarrassed and ridiculed him in front of the class for a poor choice he had made. Anger began to rise in Yvonne as she saw her son's pain and shame. They both knew that Thomas' choice had not been the best, but the consequences for him had gone beyond what was right.

Without thinking, Yvonne offered to pray with him about it. She told him that she didn't want that memory and emotion sticking to him. Surprisingly, Thomas agreed. She wrapped her arm around her son and explained that she would like to pray quickly and then give him and God space to meet about it. In a while, she would check on how things were going. Yvonne mentioned that he might want to put his hands out to show God that he was open to meet with him. Thomas nodded sullenly. 'Oh, God,' she started, 'this woman hurt and embarrassed my son and tried to stick shame on him. His heart is battered and angry and wounded. Please God, come and meet with my son. Take away all feelings and words that are holding him down, and give him your words and feelings to replace them.'

Yvonne sat next to her son as tears rolled down his face for the next five minutes, while he and God met and talked. Then his body position changed and he unfolded his arms and rested them on his sides, palms up. Gradually, she sensed peace come over Thomas and felt that it was all right to ask, 'How is it going?' Thomas nodded and said, 'Lighter. Her words weren't God's words. I'm not those things.' A weak smile spread across his face as he wiped his eyes. 'Do you want to spend more time with God?' Yvonne offered. 'Yeah, I'm gonna go and lie on my bed and think and catch and write stuff down. Call me for dinner?' Yvonne assured him that she would, and she called up after him that she'd love to hear what else God said later. With a wave, Thomas disappeared into his room, empowered to hear what God thought of him.

An exciting side-effect

A side-effect of praying with your children is that they eventually pick up the model and begin to be confident in praying with others and with you. Don't forget to create opportunities for them to pray with you or with a sibling. It is important for them to feel purposeful and powerful as ministers as well as people who receive help. There is nothing that will make you more proud than to see your children praying with their siblings, or have them help you connect with God. It is an awesome thing!

* * *

Two men chatted quietly at the back while the children gathered in small groups to catch from God and pray for each other. It was an unusual Sunday morning: the adults had gone out into seminar groups, and the children were left to meet in their groups in the main church building. Leaders huddled on the ground with the children, encouraging and supporting them as they connected with God. Two ten-year-old boys came to me to tell me that they had finished. My eyes wandered to the two men at the back of the church, and I asked the boys to follow me as I approached them.

I gently interrupted the friendly conversation, explained that the children had been growing in prayer, and asked if the two men would like the children to pray with them. They kindly agreed, and I left the boys to it. As I watched from a distance, the men stood up, and the boys began to pray with them, using the model I have described. For the next 45 minutes, the two boys stood next to the men and prayed with them, checked on them, and prayed some more. Sometimes the boys would catch something from God and feel that they should pass it on to the men. The men slowly went from standing to kneeling, to lying on the floor as they met with God, one of them crying. The boys' parents were leaders in the groups, and they fought back the tears as we all watched these children connect with God and help others to connect with him as well. After the service, the parents debriefed the boys. 'How long were we praying?' the boys asked. When their parents told them, they looked amazed and exclaimed, 'That's crazy! It only felt like five minutes.'

* * *

My husband Mark and I were leading a 'Prayer Shack' at the back of a venue for a summer camp where we would pray who children who wanted to meet with God. We had just suffered our first miscarriage and were devastated. We had wanted to name the child Grace, and we were still just beginning to process all the emotions we were feeling. Throughout the week, we prayed with hundreds of children, all learning how to hear God's voice, and we saw God do some amazing things. One of the children who had consistently come to hear more and more from God approached us on the last day. She said that she had been catching from God, and he'd told her that he wanted her to come and pray with us.

Mark and I are always happy to be prayed with, so we knelt on the ground next to this small eight-year-old girl. She explained that she would pray for us, then we would wait and see what God wanted to do, and then she would check in on us. We had no idea what was about to happen. Evidently, God had told her not only that we needed to meet with him, but also how we were feeling. With her little hands on us, she prayed, 'God, these two nice people are hurting very badly inside them, really bad, and I don't know why, but you do. They helped me a lot, and I pray that you would help them so much now. Come and meet with them loads, God.' She paused and leaned forward, whispering, 'Now we wait.' Tears poured down our faces as we met with God and he spoke to us and held us. It was the first time we had met with God as a couple about this experience. After a while, the little girl checked in: 'You okay?' We smiled and nodded as we mopped up our tears. I was worried that we might have freaked her out, but she just beamed at us. Her whole body and face were lit up. 'It's good, isn't it?' she said knowingly and skipped away. We got a brief glimpse of her name tag as she ran off. Her name was Grace.

Praying for children

I want to close with a note about praying for children rather than praying with them. This chapter has been about how to pray with children to facilitate their connection with God, but praying for your children is a wonderful thing that you should feel free to do around them. Praying for your children is an outworking of your connection to God, and it is very beneficial for children to receive that gift from you.

My favourite childhood memories are of my dad or mum praying for me before I went to bed. I was able to hear their connection with God, along with all their intercessions and the blessings they wanted for me. I felt so loved, being connected to God and them at the same time. This process continued throughout my teenage years; even to this day, I can't get off the phone with my father before he's insisted on praying for me. I love it so much, and it gives me a glimpse of how much he must pray for me when I'm not with him or on the phone. Praying for your children is important. It models for them the way your relationship with them affects your relationship with God and vice versa. Both praying for your children and praying with your children are important to their connection with God.

11

Helping children engage with church

Getting our kids to church and hoping that they love it can occupy a large part of our brain space. The subject seems full of pitfalls. If I force them to come to church, will they rebel? If I do not make them come at all, will they ever understand the importance of church? It seems that whichever way you turn is wrong, and it feels very stressful. And rightly so. A recent survey revealed that 70% of 18–22-year-olds completely leave the church when they leave home, some temporarily, some for good.[6] That doesn't mean they lose their faith, but they do lose their connection to church. When it comes to raising our children in church, we're missing something. We're somehow not connecting them well enough so that they want to continue in a church after they have left home.

Not about rules

When we talk about our children in church, often we immediately think about the rules that we want to create for them. During the service should they have to listen to the worship or could they read a book? Do they have to come every week or could they just come in the evenings? We instantly want to establish boundaries. In doing so, we may be able to control where our children are physically, but we are not necessarily going to influence where their hearts and minds are at. We first need to shift how we view church and how we communicate about church to our children.

We want our children to connect with church because it is a place of belonging, a home away from home. Church is the gift of a family of God who will love and encourage our children. It is a place for them to explore God, be needed by others and be taken care of. It is a community who will support and inspire our children to know and love God, and help them grow in connection with him. Church is more than just a service to attend. It is a deep and powerful blessing that God has given us all, and we want our children to know that.

So what do we want our children to have in their hearts and minds about church when they leave our homes? The Bible describes five foundations to the church's purpose – or, in modern terms, five church values.[7]

Exploring five values of church

1 Drawing near to God

We want our children to wholeheartedly encounter God through the worship, preaching, kids' groups and prayer times. We want our children to meet with God through the community and activities of the people that are involved in our church.

2 Radically loving others

We want our children to radically love and encourage others, and receive that love and encouragement in return. We want our children to sacrificially and joyfully put down their lives for each other, to live full of compassion and love, drawing alongside other people on their journey. We want them to receive all of that from the community as well.

3 Spurring each other into action

Church exists to enable Christians to challenge and sharpen each other; to wrestle with scripture together and share their tough questions; and to be part of a group that encourages and equips each other to live a life honouring God and what he has called each one of us to do.

4 Giving each part a purpose

We want our children to know that they are a purposeful part of the body of Christ and are needed by the whole church, and we want them to value the contributions of others. We want them to see that they are valuable, unique and useful in the greater calling that God has for his church.

5 Pursuing the Spirit

Finally, we want our children to pursue and experience the work of the Spirit, both in the internal transformation of becoming more like Jesus and in participating in his active work in the world.

If a child, a teen or an adult lives according to these values, then whether or not they use their gadgets during the service is less important. We can begin to make good parenting decisions based not on our child's behaviour in church but on their growing understanding of and participation in church.

No matter what the church is doing, I can...

When we focus on these values, it means that we as parents no longer need to feel powerless about questions such as 'Is church as fun as possible for my kid? Is it engaging my child?' It empowers us as parents to say, 'No matter what the church is doing I can help my child learn to engage with it.' We are powerful as parents, called to grow our children spiritually and train them in what church means. And as we own what church means for us, and as we grow in our children what church means for them, we can together create the church that we want to be in as a community.

Using the six-stage circle

Remember the six-stage circle (Chapter 8)? We can use it to begin to disciple our children in engaging with church. First, I would suggest that we pause to see what waves are happening in our children's lives and if we can use any of them to help our children hook into church. If our children are obsessed with sound equipment, then why not create opportunities for them to become involved in the audiovisual team? If our children are particularly intellectual and have lots of questions, why not equip them to listen to sermons and take notes so that they can wrestle with big questions? We may find that there is a wave that we can surf well to facilitate the next step for our children to engage with church.

If we feel, instead, that one of the values is something that is next for our child, then we can begin to look at exploring that value around the six-stage circle.

The six-stage circle: worship

- *Model* – Often in church we're wrangling with children, reading the notices and waving at the people we know. But one of the most powerful things we can do for our children is to genuinely worship in front of them, whatever that looks like. Whether you raise your hands, sing loudly or stay absolutely silent, create a window for them to see you drawing near to God during that time.

- *Frame* – It may be that your children don't quite understand how to connect with God in worship yet. You could take the opportunity to whisper, 'Look, can you see how the different types of people are worshipping in different types of ways? What do you think is going on in that person's heart? And that person's?' My mum took me to different denominations of churches just to begin to frame for me what worship looked like there. We would go to a Catholic church, and she would say, 'Can you see people worshipping? What does that look like for them?' And then we'd go to a Methodist church, and she would say the same thing there. I began to be able to see the relationship with God in every style of worship. Whatever is important to you, frame it for you children so they can fully understand the words and behaviours used in the worship time.
- *Equip* – The third thing you do is equip them to be able to engage in the worship. If they don't know all the words to a song, find the track online so they can become familiar with it. If they can't see the words, move them forward. If you need to explain every song so they understand what the words mean, do so. In whatever way you need to equip them to fully participate in worship, go for it.
- *Create opportunities* – If we want our children to value something, they need to have opportunities to explore it. Create times for them to experience heart-connecting worship. If they normally are in their kids' groups, allow them to occasionally stay with you. Maybe you want to do more worship at home so they can understand and grow in their ability to worship. The more opportunity they have to find their own comfortableness in worship, the more they will value it.
- *Establish boundaries* – Feel free to create boundaries. You can say, 'This is our time to draw near to God, and because of that I don't want you to play on any gadgets'; 'I'm happy for you to play on your electronics, but I'm not happy for you to talk'; or, 'This is the time we draw near to God. How do you want to do it? You can do it in all of these ways. You can't do it in these ways. What do you want to do?'
- *Give feedback* – Spend time after church talking about your experience in the worship, and why it was like that. Whether it was a great time of worship or not, talk about what got in the way, or what made it particularly special. Share your journeys with each other.

The six-stage circle: radical love

Sometimes the value we need to work on with our children isn't connected to the service at all. For example, radically loving others is different because it's not something that's dependent on the church service doing it for us. To radically love is what we as Christians are called to do. How can we help our children learn what radical love looks like in a church community?

- *Model* – Do your children see you sacrificially loving people within your church community? Do they see the impact that you have on people when you love, care for, listen to and pray for them? Do they see the impact those people make on you? Sometimes this value can be less about you needing to do more and more about letting your children see the difference the community makes on loving you.

- *Frame* – Loving people can happen very privately, and our children may not see what is happening. Rather than saying, 'Daddy's talking to someone right now; could you please go and play in the hall,' why not prepare them before the church gathering by saying something like: 'It's really important that we radically love each other, and that we give each other our time. When you see me talking to people after church, it's not because I don't love you or because I'm not hungry for lunch. I stay and talk because this is part of what we do as Christians. We love each other. When I'm talking to others after church, I'm showing that I care about them and pray for them, and that I need to be loved too.'

- *Equip* – Sometimes children need to be equipped to know how to love people within a church community. One of our church kids got hold of this value. His mother had a gift for hospitality, and he began to take it upon himself to welcome any new family to church. His mother equipped him with questions to ask people as they came in. When he spotted any new family coming in the door, he would run up and start asking the questions that his mother had prepped him with. He would find out what school the children went to, and then he would bring that whole family over to another family whose kids went to the same school. He turned out to be the best at welcoming visitors. He tied more unchurched families into our church than anyone else, because he had been equipped and been given the opportunity, and he began to love other people and make them feel like they belonged.

- *Create opportunities* – We are all able to both radically love and radically be loved, and giving our children the opportunities to do that means that they're not bored after church; rather, after church they will feel purposeful and seek ways to love and be loved. Some teens are amazing at loving older people and they go and sit with them and talk for ages. They, in turn, receive 20 grandparent figures who are always asking about them and know what's going on in their lives. Other children I know need to have opportunities opened up for them to volunteer in kids' groups to find their ability to love radically. One eleven-year-old boy volunteered in our group for three-to-four-year-olds. He had a little group of children who adored him. He ended up volunteering for the entirety of his teenage years, becoming their group leader as they grew up.

- *Establish boundaries* – Feel free to set whatever boundaries you want on radically loving. For example, your children need to talk to two adults after church. Or perhaps you say to them, 'Before church, please find one child who is not talking to anybody and chat with them for five minutes. Then you can get on with your Sunday. But I would like to see you having compassion on this lonely and lost person, because you're very, very powerful in the way that you can give your love to somebody.'

- *Give feedback* – As your children learn to love others and be loved, have conversations where you observe the impact they made on other people. 'You should have seen that boy's face as you left. He was so happy! You did sweep him up and make him feel a part of the group. Well done!'

You can do this with any value you want and whatever aspect of the value you want. Once you begin to get into the groove, you'll find you start to do it naturally and easily.

Doesn't the church need to change?

The question 'What about the church?' always comes up. Doesn't the church need to shift and accommodate children? My background is in youth and children's ministry, so of course my answer is 'Yes!' But as parents we don't have to be reliant on the church changing in order for our children to fully engage with church. We get to train our children in how to access church. We get to frame how they experience everything in church. While I would encourage churches to change and shift and grow the best they can, we aren't powerless while we wait for them to do so. Even if the church never changes that doesn't mean our children won't.

The church at home

Finally, remember that church is not just that part of the church that you belong to. Church exists whenever two or three believers gather together, and that means church can be in your home. You don't have to wait for Sundays to train your kids in worship. You don't have to wait for Sundays to show them that they are a powerful part of the body of Christ. You can utilise their gifts at home. You can train them how to do love at home. Church can be home as much as church can be the wider body that we meet with on a Sunday or midweek.

I hope this encourages you. And I can't wait for you to see the fruit of growing these values in your children. It's going to be a fantastic journey.

12

Starting well with under-fives

Elliott's four-year-old face scrunched up at me. 'Are dinosaurs from God?' he asked. 'Phew, an easy one for once,' I thought, before replying, 'Well, it says in the Bible that God created all things, and I see every day that he is still making new and wonderful things, so I would say, yes! Dinosaurs are from God.' Elliott's face broke out into a smile. 'I'm glad!' he exclaimed. There is nothing on this planet that Elliott loves more than dinosaurs, and he seems to be educated to university level in all their names and details. 'This might be fun,' I thought as an idea popped into my head. 'Hey, Elliott. People make up songs to God all the time to tell him how they feel. King David did it and we can, too! Let's sing a song to God to tell him how wonderful he is for making dinosaurs,' I suggested. Elliott giggled and agreed. For ten minutes we danced and sang and made up a song for God, as Elliott and I shared with God how much we loved him for being so creative. It wasn't the prettiest song in the world, but it was heartfelt and fun, and we both felt God's presence as we laughed and sang.

Parents of children under five years old have a wonderful chance to build faith from the beginning. I am aware that some of the ideas in this book will look slightly different if you are working with under-fives, so I want to provide some practical suggestions and true stories to encourage you as you begin your parenting-for-faith journey.

The first thing to say is that small children are like sponges, assimilating new information at an astonishing rate. They mimic the way we talk, eat, drink, process emotions and handle social situations. Everything we do serves, for them, as a blueprint for the way the world works and how to interact with it. Modelling the reality of a relationship with God is a powerful tool for those of us with young children. We can communicate so much to them merely by being ourselves and creating windows into our relationship with God, as well as framing for them and inviting them in to share our experiences with God. We cannot underestimate the power of how us being who we are is affecting our children at this age. Take advantage of it!

From birth to age two

Children at this age are just beginning to make sense of the world and their place in it. So what can we do proactively to equip them and encourage them into a relationship with God?

Building a godly 'normality'

Children of this age are absorbing the way everything works and are beginning to establish a 'normal' state of life. This is a productive time to establish for them a life filled with the presence of God, prayer, worship songs and Bible stories and verses. We have the opportunity to build into the fabric of their understanding a world with God at the centre. The best thing we can do for our children is to act as if God is in the room because he is!

Connecting with God

At one church that I worked with, our ministry with babies and toddlers had the strapline 'An encounter with God is life-changing, no matter what our age'. John the Baptist leapt in his mother's womb when Elizabeth was filled with the Holy Spirit on meeting the pregnant Mary (Luke 1:41). If children in the womb can perceive the presence of God, then no one is too young. There are many things we can do to help connect our children to God.

Pray for them

Even while you are pregnant, take the time to pray for your child, blessing him or her and asking for the Lord's presence in their life. I often prayed that my baby would know the touch of the Lord more than my own so that there would never be a moment of his life when he didn't recognise God. Our children need our prayers throughout their lives, so let's start at the very beginning.

Model chatting with God for them

They may not entirely understand at first, but when they do chatting with God will be as normal as talking to other people. They will see reality in your actions before they fully understand them. As they develop verbally, you can help them to chat with God by encouraging them at the level at which they are engaging in other relationships. I knew a mum who wanted to get her child used to the idea that God is always with us, so she began to acknowledge his real presence in the house as normal. Every once in a while, she would say, 'Why don't you show God and me your dance?' or 'Oh, should we show God your owie [a scratch or bruise]?'

Catch for them

We do a lot of things for our children when they are young, and you can start catching for them right away. I know several parents who started a book for their children as soon as they were born, and, as they prayed for them, they would include in the book words or pictures that God gave them regarding the child. I met one of their children when he was four; he very proudly told me how important he was to God and how God talked to his parents about him, and now God talks to him, too. He sat with me and showed me page after page of pictures and words, and explained each one to me. It was powerful to see a book of God's communication with this child through so many people. I was excited to see his own drawings towards the end of the book, and to recognise his catching from God as a continuation of the communication God had been sending his way since before birth.

Pray with them

Although our babies and toddlers may not be able to comprehend fully what is happening, we can still pray with them and invite God to connect with our children. I have been constantly surprised by the awareness of God that tiny people can have when being prayed for. I once visited some friends who had a two-month-old baby. She was sleeping, and, as I prayed silently and invited God to meet with her in her sleep, she began to smile and wiggle around. I also once prayed for a mother and child who both had thrush infections in their mouths. As I prayed, I watched the baby stop crying and become very quiet and peaceful. The baby then began to poke her mouth, squeezing her tongue. When we finished praying, the woman told me that she felt an overwhelming sense of peace, and immediately she began to feel her tongue grow warm and tingly. She felt that God was touching her and healing her, and I knew that the baby had had the very same experience with God. I don't think we will ever truly know what a baby's experience with God is, but we can definitely create opportunities for God and our children to meet, and trust him to reveal himself with care and gentleness.

Ages three to four

Children of this age are growing in independence and self-expression. This age requires a lot of modelling and proactive inclusion in our life with God. As they become more self-reliant, we can ensure that our inclusion times are empowering their individual relationship with God as well as our corporate relationship with him.

Building a right view of God

Children of this age are gathering information to piece together a view of individual people, situations and life in general. We can partner them in this search for life's building blocks by ensuring that we provide a wide range of biblical truth linked to relational experience, which they can use to create a right view of God.

- Give your child a wide range of Bible stories and, in the creative telling of each story, share what God was doing and thinking in it.
- Encourage your child to tell Bible stories to you, and ask questions about the relationship between the characters and God.
- Help frame life experiences by referring back to the Bible, so that your child can begin to see how you use scripture to work through issues and root yourself when life is confusing. You might say, 'Whew, I'm feeling very tired and wobbly. I wonder what God says in the Bible about what I should do?' Pick up your Bible and look up Matthew 11:28: 'God says, "If you are tired from carrying heavy burdens, come to me, and I will give you rest." That sounds great! How can I go to God? Let's lie on the floor and ask God to give me rest!' You can also pick one or two Bible verses that are particularly applicable to your family's life circumstances and refer to them throughout the day.
- Be prepared to rebalance wrong views of God. The very way in which our children's brains are maturing means that they will inevitably link things together that were not meant to go together. Keep an eye out for any mistaken view of God that pops up, so that you can correct it quickly. As we saw earlier, we can contribute to these wrong views, as we are not perfect. It is no problem; we need to be aware so that we can fix it. Once, I was teaching three- to four-year-olds at church, and we were talking about the stories of Jesus raising people from the dead. Unfortunately, I wasn't paying close attention to the words I was using as I explained that Jesus talked to the dead people and they got up and walked around again, and ate and drank. The children's reaction wasn't what I expected. After some play and craft time, a fellow leader took me aside and suggested that I redescribe the story, as many of the children were freaked out because they were under the impression that Jesus went around making zombies.
- Be aware of the difference between 'real' and 'pretend'. Children of this age are just learning about that difference, and it is helpful to be very clear with our children that God is real, and so is our relationship with him.

Connecting with God

Chatting with God

Children at this age are becoming very verbal. If you are modelling chatting with God and are proactively creating times for them to do this themselves, it can begin to grow into a habit. Many parents report that they hear their children chatting away to God while playing alone in their rooms, or in the dark while they are in bed, waiting to drift off to sleep.

Catching from God

Children of this age can begin to get a handle on how to catch from God but will make a lot of mistakes. Train yourself to watch carefully, affirm their efforts and help them to discern what is and is not from God. This is a very vulnerable time, as children's efforts can be easily squashed by us. God is faithful to speak, I promise, and you will be surprised at what happens. Here are a few experiences that parents have shared with me.

Susie and her two children were travelling in the car when the three-year-old child, Rose, started insisting that her one-year-old brother Daniel should sleep in their mother's room that night, because of the bangs and booms that God had told her were coming. Rose's mum made some positive noises but dismissed the idea in her head. Daniel had not been sleeping well, and everyone had been getting more and more exhausted. Later that night, she thought about it again and decided that she would act on what her daughter had heard from God, so moved her son into her room for the night. In the middle of the night, a loud unforecasted thunderstorm struck. Daniel stirred, but quickly Susie put her hand on his back. Comforted, he dropped right back off to sleep. Susie's husband reported the next day that, although the thunderstorm had kept him awake, both Susie and Daniel had had the best night of sleep they'd experienced in three weeks.

* * *

Jack was walking down the road with his mum, Lesley, when all of a sudden he stopped abruptly and said, 'I think God just talked to me! I felt it in my tummy!' (Lesley had not yet told him about all the ways he could catch from God, just that God spoke to people.) 'What did he say?' she asked excitedly. 'Be good,' Jack replied with his eyes glowing. Lesley was baffled. 'How do you know it was God? What did it feel like?' she probed. Jack thought for a second. 'Funny,' he replied. 'Funny-exciting or funny-scary?' Lesley enquired. Jack sighed and rolled his eyes. 'Both, because it was God!' he exclaimed. Lesley told him the story of how Samuel in the Bible heard God for the first time. Jack nodded knowingly, fully identifying with Samuel's experience.

* * *

I received a phone call from our close friend Mikel at around 8.00pm. He has two small children, and evidently my name had come up in his nightly prayers with his three-year-old daughter. Mikel gave the reason for the call: 'Um, this may sound weird, but I just wanted to check! Elizabeth was praying tonight, and she prayed specifically for your leg to get better. Is there anything wrong with it?' My jaw dropped, and I explained that, earlier in the day, I had severely twisted my leg and it was massively swollen. Mikel laughed a little bit and said, 'Well, you should know then that God told Elizabeth, and she was praying for you!'

Praying with our children

With this age group, we can easily modify the model of praying with our children described in Chapter 10. It is a matter of explaining a bit more and shrinking your waiting time to between ten and 30 seconds. You can also begin to invite your children to pray with you in the same way.

Working with children's development stages

Remember, we are working on a real relationship with a real God. It is helpful, therefore, to look at how your children are relating to other children and family members: this will be a good guide to help you understand what your child is ready for in their relationship with God and how to help them progress.

We can expect our children to display the same level of interaction with God as they do in their friendships. We sometimes mistakenly expect a more mature level of relationship with God than is normal in our children's ordinary relational lives. Don't be surprised if their entire chat time with God is about butterflies or *Dora the Explorer*. Sharing the little things opens the door for them to share bigger things. As in their everyday relationships, they might need some prompting to talk about their feelings with God. If you feel that that is the next step, encourage and guide them into doing it.

Every child is different and will progress at different rates at different times. Just as some children are adept at gross motor skills and others of the same age are adept at fine motor skills, our children may be at different levels spiritually from those around them. What matters is that they eventually emerge with a balanced relationship with God, so encourage what is going well and gently nudge them in places of growth. As you help your children to take their next step towards God, he is faithful to meet with them at each unique stage and connect with them right where they are.

Part II

Parenting children for a life of purpose

13

Identity, relationship and purpose

Her eyes were glowing as she beamed a smile at me. For the past 15 minutes, nine-year-old Jessi had been sitting on the ground, praying for an adult who had come to the side of the room during a church service to meet with God. She had confidently and gently prayed for this woman, handed her tissues when she cried, and throughout the 15 minutes whispered encouragements and prayers to her as she helped the older woman meet with God. As the grateful woman went back to her seat, I leaned over to check in on Jessi. 'How was that?' I asked. She could barely contain herself. 'It's amazing,' she replied. 'I'm normally really shy and can't say what I want to, but when it's God's words I feel strong and all the words that are in my heart actually come out of my mouth.' I asked if she wanted to continue to pray with people and she nodded emphatically, exclaiming, 'I want to do it all the time! Because I think this is what I'm meant to do. I think he made me this way, to do this – help people who hurt meet with God. I'm me when I do it. I want to do it loads.'

Purpose strikes to the core of us as humans. The search for purpose is everywhere. Why am I here? What is life all about? Who am I supposed to be? What am I supposed to do with my life? The questions resonate for all of us.

Most of us would agree that our children have specialness inside them. We can see possibilities of the future flicker in their hearts and souls as they grow. We look forward to cheering them on as they get older and 'discover' their calling in life. But what if there is more for them now? What if the flickers we see are meant for use in their everyday life as well as the future?

We all hear of extraordinary children doing extraordinary things. We see them on the news or in magazines. Billy saw a need and ran a fundraising campaign and now has enabled 600 wells to be dug in Africa. 'Good for him,' we say dismissively, as we make the school lunches in the morning. 'How much effort did his mum have to put into that?' Gemma organised a postcard campaign on child poverty. Over 100,000 postcards were sent to the prime minister. 'Weird political child,' we judge as we drive around. 'No way would a real child want to do that.' Those stories can seem to us to apply to those families who have the extra time to do it or for the unique child who cares about issues like that, far removed from our one-year-old who is mashing bananas into the carpet, our seven-year-old who adores football or our teen whose phone is glued to her hand. 'Raising children with purpose,' we think, 'takes effort, time – and someone else's children.' Or does it?

Children are designed to be purposeful, to have power within themselves and with the Spirit, and to live life heart-to-heart and in step with the Father. We often mistakenly think that purpose is the same as accomplishment, and we can become overwhelmed by the thought of facilitating such achievements in our children. But that isn't what true spiritual purpose is.

Having purpose is to exist for a reason, to live and sacrifice for something bigger than ourselves, and to pursue the will of God in our lives and in the world. Purpose is expressed by choosing to faithfully walk each day in relationship with God, knowing that we are a part of his plans today, tomorrow and the next day. Our children deserve to have a life filled with purpose. And we as parents can help them find it and live it each day.

When we begin to think about how to parent children for a life of purpose, I find that it's most helpful to look at how we were created and what we were created for. For that, we go to our Father: the first parent, the ultimate parent.

Genesis 1 and 2 tell us the story of the creation of people. God was in the process of creating the world and he had the idea to make people: children for himself. He carefully and lovingly made them in his likeness, and then he spoke to them. 'So God created humans to be like himself; he made men and women. God gave them his blessing and said…' (Genesis 1:27–28, CEV).

We assume that God's initial doting was similar to ours. When we first meet our children, we often want just to hold them and watch them. We tell them how beautiful they are, and we want to protect them forever. But look at what God does with his new children. He blesses them, which I'm sure was lovely, and then says to them, 'Have a lot of children! Fill the earth with people and bring it under your control. Rule over the fish in the ocean, the birds in the sky, and every animal on the earth' (v. 28).

His children are brand new, and the first thing he does is give them a job! They are fresh out of the package, and yet they have been given a purpose for now and a vision for how to develop that in the future. God considered it vital to impart to his newly formed children their purpose.

Identity, relationship and purpose in the Bible

Adam and Eve were created in God's image, directly able to see and experience their own similarities to him. They knew who they were and what their identity was: they were created by the Creator, and were his children.

They were also given a relationship – a relationship with God as his children, able to hear his voice, interact with him and know him. If you look at Genesis 2 and 3, you will see that Adam and Eve conversed with God and knew his voice well. They even knew the familiar sound of him walking in the garden. They had a natural and real connection to God.

And almost immediately, they were given purpose: a task, a vision, a thing to give themselves to. All three are important in their own right but are also inextricably linked. God gave them their identity and lived in relationship with them, and that experience shaped how they found and walked in their purpose.

We can see this pattern throughout scripture. The people we most admire tend to have identity, relationship and purpose emblazoned in their spirits.

Abram's *identity* was shaped as God told him who he was and would be: a blessing to nations, the father of many nations, and fruitful. God even changed Abram's name to reflect the new identity he was shaping in him, from Abram (which means father) to Abraham (father of many). God drew him into a covenant, a formal binding *relationship*, and talked with him openly and often, in direct conversation with him throughout his life. God gave Abraham a mighty *purpose*, and he obeyed faithfully (and sometimes not) as he pursued his purpose in response to God's direction and in confidence of who God made him to be. Abraham lived his purpose walking the length and breadth of the land he was given, interceding for people, and holding firm to the tangible promises of God (see Genesis 12, 13 and 17).

Jeremiah was only a child when God told him that before he formed him in his mother's womb, he had appointed Jeremiah as a prophet to the nations. His *identity* as a prophet had been planned even before he was created. God added to his identity, saying that he also made him as a fortified city, an iron pillar and a bronze wall to stand against the whole land. God promised his constant voice in *relationship*, his presence and his faithfulness to rescue Jeremiah. God also laid out clearly Jeremiah's *purpose*: to go boldly and without fear, speaking the words he would give him to kings, priests and people in order to change the nations. Without his purpose, Jeremiah wouldn't have his identity. Without the tangible relationship with God, he would have nothing to speak and no purpose to fulfil (see Jeremiah 1).

In the life of Jesus we see the intertwining of the three. When Jesus was baptised, God spoke and named Jesus as his Son, affirming his *identity*. Jesus walked confident in this every day, accomplishing all his Father had for him to do because of his unique identity. He lived life in *relationship* with the Father and the Holy Spirit, ministering with the Spirit and often spending time on his own in prayer to the Father. His *purpose* on earth was clear: to redeem us to the Father and to show us how to walk in relationship with him. Identity, relationship and purpose are expressed best in Jesus showing us the perfect balance of how to live healthily with all three (see the gospels, for example Matthew 3:17; 9:13; Luke 4:16–21; John 3:16–17; 17:1–26).

The examples can go on and on: Moses, Joshua, Gideon, David, Peter, Mary and Paul. Identity, relationship and purpose gave people strength and ability to live great and significant lives.

An entwined approach

This entwined and balanced approach is something we naturally do as parents. As our children grow, we deliberately help them to understand themselves and their place in our family (*identity*). We help them to feel secure in their relationship with us and assist them in navigating their relationships with others (*relationship*). We also give them the skills and understanding to be productive, conscientious and independent members of society (*purpose*). We do it so naturally that we often don't notice how holistic our approach really is.

When it comes to growing our children spiritually, though, we can often lose confidence in our holistic approach. We can lean towards focusing heavily on identity and relationship. Our instinct can be to want our children to know that they are loved by us and by God and be comfortable in that. But when we begin to face spiritual purpose we can shy away, leaving it out almost entirely for the first decade of our children's lives, not wanting to drop the bombshell that there are other requirements that we have to 'do' as part of the Christian deal. We don't want to stress them out or make them feel pressured to perform, so we often leave purpose on the sideline, to be picked up at a later time when it is convenient. In doing this, I believe we are stunting the spiritual growth and happiness of our children.

Without purpose, children's faith can become insular and selfish, focusing on their experiences first. Boredom and confusion can creep into their faith because it has become purely about what they are getting out of it.

Without purpose, children are robbed of the power of their God-given identity. What is the use of having authority in Christ, if you have nowhere to use it? What is the use of being unique, if you cannot apply it to something?

Without purpose, children's relationships with God will be limited. God is a God of action and creation, as well as of love. He has purposes and plans. He is in the world accomplishing and doing. Purpose reveals a different side of God, adding depth to our understanding of God's heart in action. It is important for our children to know the fullness of God, which includes his purposes and actions, so that they can learn to see him in the world and choose to join him in his plans.

God is a God of completeness. When identity, relationship and purpose exist side by side, our children can walk in spiritual health, thriving confidently in their relationship with God, and in being an essential part of something bigger than themselves. We cannot and should not teach one without the others.

14

Telling the whole story

Eleven-year-old Hannah scrunched up her face at me. 'I'm not sure I even want to be a Christian any more,' she admitted. 'It's so boring. Do this. Do that. Make God happy. And it doesn't make any sense. If God was real and actually here, why did the tsunami happen? If he loves everybody so much, then why doesn't he help?'

Over and over again, I have run across parents whose children struggle with the same questions. Children look at the world and see so much that confuses them when they try to match up what they see to their faith. They can't see God's purposes, nor can they find their own purpose within them.

We can be faced with this barrage of questions on a daily basis. Our own life circumstances and difficult stories about our friends, our communities and our nation often swirl around in our thoughts. These stories swirl around in our children's minds, too. We are desperate for our children to have an anchor that will help them to weather these storms in life – and not just to weather them: to flourish in them.

An incomplete foundation

All of us want the best for our children's faith, whether our children are one or eight or 14 or 35 years old. In our efforts to help our children connect with God and acquire faith, we often shelter them from the whole story, the complete story of the gospel. By giving them only an incomplete understanding of the gospel story, we actually disconnect them from God, who would be their anchor and who wants to hold them firmly and empower them with faith and purpose through the storms of life.

The problem is that sometimes we find it difficult to break down the whole gospel story – and so we end up leaving out key elements rather than trying to find ways to translate them into simpler concepts. We decide that we will add them in later, but we rarely do. It sounds harmless enough, but the results are significant: many children grow up in the church with only a partial understanding of the gospel story, with an incomplete foundation.

It can sometimes look like the diagram below:

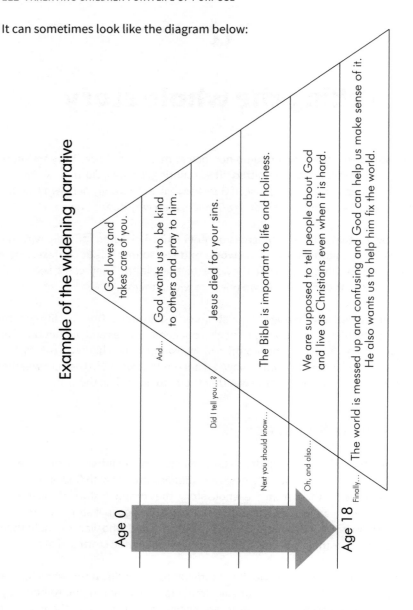

Example of the widening narrative

God loves and takes care of you.

And... God wants us to be kind to others and pray to him.

Did I tell you...? Jesus died for your sins.

Next you should know... The Bible is important to life and holiness.

Oh, and also... We are supposed to tell people about God and live as Christians even when it is hard.

Finally,... The world is messed up and confusing and God can help us make sense of it. He also wants us to help him fix the world.

Age 0

Age 18

When we first begin to talk to our children about God, we often start by telling them that they are loved, welcomed and precious to their Father. We really want them to bed down in that safeness. Then we add a bit of the story: because we are loved, we should try to please God. After a couple of years of space, we gently slide the gospel in, trying to explain salvation and Jesus' sacrifice lightly. We add the 'shoulds' of being a Christian, with spiritual disciplines and lists of what God requires. We let that bed down for a while. And then once they start looking bored, we talk about holiness and evangelism and mission and try to excite them about the obligation of 'spreading the gospel'. Eventually, as our children approach adulthood, we feel safe to suggest that maybe they may want to get involved with doing something about the hurt in the world and begin to discuss the more grey areas of being in the world as a Christian.

By the end of this journey of childhood, the initial message – love, safety and unconditional approval – has turned into something totally different. It is now about behaviour obligations and restrictions, responsibilities, ritual, tradition, and a pressure to 'share' with others and do something about the broken world if they want. And being loved, and occasionally safe. Meanwhile, the world is happening around them and to them and they don't have a framework for understanding it, their place in it, or where God is and what he is doing about it.

If we want our children to be able to stand firm in this life and find their place, then we need to tell them the whole story of the gospel from the beginning. If we tell it well, then everything can be tied to it. The whole story will provide a theological framework for them to grow in understanding of God and the world. It will provide a story big enough to live in and to be a part of. It will provide a story in which all things can be understood and next steps can be known. Telling the whole story is important. As they get older, the story of the gospel will deepen, but not change. There will never be a surprise that leaps out, just a deepening of understanding.

We instinctively know how to do this. No matter what the story, it can be told simply in six sentences in a baby's board book or it can be expanded into an entire three-hour movie! The story is the same, but the depth of understanding and detail grows with the telling.

So what is the whole gospel and how does it relate to reality?

At every age, we can translate the gospel story into language and concepts that children can begin to understand. I find using the following six points, which are inspired by the structure and content of John 3:16, a helpful way to make sure I am telling the whole story:

1 God is love. He made all things from his vast creativity and love. He created man and woman to be loved by him and to respond to that love, and, in turn, they are to love all those around them. God loves and fully knows each individual – us, and everyone else.

2 People walked away from God. The world and its people chose, and keep choosing, to separate themselves from God. Instead of loving him and loving other people, we choose to love ourselves, to love our stuff, to love getting our way, and to love only the people who give us what we want.

This makes us move further away from God and further towards evil. Even people who try to love God and other people do this sometimes. It isn't good for us or for other people. It affects decisions and the very way we build society, because if people in power act this way, it has even more impact. It creates lots of bad consequences in the world: people in pain, people not having enough to eat, people being treated badly just because of where they live or what they look like, people being isolated, or people trying to fix problems with things that don't work and simply make them sadder or more selfish.

This separation between the world's way and God's way is so big that some people don't even believe God exists any more, especially when they look at the mess we have all made.

3 Jesus cleared a way back to closeness with God. Living in a broken world can be hard, but we don't need to be afraid or give up hope, because God is bigger than all of this. Through Jesus, and through what he did for us when he died and rose again, we have a way back to love and the relationships with God and other people that he intended at the start.

4 God is active in the world and we can partner with him to transform it. Knowing God and being his friends means that we can love him. We can be forgiven for all the clutter that gets into our hearts and can love other people again properly. If

we follow him, he invites us to work with him to help ourselves, other people and the whole world to move away from evil to good. That means working with him to share his story with others, to stand up for what is fair, to care for the poor and hurting, to pray for others, to be generous; and much, much more.

5   He gives us his power through his Holy Spirit to join with him in putting love at the centre of everything again. All that is broken in the world is being changed. None of it is as big as God or beyond being changed by his love as we join in with that work. No one has gone so far that he or she can't come to know God again.

6   One day, it will all be the way God meant it to be forever. One day, when Jesus comes again, the whole world will be completely good and loving again, and there will never be anything else that gets in the way of us loving God and each other.

This is the whole story. It's still not the full story – there is a lot of depth still to come – but there are no surprises left for later. There is also a clear sense of humanity's purpose: to love God, to live in community, to experience the abundant life Christians are called to in loving God, and to work with him to change themselves and the world.

There will be better ways to summarise, translate and explain the whole story for different ages, backgrounds and personalities, but it's important to ensure that none of these core elements is missing. When the scriptural story is the core, our experiences and reading of scripture and theology can be tied to it, so that nothing exists in isolation from the adventure story of God. Instead of the triangle model of a widening story given to children and teens as they grow, they can have a consistent simple model with the core story always at the centre. As children and teens grow, more knowledge and experiences can be tied to the core story that deepens as the child gets older.

For instance, a four-year-old will know the core story and will have a few theological points and life experiences to tie to it.

By the time the child is ten, the story stays the same, but the child is able to tie to it more and more of his knowledge and experiences of God and life. See the diagram overleaf.

4 years old

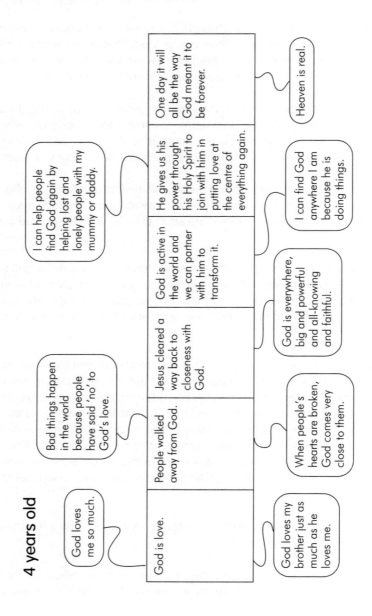

God loves me so much.

God is love.

God loves my brother just as much as he loves me.

Bad things happen in the world because people have said 'no' to God's love.

People walked away from God.

When people's hearts are broken, God comes very close to them.

Jesus cleared a way back to closeness with God.

God is everywhere, big and powerful and all-knowing and faithful.

God is active in the world and we can partner with him to transform it.

I can find God anywhere I am because he is doing things.

I can help people find God again by helping lost and lonely people with my mummy or daddy.

He gives us his power through his Holy Spirit to join with him in putting love at the centre of everything again.

One day it will all be the way God meant it to be forever.

Heaven is real.

10 years old

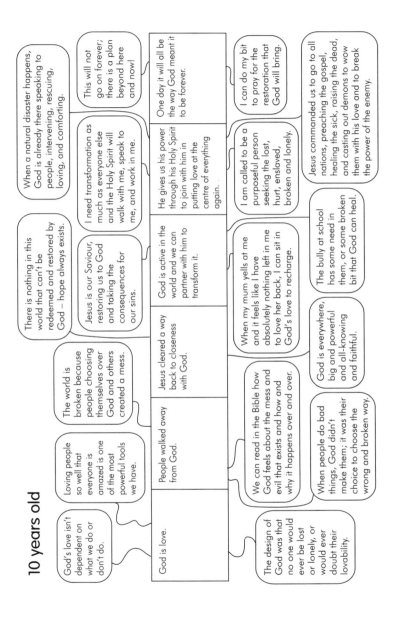

Orienting to the story

This core story approach means that our purpose and our actions can be easily linked in to the identity, relationship and calling we have within the whole story. When we talk with our children about the importance of generosity and sharing, the reason is not just because God wants us to do so. It's because God loves other people as much as he loves us, and other people have needs and wants and are hurting. When we are willing to love God and other people more than we love our belongings, we can partner with God to lift others up and help minister to those more in need by giving them what we have, happily and freely.

When we look at the news and see the horror of what is happening, we don't have to be confused by the 'why?' questions. We can say:

> I'm reminded of that verse in the Bible when Jesus says, 'In this world you will have trouble. But take heart! I have overcome the world' (John 16:33). This world is so full of awful trouble, isn't it? My heart just wants to pray for those people right now. God, thank you that you have overcome this world, and those people need you. Please rescue them, and send your angels to protect them and comfort them. Create safe places for them. Help them, God.

We can then empower our children to connect with God, heart-to-heart, about their feelings.

We can highlight how life scenarios fit into the whole story and what that means for us and the people involved. In the case of a natural disaster, we could reassure our children:

> God didn't send this tsunami. Earthquakes are a natural part of how the world works, and horrifically the consequences for people living in the impact zone are huge. But God is always at work being who he is: the rescuer, redeemer, comforter, protector. Can you see where God is and what he is doing in the midst of the mess? How can we help? What can we do?

When our children know the whole story, they can find every experience in life in the story, and they can be empowered in their place within it.

15

Foundational purpose

In the novel *The Lord of the Rings*, there was a quest. An evil enemy was attempting to conquer the land, and the good guys had discovered the way to defeat him. An essential journey had to be undertaken in order to destroy an object for the good of all the world. A core group of people from different societies were so captivated by this purpose, by the fundamental goodness of its goal, that they voluntarily chose to sacrifice all to achieve it. The quest required them to shine individually, to support each other, and to sacrifice personal goals for the good of their purpose. Sometimes alone and sometimes together, the core group finally achieved their grand purpose and saved the world.

What would have happened if one of the characters had refused to participate until he was individually given a plan for exactly what would be required of him on this quest? What would have happened if they stopped each time a question or crisis arose, or waited until someone told them exactly what to do based on their individual strengths and weaknesses?

The reason the core group achieved their purpose was that their eyes were fixed on that grand purpose. They applied themselves to achieve that goal, in community with each other. Together they were stronger than when they were apart, and it needed each one of them to succeed.

Throughout scripture there is a whole host of purposes outlined for people following God. Jesus simplified it beautifully for us: '"Love the Lord your God with all your heart and with all your soul and with all your mind." This is the first and greatest commandment. And the second is like it: "Love your neighbour as yourself." All the Law and the Prophets hang on these two commandments' (Matthew 22:37–40).

When Jesus came to earth, he lived that purpose, and we see the power that a life lived well can truly have. Jesus brought God's love to earth, and that love set people free and brought joy and fulfilment and healing to a broken world, reconciling people to God. When he returned to heaven, he tasked his followers with doing the same as he had done.

It is this purpose that we need to own for ourselves, this purpose that will fulfil us and give us a goal each day of our lives. Too often we dismiss that grander purpose as too impersonal, while we are waiting for God to give us our own individual detailed step-by-step plan.

For a long time I searched for my calling, the unique plan that God had for my life, the journey that was designed for me and my wonderfulness. To be honest, I dismissed the purposes laid out in scripture because I found them boring.

I looked at scripture and was overwhelmed by the list of things to do: act justly, love mercy, serve the poor, take care of widows and orphans, proclaim the good news, set captives free, bring sight to the blind, make disciples of all nations, destroy the works of the enemy, visit those in prison, clothe the naked, feed the hungry... That couldn't all be my purpose!

I had confused the commands in scripture with purpose. In my head, purpose had been reduced to dos and don'ts. Purpose was robbed of power and replaced with obligation and obedience. I found no appeal in that. I wanted to know my destiny, not a list of things that everyone should do.

I think that is common for many of us. We look first to see our path in the midst of the grander purpose, and by doing so, we miss out. When we choose to follow Christ, we choose to be part of the core team set to achieve the purposes of God on this earth. And what are those? Nothing less than the rescuing of each individual in the world, the breaking of the darkness over people's lives and the reconciliation between them and their Father, a restoration of his kingdom on earth.

No matter what job or ministry we have, this purpose will still stand. No matter what particular calling the Lord gives to us or spiritual gifts we receive, they will be a part of this purpose, and that is wonderful.

All the dos and don'ts detailed in scripture are to help us understand how to pursue that purpose and be effective in it. I do believe that God has specific tasks for us to accomplish as part of the grander purpose, and we will be talking about that in Chapter 18. Growing in our children the foundational purpose of love and freedom we are all called to is absolutely crucial to their ability to feel and be effective and purposeful each day. Without this understanding of our foundational purpose, our children can feel paralysed and unsatisfied in their search for what God wants them to do.

So how do we train our children to embrace and pursue this purpose Jesus passed to them? In the next four chapters we will be exploring how to help our children to:

- see how powerful they really are;
- live a life of compassion and courage;
- run their individual path well and confidently.

In doing so, we will look at how we can apply the six-stage circle, introduced in Chapter 8, to instilling these values in our kids.

16

Seeing power in the mirror

At a weekend away, the children were having their own time to connect with God in prayer, and a nine-year-old girl beckoned me over to tell me about her time with God. She told me that while she was chatting with God, a picture popped up in her mind of his giving her a crown at school for her to wear. As the story progressed in her mind, she walked around with the crown on her head, and people moved out of the way and listened to what she had to say. She told me that she thought it was because God is a king and her Father, and we chatted a bit about what that means in scripture. I asked her if she felt God was asking her to do something specific with the influence he has given her as his child. Instantly her thoughts went to a 'weird' girl who had no friends and was very lonely. She talked about how she could totally change how that girl feels every day if she decided to be faithful friends with her and connect her into other friends.

A shadow crossed her face. 'What if she becomes really clingy because she doesn't have other friends? What if my friends don't like her because she is weird and they stop being my friend because of it?' she wondered aloud. I nodded and told her that there is a lot to weigh up when choosing what to do. Her face wrinkled up. 'Oh gosh, it is hard sometimes having so much power and responsibility as the child of the king, isn't it?' she mused. I assured her that it is, sometimes. After a pause, she nodded solemnly and said, with a smile spreading across her face, 'I choose to change her life. This is going to be gooooood.'

We live in a world that tends to disempower children. Our culture communicates that power comes through titles and roles, through being a 'leader' or controlling our environment or our peers. Social status and being famous give us power, our culture says. Physical intimidation gives us power. Being the smartest, the prettiest, the strongest are all ways to gain what we don't have: power. Children want to play with the right toys, to dress in a certain way, to fit in and be clever, or louder or less weird or anything else that will allow other people to find value in them. They feel the pressure to change themselves to what other people like so that they can be endowed with power by others.

What our children often don't understand is that they are powerful without all those things. They were given power when they were created and have been given a powerful identity because of their relationship with God. They have somehow been lied to about how powerful they are, and so they chase after regaining something they never lost.

The first step towards building purposeful children is to shape powerful ones. This process is about helping children to discover their natural power as people, and then linking their understanding of how powerful they are to who God made them to be on this earth. They need to be trained to see power in the mirror, to be able to look at themselves and see a powerful person, and to be equipped to know how to use it well. Purpose is just a directed application of the power they already have.

Too often we try to push children into purpose when they don't understand how powerful they are. This leads them to feel inadequate and stressed, feeling the 'shoulds' press on them to perform religion well instead of confidently living who they truly are. For children to understand power, they have to know that who they are matters as well as what they do. They need to know that:

- They are heavy: their presence carries weight.
- Their voice is powerful.
- They are an influential follower.
- They have spiritual power and authority because they are God's child.

I am heavy: my presence carries weight

Often children and young people are used to being the 'add-on' to the more powerful people in the room. Usually these people are the adults or the natural leaders among their peers. They have learned that other people are the ones who decide if they are or aren't valuable and significant in a certain context. They have to wait to be given power by the people who hold it.

Some of this is a right understanding of how certain social situations work, and that is perfectly proper. We do not always have the position to speak or influence in situations. If I attended Prime Minister's Questions in the gallery, I would not have the right to speak because I have not been given that position. While there is a right teaching of respect and position, though, sometimes children can internalise that to help shape their identity as always powerless unless someone gives them power.

Children need to know the many ways that they are always significant, which is the power they carry just by being themselves. I describe it to children this way: they are heavy. This heaviness comes from being a creation of God. They were designed with the ability to be powerful.

Sometimes children feel as if they are a feather. They can't really make a difference to the societal or spiritual scales either way. But when we teach our children to view themselves as having weight, they begin to learn that where they put this weight can shift the balance and make a huge difference. Their weight can tip the scales. They need to know that when they are part of a crowd, they still can have an impact. They don't stop being who they are because they are in a crowd. When they are in a room and something wrong is happening, simply by standing by they are saying that they approve and agree that it's okay. When we agree with people, we add weight to their choices.

Children need to know what to do with their weight when they are in a large group. If they think they are a feather, it's easy for them to go along with the wind. If they think of themselves like a lead weight, they have to make a choice to move their weight.

This is the way I often talk children through a scenario of being in a large group:

> Sometimes, when you are in a group, you choose to put your weight behind the leader. But if your group starts to discuss or do things that squish your integrity, what should you do? 1) Use your voice and then 2) decide where to put your weight. If people want to do something with which you don't agree, put your weight somewhere else. You can be the one who says, 'No thanks, I'm going to go over here and do something else.' If a group is bullying, then you can move your weight over to the one who needs help. Be the one who stands next to him and tells the bullies to back off, or invite the child to leave and play with you.

I tell children that if you stay part of a crowd, you have chosen to keep your weight there, and you are responsible for the power you have added to it.

My voice is powerful

As babies begin to talk, they grow in their understanding of the usefulness of words. As they grow older, though, life can teach them that their words are not valuable or powerful when dealing with other people. In order for children to feel able to affect the world around them, they must feel confident that their voices, their words, are influential.

The truth is that everyone's voice is intrinsically powerful. You don't have to be in charge to be influential. That's why what we say matters so much. Encouragement and compliments lift people up, and insults and mean observations hurt. Scripture talks about how our tongues are like a spark that can start a forest fire (James 3:1–12). Solomon went so far as to say words can bring death or life (Proverbs 18:21). Part of human design is that the words we speak out about ourselves and others impact on other people's self-perceptions and relationships and on society itself.

Each one of our children has a powerful voice. Their opinions, insights, thoughts and ideas are valuable and important, even in disagreement. They have a unique view that needs to be heard and counselled with, and it is important that they learn to use their powerful voice responsibly and positively.

I am an influential follower

Our children can sometimes feel that unless they are the leader, they are nothing. I believe that this is because we haven't trained them in the immense power of being a follower. Derek Sivers drew our attention to this phenomenon at a TED conference (see sivers.org/ff). He showed a YouTube video taken at a music festival. There was a sea of thousands of people sitting and listening to a performance on the side of a large hill, and on the fringes of the crowd was a man. He was a tiny, skinny man in little shorts dancing with ridiculous and complete abandonment, like I used to do as a child in front of my mirror in my bedroom. This man was on his own, having a great time, while thousands of people rolled their eyes and judged him. He did this for over half an hour, just as wacky, just as weird, totally revelling in the music.

And then it happened. One guy leaped up out of the crowd and joined him. He didn't join in shyly; he went for it, just like the original dancer. About 30 or 40 seconds later, a second man joined, and then five and then 20 and then 80 and in the span of three minutes, over 100 people were dancing and laughing and having a great time surrounding this man, dancing just like him. As that song ended, a huge cheer went up and they lifted the original dancer in the air.

Derek Sivers asked the questions: what made the difference? What created this moment? In his view, it was the first follower. The first follower turned the wacky guy into a leader. He showed others how to follow and broke down barriers for others to join in. The second follower was also important and the subsequent followers added momentum, but it took a lot of bravery for the first follower in particular to throw his weight in with the original lone dancer. The first follower's choice changed the dance of one man into a movement.

We see this in scripture over and over again, but never more so than with Jesus' disciples. Jesus was one man doing great things, but it was his disciples, empowered by the Holy Spirit, who took his message around the world. Being a follower is a powerful thing. Our children need to know that they are just as powerful when they are a follower. They can add their weight to someone or something and make a huge difference.

They can be the first follower. Who do they see at church, at school or in the community who is doing something good but needs someone to believe in her, to join her, to have someone add weight to her voice? What ministry needs their support financially or physically? What lonely child with a great idea needs someone to go to his meeting? Who is God asking our children to stand by and be the best follower there is? Rather than thinking, 'Who else will be there?', could they think, 'What would I add if I went?'

I have spiritual power and authority because I am God's child

When we know who we are, we naturally live by the permission and authority that this gives. A child knows the rules of the house and also knows the permissions of the house granted to her because of who she is. She can walk into the house, dump her clothes in her room, grab some food, plonk down on the sofa and whack on the TV because it is her home – not because she did anything to earn it, but because she is her parent's child. That identity gives her authority to live in her home and special permission to access most of it.

Children know how this feels, because every day they act as your children. They know what that requires, what permission they have, and what authority they carry because of it. My dad was a police officer as well as an instructor at the police academy. As a teen and young adult, I could confidently walk through the gates of the police academy and into rooms with intimidating men and seas of cadets and feel totally comfortable – not because I had any right to be there or do anything, but because of who my dad was and the identity I had through him. I had a right to be there because of my father. It was his authority of which I was able to be a part.

When we came into Christ, we became children of God. Our identity as children of God gives us not only access to our Father but also a confidence in the freedom and permission we have because of who he is, not because of who we are.

When Jesus was ministering on earth, he had the authority that his Father gave him. 'All authority in heaven and on earth has been given to me,' Jesus said (Matthew 28:18). Because of his authority and the power of the Holy Spirit that empowered him, he worked out his purpose on earth, accomplishing great things. Then Jesus gave his authority to us, and now we can do the same.

Our children can have a solid sense of identity and authority in Christ in order to accomplish what God has called them to accomplish on this earth.

When our children know that they have weight, that their voices are powerful, that they are influential followers and that they are children of God who carry spiritual authority, then they are able to work out their purpose by simply choosing where to apply the power they know they have.

The six-stage circle

So as parents, how can we instil these truths in our children? Let's explore some ideas using the six-stage circle tool.

Model

Tell stories of times when you were in a crowd and disagreed with what was happening. What did you do, and why? How did you feel about it? How do you think God felt about it?

When you are all together as a family, let your children see you being 'heavy' and making a difference. Help a struggling single mother to load her car with her groceries, help a family move, give a homeless man your umbrella even if it is raining and this leaves you wet, cook meals for a grieving family. Let them see you making a difference in people's lives, just by being there for others when no one else is.

Let them see you use your voice in powerful ways. Deflect some gossip or defend someone who needs it. Encourage and build up someone who is upset or praise others in their failure. Let your children see the impact a voice can make on people and situations.

Do some reflecting on your experiences as a follower. Where are you adding your weight? Where are you going for the purpose of following well or for being that key follower who adds momentum? Invite your children along. Create a window for them to hear your feelings about it and why you go.

Create windows into how you live as a child of God. Chat to God informally in front of them. Share your favourite worship song or Bible story. Tell them a story of when you first realised what it meant to be a child of God.

Pray for people in front of your children, so they can learn what it means to pray with authority as God's child.

Frame

When you are heading out to attend a meeting, frame the power of your presence, your heaviness. For example, 'I really want to go because it's important for Susie to see that I support her. I want to be a positive person in the room to help other people join in. What she is doing is important, and I want to add my weight to what she is doing. I can really help by going.'

Wonder out loud about the people in the Bible who used their weight to tip the scales. Daniel was one man disobeying an unjust law (Daniel 6). Shadrach, Meshach and Abednego put their lives on the line to put their weight with God (Daniel 3). Esther weighed in with the king and saved a nation (see the book of Esther). Tell stories of people in the Bible who used their voice powerfully. John the Baptist showed Jesus to people (Matthew 3; Mark 1; Luke 3; John 1). Gamaliel stopped a crowd from killing Peter and a group of disciples just by speaking wisdom (Acts 5:34–40). Jesus' words brought spiritual and emotional freedom to people.

Debrief with your children why you speak the way that you do in certain places. For instance: 'Have you ever noticed that when we are at Scouts and your leader says things that you know I disagree with, I just smile? It's because I don't want to embarrass him. Sometimes I chat with him about it afterwards if I think it's important. It's good to make sure that, if we can, we use our voices in a way that doesn't embarrass people.'

Watch movies together and discuss the 'sidekicks' and key followers who empower the leader. Could the leader have accomplished all that hero work without them? Why, or why not? Why don't followers get as much attention?

Go to places with your child, and instead of chatting with the leaders, chat with the key followers. Praise them in front of your children and acknowledge their key roles.

Point out when people are being the first followers or part of an initial group. Notice how the situation changes because of what they do. Notice when a situation really needed a first follower to participate in order to take off, but no one stepped up. How did the leader feel? How would it have been different if followers had joined in?

Verbally frame aspects of your relationship with God when you act out of that place of God-connection. For example, before you head into Nanny and Grandad's house, take a minute to pray as a family, thanking God for being your Father and asking that he come with you into the house so that they may know him better through you.

Equip

Chat over possible scenarios that would require your children to make a tough decision about where they put their weight. While you are doing dishes or driving around, pose hypothetical situations and ask what they think they would do. For example: 'When I was your age, I went to the toilet at school and found three children making fun of a little child while he washed his hands. I'm not sure I handled it very well. What do you think you would do in that situation? What are the choices?' There is no right answer to these questions, but it can help your children to work through all the different scenarios. They could ignore it and just go to the toilet. They could distract the bullies by asking a question. They could join the small child and wash their hands and leave with him, and be able to use their powerful voice to encourage. They could tell the bullies to stop and defend the small child. They could leave and get a teacher. They could just leave and do nothing. There are many choices, with different consequences for each. Have a great conversation!

Wonder out loud what makes a good follower. Invite the curate or assistant minister to your home and ask about his or her journey in that supporting role.

Plan together to attempt to be the best followers ever during something (sports practice, church, Scouts) and then discuss how it went. What worked? What didn't? How did it feel?

Notice when your children are following well or bravely choosing to be a first follower or part of an initial group. Help them to see the impact it made on other people.

Continue to help your children develop a deeper heart-to-heart connection with God. Ask them about how it feels to do life with God together, and chat with them about all the precious moments you cherish with God throughout the day. Suggest that they find a similar moment with God each day.

Create opportunities

As a family, stop when you enter church, look around and decide if there is any place that needs your family's weight. Is there a new family that could use some companionship? Is there a family with several young children that could use some extra hands during worship?

Come home from a tough day and ask your child's advice on a work scenario. For instance: 'Someone at work is very cranky and is hurting people with her words. I want to say or do something to help the situation, but I haven't quite figured out what. What do you think?' Ask follow-up questions and chat about the consequences of the possibilities. Don't forget to give feedback once you do something about it!

Help your children to spot opportunities to be excellent followers for someone. Help them to find some cause that touches their hearts and to which they would want to add their weight. Encourage them to pursue it or offer to go with them. This could be anything from hearing a friend mention a good idea to solve a problem at school, to being moved to go on a mission trip. It could be volunteering to join a team on a new ministry at church or writing encouragement letters to persecuted Christians in China. The more you expose your child to good leaders with passion, the more their hearts will have the variety to chime with!

Invite your children along to be influential followers in something you are leading. Chat before the event about where you need support and how they could help the situation. After the event, help your children to see how they influenced other people to engage by being brilliant followers. Express your gratitude and appreciation.

When your child has a nightmare, remind her that, as a child of God, God is with her always. God is right next to her, and so she can tell the dreams to go away in the name of Jesus because she is God's child. Share with her that the Bible says that 'perfect love drives out fear' (1 John 4:18) and invite God to hug your child and sweep all the fear away.

Expose your child to needs in your community and in the world, and suggest that you would support her if she wanted to add her weight to do something about it.

Coach her through the process of finding out more information, planning a way to help and accomplishing her goal: this could be anything from a collection for orphans in Uganda, to gathering toys for the poor in your town, to a sponsored silence for a disabled child at her school, to visiting the elderly at Christmas.

Establish boundaries

How do you want to guide your children in the development of understanding their own power? What are the boundaries for their behaviour? Some parents set boundaries for their children's external behaviour. It might look like this: 'If you are part of a group or being a follower, then you should do it well. If you can't keep your integrity as part of a group, we can give you some time off to think about how you want to deal with those situations when you return.' Maybe it is simply watching your children's internal development and knowing when you want to step in to coach a bit more. If you notice that a particular group or leader is making your children feel powerless and out of control, then you might want to step in to coach your children to find their voice again. If you see them standing by while something bad happens, do you want to hold them accountable for adding their implicit weight to it, or, rather, ask them what they did about the situation?

Check the messages that are going into your child's head from both the secular and Christian scenarios of which they are part. Is your child being surrounded by the message that power is found in violence or in beauty? Are the media that he watches reinforcing his God-given power or redefining it? Are the friends she is playing with making her feel powerful or powerless?

Children are designed to be part of God's plan on this earth. It is part of how they were created. They have the power to impact people's physical, emotional, mental and spiritual lives significantly. We want them to know this for themselves, but we also need to ensure that they understand that all of this is true of others. As they learn how to exercise their power, they will need to learn how to respect and honour other people's power as well. Many of your house rules may naturally fall within this idea. For instance: 'Please don't pull at your brother. He has chosen not to play and we respect people's decision to say no. Why don't you go and play and we'll see where he chooses to be,' or 'Please don't yell over people. It is important that everyone's voice is allowed to be powerful. We don't use our powerful voices to squish others.' 'Please be careful of your bossiness. Your friends chose to be followers when they said "yes" to your game, but it is important to honour our followers and treat them well. They could choose to follow someone else.'

Give feedback

Raising our children to be powerful people requires them to have a safe place to be part of a consistent and loving feedback loop. Our families are the perfect places for this to happen.

Would our parenting change if we treated our children as significant people whose presence and voice carried weight in our lives and in our family? Could we consult them more or ask their opinion? Often we just get on with life, taking all the decisions for our family, big and small. Our children get used to not having a voice in the group of our family, with the power resting solely with the parents. How can we adjust our parenting so that we still hold leadership without disempowering our children? Here are some ideas.

Notice and acknowledge when they enter a room. Look up, smile, wave and pat them on the back. Let them know you see them and are glad they are there. Often we spend significant chunks of our time with our children while tuning them out. Let them know that their presence is important to you.

Give your children significant roles in an activity. Arrange it so that their contribution makes a difference or that the task would have been harder if they hadn't been there. After the activity is done, be specific about how they not only helped you but also enabled other benefits. For instance, by helping you to shop, the errand went faster, so you had more time to be peaceful, and the whole family was less stressed. The result: they helped to change the home atmosphere by helping you. Or, because they planned and cooked a meal for you, you were able to meet up with a struggling friend and help her through a difficult time. The result: their powerfulness enabled a person they don't know to feel blessed. When we not only let them help us but also show them the impact of their efforts, then we remove the word 'just' from their sentences ('I'm *just* a helper, not a leader,' 'I *just* pushed the trolley'). They will begin to learn that their weight added to the whole, so that they were a part of the result.

Allow your children to come up with the solutions to their own problems. Instead of rushing to help or sorting it for them, say, 'Oh no! What are you going to do?' This communicates to your children that you are confident that they are able to respond to a difficult situation.

Choose situations during the day in which your child can participate in the decision-making. For instance, invite your child to run errands with you and give them the choice of which shop to visit first, or ask their advice on what vegetable to serve for dinner. Ask their opinion about situations and take their advice. Often we ask their opinion and then ignore it or do something different. From little to large situations, the more you genuinely allow them to influence decisions, the more comfortable they will be in their voice having power and in the consequences this will have.

Make your home a place for your child to exercise her authority as a child of God. Empower her relationship with God daily and give her the honour of leading the family in prayer at the Christmas meal.

17

Learning the way of love

I was praying with nine-year-old Lucy, who was being badly bullied. She came to pray with me that God would stop the verbal abuse. We prayed for God to help heal Lucy's heart from the mean words spoken to her, and for God to protect her at school. As we chatted together afterwards, I mentioned that often people become bullies because something is going on in their lives. I gently suggested that if she was up for it, she could ask God about it. She looked surprised at the idea and wanted to ask him right then.

We sat back down and she settled in. She asked God what was going on in the bully's life. In the silence that followed, God showed her a picture of the bully sitting alone on the ground in the middle of a field, bleeding, next to a fallen bike, and her family far away laughing at her. Lucy was disturbed that no one was helping her, and she felt that God was showing her how the other girl felt lonely, unloved and hurt. Something welled up in Lucy as she told me about what God had showed her. She said, 'I just want to pray some more right now.'

As I sat next to her, she prayed earnestly for about ten minutes, asking God to give friends to the lonely and hurt girl, to help her feel God's love and smile, to change her life circumstances and to heal her hurt heart. When Lucy finished, she was totally changed. She was no longer focused on the hurt of being bullied but was filled with compassion for this other child. She sat and thought for a bit and decided that she was going to make it her goal to show this other child that she was loveable: 'I know that she will probably just keep being mean to me, but I will keep reminding myself of how she feels inside. I won't let her hurt me or push me, but I'm not going to ignore her or be mean back. I'll still protect me, but I'm also going to attack her with niceness and love. All year. Someone needs to make her feel that she isn't alone.'

We must remember that at the root of purpose is simple love. Jesus answered the question 'Which is the greatest commandment?' with 'Love the Lord your God with all your heart and with all your soul and with all your mind,' but he did not finish there. He went on to summarise the rest of the law as 'Love your neighbour as yourself' (Matthew 22:37–40). 'Neighbour' here literally means anyone you have anything to do with. To Jesus, expressing love for God is inextricably linked with loving others. Ignoring or retreating from the world is simply not an option. Multi-directional love is at the very centre of the Christian purpose.

Cultivating our 'heart garden'

In our modern Christianity we have begun, wrongly, to separate the idea of 'acting lovingly' from the concept of actual 'love'. 'Love is an action,' I have heard said in churches. 'We don't need to feel full of love to act out of love.' In another sermon I heard, 'We can't just wait for the fuzzy feeling of the emotion of love to come; sometimes we just need to act lovingly first.' I even read in a children's curriculum: 'Love is a choice, not an emotion.'

I think this separation is a false one. This concept has allowed God's command to love to become mere religious duty. When it says in scripture that God is love or that God's love is abounding and everlasting, it is not talking about him just acting lovingly without feeling it. When Jesus walked on the earth, he didn't merely act as if he loved people. I believe that the heart of the Father, the Son and the Spirit is love. I believe that when we were commanded to love God and others, it was a genuine command to cultivate a heart full of love from which our actions would naturally flow.

I am responsible before God to love him authentically from the depths of my soul and being, and to love my neighbour authentically from that same place. It is my job as a parent, with the help of the Spirit, to tend my heart garden to produce the fruit of love – to remove the weeds that choke the growth of love, to feed and provide for the nourishment of my love, and to protect and guard it so that it doesn't become scarred or unusable. It is my job to ensure that what my heart grows and pours out *through* my choices and actions is love.

So often we tell our children to think of what would be the loving thing to do in a situation and then to do it. This isn't what God is talking about. In every situation, we are called to *love*, not just to perform. Love isn't a thought process. Love isn't an action first. It is a heart attitude, a spiritual fruit of a walk with our Father. Love is an emotion; a powerful, motivating energy generator that powers our actions. If we disconnect that generator, if we deny the necessity of the motivational cultivation, we are left merely with striving and religious duty, attempting to fulfil tasks he never gave us.

We are called to love the way Jesus loved. We need to start noticing how he cultivated his heart, instead of how to replicate his actions.

When a conflict arises between children, we often try to help them problem-solve what to do. We focus on their behaviour instead of their heart. When the name-calling or the shoving starts, we often try to stop this behaviour and reinforce better behaviour. All well and good, but how often do we pull our child aside and say, 'What's going on with your heart? It seems that it only took a little thing for you to get very angry with Daniel. Why do you think you are so angry? What pushed the love away?' It is our job to help our children to learn to reconcile and live with a heart of love instead of a muddled heart of anger, pain, fear or stress.

It is our job as parents not only to grow in our children a heart of compassion, but also to give them a worldview of love. It is our job to teach our children how to be in charge of their own heart gardens. Too often our children feel victims of the world. People hurt them and disappoint them and their hearts get battered, and their only way to fix it is to lash out or strike back or shut others out or try to control the other person. We are able to coach our children in how to defend their hearts well, maintain love with strength and forgive others in order to keep their hearts in a healthy state. It is training our children to pause before they act; to notice that 'I'm filled with hurt and bitterness towards this person' and sort that heart position out first. It's restoring love before they act lovingly, instead of the other way around.

Why? Because real love is transformational for all involved. The Bible tells us that love chases away all fear (1 John 4:18), and causes us to lay down our lives for each other (John 15:13). It is how we will be known to the world (13:35) and it is how Jesus provided a way for us to reconcile with the Father and how he bought freedom for us (3:16). Love is at the core of how we as humans respond. It is the key to our hearts and to this broken world.

So if we are called to love as Jesus loved, how did he cultivate his heart garden, and how can we do that with our children? Scripture gives us some clues of how Jesus grew and operated out of a pure love for his Father and for others. He:

- drew close to God;
- saw people through God's eyes;
- maintained compassion for people and loved them as himself;
- walked in forgiveness.

Drawing close to God

When Jesus' disciple John was talking about love, he pointed directly to the source of all love:

> My dear friends, we must love each other. Love comes from God, and when we love each other, it shows that we have been given new life. We are now God's children, and we know him. God is love, and anyone who doesn't love others has never known him… We love because God loved us first.
> 1 JOHN 4:7–8, 19 (CEV)

Jesus often carved out time to spend with God, one to one. He went to his Father for comfort and counsel, to worship him and to draw near to him (see Mark 1:35; 6:45–46; 14:32–34; Luke 5:16). Throughout his life, Jesus was so aware of the presence of his Father that he told his disciples that he did only what he saw his Father doing (John 5:19). Jesus rooted himself in the knowledge, presence and love of his Father.

It is absolutely essential that children know the intensity of emotion the Father feels for them, especially children who come from broken circumstances or painful home lives. They must also understand that God's love is expressed in an active pursuit of us. It is expressed in Jesus' laying aside his majesty and coming to dwell with us; in giving up his life on the cross to reconcile us; in reaching out in acts of mercy throughout history in order to see lives transformed.

Children need to know that because of what Jesus did, we can be God's children and experience a personal and daily life with him filled with his joy, presence and love. They deserve to grow to know God and his love for them deep in their being, so that they can't be shaken from it by the world.

When children are God-connected and not just God-smart, their understanding of love comes to life. Since God is the essence of love, the best way to define it for them is to connect them in relationship with him! If love flows out of our relationship with God and how we see each other in the light of this, love is a worldview to cultivate, not a rule to enforce.

Seeing people through God's eyes

When Jesus met people, he rarely responded to what he saw with his own eyes. Most of the time, he saw people through his Father's eyes as precious, lost, needy and loved. Often he would hear his Father speak specifics about people's lives, hearts and circumstances, even before the people themselves shared them.

Jesus was able to love people extraordinarily because he saw them through the eyes of the one who loved them most.

We can empower children's purpose by helping them to learn to see people and situations from God's viewpoint. It is so hard in our humanness to understand, but God's view is different from ours. 'People look at the outward appearance, but the Lord looks at the heart' (1 Samuel 16:7). To us, situations and people can look broken and messy, mean or unfixable. We can see no way forward with our own eyes. God sees differently.

God looks at people's hearts. He sees the whole: the actions and what is deep in the hearts of those who act. When we choose to look from his point of view, we can begin to understand how to love people.

For children, I find it helpful to explain that God has the ability to see into the very centre of people's hearts and minds. That he loves each person on earth deeply and faithfully. That it makes his heart ache with sadness when he sees the people he created hurting each other, suffering, and getting lost in sin and darkness. That he longs to set each one free from all brokenness and give them a hope and a future. I encourage children to go to God with their questions about people and situations, so that they can talk together about how to love best.

It is our honour as parents to be able to frame for our children how to see, not only with our eyes but with God's eyes. We can help them to learn to pause and consider who the person in front of them is to God and then respond out of that understanding. It is also important to be mindful to coach them in how to protect themselves emotionally, spiritually and physically while still loving people with the love of God.

Developing compassion for people

Compassion is a key part of God's heart. Over and over in scripture, we see that compassion is essential to Jesus' character and motivates him to intervene in people's lives. When Jesus walked on earth, he was often moved by compassion to heal or feed or teach.

Compassion comes from understanding and empathising with someone's situation. It requires allowing oneself to hear, see and truly understand what another person is going through and to be emotionally moved in response to it. This natural trait is something that is being eroded by our society and its values. The media allow us to watch people's suffering as entertainment through movies, television crime programmes and children's cartoons. Violence, verbal abuse, rudeness and bullying are all sources of enjoyment as we laugh our way through some 'light entertainment'.

On the playground our boys try to enforce toughness because they don't want to be seen as soft or 'girly', and our girls often get sucked into using emotional and verbal abuse and manipulation with each other.

Compassion isn't a gender issue or an entertainment issue. I'm not arguing that everyone needs to shelter their children in a media-free environment. What I am saying is that compassion is a crucial part of God's character and one of Jesus' main motivations; therefore, it is up to us to shape and help to guide our children in valuing it and operating out of it. It takes deliberation on our part to protect and grow our children's compassion for others.

Walking in forgiveness

Forgiveness was a major theme in Jesus' teachings and in how he lived his life. Jesus even shared with his disciples that before they offered gifts and prayers to God, they needed to forgive others (Mark 11:25; Matthew 5:23). He urged them to sort out their heart gardens on the spot, even in the midst of praying. For Jesus, forgiveness wasn't an occasional thing but a continual process of weeding. Even while experiencing the agony of crucifixion, he still managed to ensure his heart was right and asked his Father to forgive those who were hurting him.

Forgiveness is a big part of maintaining a heart garden of love, and we need to ensure that we are training our children in it well. I describe forgiveness to children like this: if someone broke into your house and stole your stuff, you do not get to go and find him and then kick him in the shins over and over again until you feel he has been punished enough. If someone broke into your house, what would happen? He would be arrested by the police. The punishment for his crime, the consequence for his actions, would be given to him by our justice system. He would be put in prison or made to pay a fine. You would not get to punish the person. Even though the person stole your things, it is the justice system's job to punish, not ours.

When people do bad things to us, something inside us wants to punish them. We want to hurt them back and be the ones to do it. But God says that that is not our job. He is the one who deals with justice. He is the only one who gets to judge people.

So what can you do? First of all, if you are hurt, or if a crime has happened, you need to tell an adult. God put parents, teachers, church leaders and governments there to keep people safe and to help carry out his justice. But what do we do with our hearts and our relationship with others?

Well, we can keep carrying around our emotions, wanting to punish those people and trying to hurt them and get at them, or we can let God help to heal our hearts and trust him to be the judge of those people. We can trust that God will judge them. It's our job not to let that hurt and fear and upsetness damage our heart garden and interfere with the love we are growing or with our ability to live our purpose on earth. Those things can choke our joy and happiness and love. We need to forgive, not because other people deserve it, but because God wants us to live free and humbly before him, letting God be God. Forgiving means saying to yourself and to God, 'I am really hurt and upset, God. What happened to me wasn't right. But I leave it with you to deal with, whichever way you want to. I let go of my anger and my desire to hurt them back. God can help to heal my heart garden so that I can live a life of love and joy and peace again.'

Jesus' ability to forgive and love was so great that he not only didn't desire to punish the people who hurt him, but he even asked God not to punish them. True forgiveness allows love to triumph over all. Because of the lifestyle of love and forgiveness Jesus lived, he was able to fulfil his purpose to bring us freedom from sin and death.

The six-stage circle

So how do we begin to cultivate our children's heart gardens and train our children to maintain their heart gardens for the sake of living out their purpose on earth? Let's explore some practical ideas through the six-stage circle.

Model

Allow your children to see you on your journey of loving God. Let them peek into how you chat with him and access his voice. Talk about your feelings about God and how life with him works. Display to them what an authentic everyday relationship with God looks like, not a fantasy of an ideal one.

Voice your thoughts out loud about people you encounter, sharing how you can see them with God's eyes. As you walk past the homeless man on your road, smile at him and ask how he is getting on. As you walk away, say briefly to your children, 'God loves that man a lot. I was praying for him the other day on the bus.'

Occasionally let your children see some of the ordinary sacrifices of compassion and love that happen in your everyday life. Often our children don't know that you do these things, but unless they see a glimmer of it, they don't know that it's part of the average everyday life of a follower of Jesus. Let them see you opt to buy a cheaper meal for the family so that you can buy a 'special extra' as a gift for someone at church.

Tell stories of when you were wronged and either forgave someone or didn't forgive. Share your experience and the impact your choices made on you and others.

Frame

Be aware of when you tune in to God throughout the day or week. Notice when and how it happens. Share about that experience with your child. For example: 'You know, I never noticed before, but my best times with God are when I am just chatting with him in the shower.' If you think your child is receptive, ask, 'When do you think about God or chat with him?' Don't worry about 'teaching' the answer or correcting your child. This is just to frame experiences, not to nudge your child towards compliance.

While you are sitting in a public place waiting, lean over to your child and ask, 'Who do you see?' Spend some fun time people-watching the way you normally do. Then say, 'God sees people a bit differently. How you do think he sees these same people? What about that man?' If you are both feeling brave, you can ask God directly, 'How do you see that woman in the green coat?' Sometimes you may feel that you want to pray quickly for that person as you watch him or her walk around.

Verbalise when something hits your heart on the news, in your family or circle of friends, or as you walk around. When you drive past a car accident, instead of just saying, 'Oh, here we go. That's what the problem was!' take a moment outwardly to process the flicker of compassion that happens internally as well: 'Oh, here we go. That's what the problem was! Gosh, look. Those people are standing out in the cold and their car is crunched up. They must be feeling very scared, cold and shaken. God, please send your peace to surround them and help them.'

Sometimes conflicts in our friendships or marriages happen in front of our children, but the making-up happens somewhere else. How to resolve conflict and forgiveness healthily is something that often children don't see. On the occasions when your children see part of the conflict, it may be a good opportunity to tell the story of how you resolved the issue and forgave the person. For instance:

Remember the other day when Liz said something that made me feel hurt and I got snappy with her? I'm sorry we did that in front of you. Did that make you feel uncomfortable? Sometimes when my feelings get hurt, I let my words talk out of the wrong place. I was talking out of hurt, not love, and that's never good. I said sorry to Liz, and she said sorry to me. I had to spend some time with God forgiving her, so that next time we chat I'm not thinking, 'You said mean things to me,' but I can think, 'I love Liz.' I feel much better now. I just wanted you to know that I'm okay, and Liz and I are getting on fine.

Equip

Take your children to the local park or to someone's garden and show them how growing a garden works. Maybe invite a friend along who knows about plants and can tell your children about all the work and effort that goes into producing a beautiful garden. Share how our hearts are like gardens, and that it's our job to tend them with God's help so that we can do great things with our lives. We have to be careful what we let grow in our hearts.

When your children are upset about a situation, listen to them and give them compassion and understanding. Validate their feelings, and then ask them: how do they think God sees the situation? Maybe ask God for some wisdom for a way forward. Pray with your children, if they are willing, that God will heal their heart and grow more love that will push out any bad feeling that has taken root in their hearts.

Expose your children to different needs in the world so that they can grow familiar with the struggles people have. Watch documentaries, visit museums or look in magazines. Chat about other people's lives and draw parallels between their experiences and yours. Ponder together why people behave as they do, and to what emotions, worries and fears they might be responding. Compassion is empathy, the ability to understand and feel what other people are feeling. It is important to help to train your children to be able to see others' experiences reflected in their own.

Be a positive and loving mirror for your children as they process hurt. As you support them in their journey, notice when they are acting out of hurt and pain. Highlight for them how stressful and painful it is for them, and how it is affecting others. Gently open up a conversation about how they feel, and why they do or don't want to get rid of that anger by forgiving. Listen to their concerns and allow them to go on the journey of forgiveness at their own pace.

Invite your children to join you as you meet up with a mum and her special needs child who is lonely. Share a story of when you were lonely and how you can see that they are feeling the same way now. Chat about how you wished someone had done this for you, and now you can do it for someone else. Whatever you normally do, just create a little window for them to see in.

Avoid pairing up 'forgiveness' with 'getting along'. Often we set up a scenario where one child apologises to the other one, and then we communicate an expectation that forgiveness will happen automatically. If one of our children is moping, we can accidentally try to force him into 'forgiving' his sibling in an effort to end the conflict. Instead, try communicating that it is all right if he is struggling to forgive, but while he is sorting out his feelings between himself and God, you would ask that he is at least polite to his sibling. This enables the child to see the difference between a heart change and the behaviour you expect.

Create opportunities

Resource your children's heart connection to God. If you notice that they love music, buy them a worship CD. If they like reading, get them a devotional or testimony book. Send them to a midweek children's group at church or ask them to journal with you as you do your time with God in the mornings.

Invite your child to be more active in church, seeing people from God's view and helping those who need help to find a place to sit or people to talk to.

Stay tuned into your child when everyday opportunities arise to foster compassion. If there is an older person struggling with his trolley, point it out to your child and ponder how you feel when you are physically struggling. If your child seems to be engaging with the idea, wonder what you both could do to help lift his burden, and do it together. No matter where you are, take the natural opportunities to foster compassion and connect it to action.

You won't need to create opportunities for forgiveness. The world will provide those!

Establish boundaries

Lay a foundation of conversation with your children about 'heart gardens'. Chat to your children about how Jesus once said that the words that come out of our mouths come from the overflow of what is in our hearts (Luke 6:45). Let them know that if you notice their words are telling you and other people that something is not going well in their hearts, then you are going to ask them about it, and you would love to help them sort it out. They won't ever be in trouble about what is happening in their hearts. You are their parent and love every bit of them. You want them to have all the great things God has for them, and that includes freedom, peace, joy, love and happiness in their hearts.

Children can get confused about the difference between forgiveness and trust. When talking through forgiveness with children, it is helpful for them to know that just because they forgive someone doesn't mean they have to trust them again immediately. Some people aren't trustworthy with our hearts or with our belongings. Some people aren't safe to be around or haven't yet earned our trust. Forgiving people who hurt us means that we let go of wanting to punish them. God helps to restore our hearts to the place where we can live our purpose well. Forgiving people does not mean that we stay in a place or relationship with people who hurt us.

Give feedback

If you notice your children changing because of their encounters with God and their life walk with him, let them know! 'Son, you have made me feel so loved recently. Thank you so much. It just seems to flow out of your heart.'

Draw your children's attention to the impact they are making on their relationships and on those to whom they minister. Tell stories in front of them of the impact they are making on friends or family members.

Notice when your children do something out of compassion. Don't necessarily thank them, but simply say, 'I saw it when you slowed down while you were playing after school to let your friend win. He had come in last each time, and I saw you wanted him not to feel sad. That was a fine bit of compassion you did right there. Did it work out the way you thought it would?' Invite him to tell you the story of why he chose to do that and what impact he saw. Training children to create their own feedback loops is essential for the inevitable day when you can no longer debrief every situation in life with them.

18

Finding our calling

I was chatting with ten-year-old Ben over ice cream, and he was conflicted: 'I don't know what I'm supposed to do when I grow up. I'm good at singing, so I guess I could be a pop star or worship leader or something. My mum says I have the gift of helping, so I guess a waiter or whatever? I don't know. I don't have to decide yet, I don't think. I'm still a child, but I want to know.'

Finding our calling, our individual path on our journey of purpose is something that we all ponder. It matters to our children as well as to us. If we can learn how to talk to our children about it and to help them feel confident and peaceful about finding their individual path in life, we will be giving them a huge gift of empowerment.

My family and I love watching sports. There is just something about it that gets me very excited: the variety, the pageantry, the high stakes and the gathering of people from around the world. The event that fascinates me most is the marathon.

Lining up together, a sea of individuals stretch, jump and prepare themselves for the ordeal ahead. They all look the same to me, but they are vastly different. Their journeys to get to this moment in time defy categorisation. The race before them isn't really about beating each other, but running the race they have set out for themselves. Each one will have particular weaknesses to watch out for, strengths to rely on, dangers to overcome, temptations to fight. Their motivations are different, their strategies will vary, but the goal is the same: to complete their own race in their own marathon.

The author of Hebrews talks about our life's journey as something similar. 'Therefore, since we are surrounded by such a great cloud of witnesses, let us throw off everything that hinders and the sin that so easily entangles. And let us run with perseverance the race marked out for us, fixing our eyes on Jesus, the pioneer and perfecter of faith' (Hebrews 12:1–2).

We are all on this journey of a life of faith and purpose, adults and children alike. We run alongside each other.

Problems can arise when we become so focused on discovering our individual path that we forget that the goal of the race ahead has been clearly declared: to stand before God at the end of our lives and look back with him and see that we have run our race well; to have accomplished what God has asked us to do; to have lived a life loving the Lord with all our heart, soul, mind and strength, and loving our neighbour as ourselves. Our children can spend a lifetime ignoring the foundational goal of their lives while trying to search for their individual path.

Look at the disciples and those who followed Jesus. They all came from different places and different life experiences, and they shared the common ground of being with Jesus and being trained by him. After he ascended to heaven, they lived their lives. Their individual paths were vastly different: some were apostles and travelled around the world, some stayed at home and cared for orphans and widows, some continued as parents and husbands living transformational lives at their everyday jobs, some were publicly martyred, some preached to thousands, and some were mothers who raised a generation of children who loved God and lived purposeful lives. All of them shared the same foundational goal, but it looked different for each person. All of them shared the same experience with Jesus and were sent out to live lives of purpose, following Jesus' teachings and being empowered by the Spirit. But their individual paths were very different from each other as they each pursued the goal to the best of their ability.

Children are not all the same. Our children are vastly different from each other, and their paths will turn out to be unique. How can we as parents keep them focused on the foundational goal we are all commanded to pursue, prepare their hearts, and still encourage and support them as they run their individual journeys?

Determining a path

In this highly individualised society, we tend to be very good at self-analysis. We crave it. There are seemingly a billion different ways to categorise people. We seek to know ourselves more and more and, by knowing ourselves, we hope to express ourselves more fully. We have personality tests, magazine quizzes, learning styles, leadership strength tests, compatibility analysis and so on to help us know who we are. The design worlds try to convince us to express ourselves through our clothes, our homes and our choices of music and art.

Self-knowledge and self-expression are seen as essential in our modern world. So naturally an intense desire arises in us to help our children self-analyse spiritually.

What are their spiritual gifts? What is their unique path and calling in this life? How do I help them find that? The big questions ring in our children's heads strongly: 'What am I going to do with my life? What is "God's will" for me on this planet? What is my calling?' Often, in Christian circles, we place an emphasis on the unique shape of the individual and the unique 'calling' people have in their lives. The problem is that the answers seem so illusory that the search can paralyse children and teens as they look for their tiny thread in the massive tapestry of the world.

When my son was two, I became the world's best day-bag packer. I could look at what we were going to do on that day and pack the perfect bag to facilitate it. Breakfast on the road, followed by a swimming lesson, followed by a lunch meeting with a volunteer, afternoon shopping, attending a birthday party and then home. No problem. The bag would be perfect, ready to facilitate everything we had to accomplish (adjusting even for what his personality would be like at certain times of day).

My son became accustomed to the magic of the day bag. We would arrive at a location, and before he even asked, the relevant tools would appear. If they didn't appear, then at any moment he could look up to me and sign (he had profound loss of hearing): Apple? Car? Sticker book? Swimming? Cereal? And I would smile and go into the bag and get it. The bag was packed to facilitate the day. He would have everything he needed to accomplish the journey of the day and the tasks we had to achieve.

Our personality, skills and spiritual gifts are similar to the items in my son's day bag. God gives them to us. When we get them is not really relevant; the important thing is that we have them to accomplish the journey of the day and the tasks before us.

It would be very frustrating for my child to rip open his bag at the beginning of the day and see swimming shorts, toy cars, a present with indecipherable writing, my wallet, my phone, his sticker book, my tablet, a bag of cereal, a towel, two nappies, my notepad and his headphones. He could guess some of the events of the day, but about others he would have no idea, and he certainly wouldn't know the order of events.

So often we do that with our spiritual gifts! We stare at our individual make-up to try and find out what the journey of our life will be, and what great things we should accomplish. We rummage around in our spiritual day bag and try to solve the mystery of our purpose by analysing the contents.

We often do this to ourselves and to our children. We try to figure out our gifts. We analyse ourselves and our children. We take the quiz.

It is a frustrating place to be for two reasons: 1) spiritual gifts are not designed to forecast our future, just to facilitate it, and 2) we could be wrong in our assessment of ourselves or we could limit ourselves. God designed us. He knows all he put into us already, and he will continue to give us what we need as we go along (1 Corinthians 12:4–7). If we decide what gifts we have and don't have, we may miss what God is prompting us to do because we have already judged our lack of suitability instead of confidently moving in the opportunities God has created for us.

I take my child to the leisure centre for the purpose of swimming: to enjoy himself, to learn how to swim and to meet with friends. I pack everything he needs to participate fully. I go with him into the pool. If my child refused to go into the leisure centre because he didn't see the swimming shorts in his bag, it would be ridiculous. He goes into the leisure centre full of excitement because we are together and I have taken him there. He doesn't even think about whether or not I have what he needs.

Often we are more like Moses. He had been raised in Pharaoh's household, and his character had been shaped by God. God drew Moses to a place to talk with him about the next step.

> The Lord said, 'I have indeed seen the misery of my people in Egypt. I have heard them crying out because of their slave drivers, and I am concerned about their suffering. So I have come down to rescue them from the hand of the Egyptians and to bring them up out of that land into a good and spacious land, a land flowing with milk and honey – the home of the Canaanites, Hittites, Amorites, Perizzites, Hivites and Jebusites. And now the cry of the Israelites has reached me, and I have seen the way the Egyptians are oppressing them. So now, go. I am sending you to Pharaoh to bring my people the Israelites out of Egypt.'
>
> But Moses said to God, 'Who am I that I should go to Pharaoh and bring the Israelites out of Egypt?
> EXODUS 3:7–11

This is a very understandable question to ask. It is probably one I would ask as well. This is a huge and terrifying undertaking, and Moses seeks some sort of affirmation of identity, some sort of assurance of his ability to accomplish what God is asking him to do. So how does God respond?

> And God said, 'I will be with you. And this will be the sign to you that it is I who have sent you: When you have brought the people out of Egypt, you will worship God on this mountain.'
> EXODUS 3:12

I find it fascinating that God didn't respond with, 'I have given you the skills and gifts to be able to do this. You are perfect just the way you are.' Instead, he said, 'I will be with you.'

Moses asked more questions about how it would work, and God promised miracles and riches for his people and a guarantee of God's fulfilled purpose. But Moses wasn't done. He spotted a flaw in God's great plan: his own personality and gifts.

> Moses said to the Lord, 'Pardon your servant, Lord. I have never been eloquent, neither in the past nor since you have spoken to your servant. I am slow of speech and tongue.'
>
> The Lord said to him, 'Who gave human beings their mouths? Who makes them deaf or mute? Who gives them sight or makes them blind? Is it not I, the Lord? Now go; I will help you speak and will teach you what to say.' But Moses said, 'Pardon your servant, Lord. Please send someone else.'
> EXODUS 4:10–13

You see, even after seeing those miracles in front of him, Moses still didn't believe that God could use him. He trusted in what he could see over what God had planned and provided. God simply asked Moses to trust that the 'day bag' he would provide would have everything he needed, but Moses wasn't able to do so. He tried to bail out of the whole calling, refusing God because of his own judgment of what he was capable of doing.

Gideon had a similar experience. God came to him to draw him into the exciting task of defending his people from severe oppression.

> 'Pardon me, my lord,' Gideon replied, 'but how can I save Israel? My clan is the weakest in Manasseh, and I am the least in my family.'
>
> The Lord answered, 'I will be with you, and you will strike down all the Midianites, leaving none alive.'
> JUDGES 6:15–16

I love how Gideon even details how ridiculous he is. I do this often to God: list my terribleness, waiting for his affirmation to rush into my insecurity and to confirm to me why I am the perfect person for this. But God doesn't respond by convincing Gideon of his suitability. Later, we learn that God's whole approach to saving Israel was to keep them as weak as possible so that they would see God more clearly. When Gideon responded to his call with fear and seeking affirmation, God replied by declaring his presence and power.

Over and over, it is God's presence and power that makes the difference. God drew Moses and Gideon closer into relationship to facilitate their purposes. Our children need to take more comfort and confidence from God's presence than from their belief in themselves.

When Samuel was choosing David to be the new king, he said, 'People look at the outward appearance, but the Lord looks at the heart' (1 Samuel 16:7). We will never see the way God sees. We all have strengths and weaknesses and spiritual gifts, but God's evaluation of what those things are and how he chooses to use them are his alone. He may ask us to operate out of what we see as weaknesses because it puts us in a place of spiritual and emotional vulnerability to his guidance. Or he may call us to a place where we discover strengths we never knew we had. When we over-focus on trying to define and know ourselves for the sake of knowing our purpose, we limit our trust in the Creator who calls us to that purpose.

Children are used to this idea of destiny: this end point towards which we are headed. Our stories are full of it. Romances end at the wedding. Movie hero stories end at the success of the task or the full embracing of a hero's identity. You figure out who you are and then you act on it, or you focus on the task you are set to accomplish and you succeed. Our children have responded most often in either one of two ways: 1) that they are not a hero or someone extraordinary, and so aspire only to live a fairly ordinary, mundane life: get a job, have a family, and live; or 2) that God has a specific and significant thing he wants them to do, and they have to work hard to find it and accomplish it, like a secret agent – neither of which is true.

If you look at hero stories in the Bible, a life calling really was a series of relationship-based decisions in response to God's voice. We can see the whole arc of the story, but for the main hero at the time, it was one step in front of the other, living out her purposefulness in God's story the best she could each day.

I think our desperate desire *to know* is a fairly modern concept. We want to know where we are headed. We want to know the end point before we begin. We want to line up our life and be in control of its steps. In some ways, we want to know what the big calling of our life is so that we can take control and plot how to achieve it. We want our assignment so that we can get on with doing it. I think, more often than not, God says, 'Follow me' and promises his guidance and clear voice. As we follow, our unique purpose and path unfolds before us.

When we look at how Jesus led his disciples on their life journeys, there was no one way. Most of the time, he said simply, 'Follow me.' He told a few that they would be fishers of people (Matthew 4:18– 20), but to others he simply extended an invitation (see, for example, Matthew 9:9). He didn't say, 'Bartholomew, follow me and you will be the admin guy for this ministry for three years, and then grow in your business career in Jerusalem after I've gone, and then switch it for a life as a tanner later in life to please your wife and because you like working with your hands.' He simply said, 'Follow me.'

The promises from God about the direction of our lives aren't that he will supernaturally appear or give us a 'sign' every time we have a decision to make. He promises simply to lead us in the ordinary, everyday way. 'If you go the wrong way – to the right or to the left – you will hear a voice behind you saying, "This is the right way. You should go this way"' (Isaiah 30:21, NCV). 'But when he, the Spirit of truth, comes, he will guide you into all the truth. He will not speak on his own; he will speak only what he hears, and he will tell you what is yet to come' (John 16:13, NIV).

My prayer for my child is not that he will accomplish one great big thing, but that he will live in relationship with God each day, impacting others and living his place in God's greater story.

The purpose of our lives isn't to find the career that is right or the one big thing God is asking us to do. Our purpose is to love God with all our heart, soul, mind and strength, and love our neighbour as ourselves. We are to flourish in relationship with God and partner with him to transform one life at a time in love, one situation at a time. Sometimes the task looks huge, and sometimes it looks small, but it is always, always, significant.

This is why our children have a purpose from birth. They are capable of being significant always, capable of transforming moments always, capable of walking in relationship with God and following him in the world always.

Our journeys of purpose are often much more winding and erratic than we instinctively think they should be. We have a fantasy that one day we will wake up and know our one big calling in life and then pursue it relentlessly until it is accomplished. I don't know where we got that idea, because as we look around, there is virtually no one who does that! Look at the people in the Bible. Look at your friends. Look at your own journey.

In the end, our unique, individual life path is just a series of decisions to live the purposes God has called us to each day. Some days, this will include big, life-altering decisions, and other days, it will include ministering peace to a small child. The process is the same. Each day we wake up determined to love God and love others, responding to needs and opportunities in relationship with him, and it is up to God to guide us. Moses didn't know his entire future at the beginning, but at the end of his days he could look back across his life and see the grand path that he was on, and one day our children will too.

As parents, our job is to prepare our children not for the one big thing that they will do or the career they will have. Our children are constantly changing and adapting, adding skills and growing in their sensitivities and character. Any time we look at our children, we see only a snapshot, one moment in their life's journey. Our job is not to build a path around that single snapshot, but to prepare our children to live their daily purpose in better and better relationship with God and to empower them to follow him wherever he is asking them to go. The next two chapters will explore some practical ways we can position our children to respond to the daily opportunities of calling that each of us is given.

19

Shaping our response

'MUMMYYYYYY!' the tiny one-year-old screamed as she saw her mother leave the crèche room for the main service. Her little body shuffled towards the door and she pressed herself up against it, straining for the door handle.

Other children ignored her agony and played with the array of toys scattered about as a crèche leader attempted to distract her and draw her into the play area, to no avail.

Eli, aged two, stood frozen, looking at the distraught girl. 'Lost. Sad. Oh no!' he exclaimed and glanced up at me. 'That's right, Eli. She is feeling lost and sad. What can we do to help her feel happy?' I responded. He tentatively approached the sobbing child and wrapped his arms around her. She paused in her screaming, then turned to him and pleaded, 'Mummy!' The tears returned.

'Idea! Toy!' said Eli. He ran over to the toys and grabbed his favourite one, returning to the girl, car extended. 'Look! Car! Happy, go fast! Brrmmmm brrmmmmm,' he enthused. The girl froze in surprise, tears flowing, and looked in confusion at this small person waving a car in front of her. She took the car and then shuffled close to him. Eli hugged her and patted her head gently. 'Happy. All right! Sit,' he said quietly. He sat down and started playing with the toys, and she sat down next to him, their sides touching. Her breathing slowed. 'All right. Safe,' Eli said. He patted her leg, repeating the words. 'Look! She happy! All better,' he exclaimed. His face beamed with pride. 'I did it! Nice and happy,' he finished. He patted her again and they played together.

Purpose is part of our birthright. It is part of the make-up of who we are. We have been created with a call to be purposeful, both now and in the future, and we can position our children to be ready to respond to the daily calls of purpose that God lays in front of them.

One life matters

One of the most important ideas we can impress upon our children is that one life matters. The difference we can make in the life of one individual is remarkable and worthwhile. The world tells children that success is about the big and the many; that helping thousands of people at one time is much better than helping just one; that running a big fundraiser is more important than giving your pocket money away; that big impressive purpose is more important than hidden yet significant purpose.

Thinking that 'big' purpose is better than 'small' can trap our children into believing that they must strive to impact multitudes to be purposeful, when the reality is that every life matters. Every individual is cherished by God, and every day we can bring significant and real blessing and love to someone who is hurting. That is the work of Jesus. He healed people one by one when he met them, face to face. He eased emotional brokenness one person at a time. He died for humankind, but he came to earth to meet and minister to the individual. When we begin to raise the profile of ministering to individuals, a life of purpose becomes possible and significant. I would be happy if my child worked in a low-status job his whole life but loved God with his whole heart and daily transformed lives around him.

This is where the whole story of the gospel is essential. When we seed into our children the whole story of a broken world and Jesus' desire and power to restore and reconnect, then they can see that pattern in people's lives around them. The shepherd went after one lost sheep. God went after his lost people. And Eli went after one lost toddler in the crèche. Each life matters. Each day of purpose matters.

The character to do it well

Character is something that we are growing in our children already. It's the job of every parent. Each one of us is already trying to grow humble, loving, strong children who love God and act respectfully and kindly. It is helpful to remember that character matters for spiritual purpose as well as for daily life in the world.

A key aspect of parenting for our children's specific purpose is to focus our parenting on growing our children's characters, so that they are able to fulfil the opportunities that God has for them. In the Old Testament, both Moses and Joseph were taken on a journey of character refinement before they were able and ready to take the big step to a greater level of influence.

Look at Moses when he lived in Pharaoh's palace. He was compassionate, quick to anger, rash and impulsive. One day he saw an Egyptian beating a Hebrew. He looked around, thought that no one was looking, and then killed the Egyptian and buried him in the sand (see Exodus 2:11–12). Didn't regret it one bit. Impulse to defend the weak and powerless? Fantastic. Character that solved the problem by deliberate murder? Needed some work. At that point, this man was not ready to lead the Hebrews out of Egypt with wisdom, humility, grace, and holiness. God needed to refine his character to make him ready for a future season of daily purpose.

As our children's character grows, so will their ability to bear larger roles as they live out their daily purpose. That doesn't negate their current usefulness to God. Each season of purpose is precious and effective. It simply means that as they grow and as their character strengthens, so will their ability to step into more influential or complex opportunities. Our goal is to cultivate a character that will be able to respond humbly to whatever God-opportunities may arise, small and large.

Some of the most unsung heroes in the Bible are the parents of the people whose stories we know. The parents grew in their children a sense of purposefulness and the strength of character to be ready for God's prompting and calling. I wish I knew what Mary and Joseph's parents were like. Think of it! They managed to grow children who as teenagers loved God enough and had the cultivated character to respond faithfully to God's calling to bear scorn and shame and to raise the child of the living God. The decisions Mary and Joseph made were just the next steps in a series of purpose-filled decisions they had made up until that moment.

We can't predict what our children's paths on earth will be but we can prepare our children. God will lead them through their journey.

Responding to their developing sensitivity

Throughout our children's lives, and as their personalities and characters develop, their hearts will resonate with particular topics, and personal interests will emerge. Our goal is to facilitate the growth of their souls as they encounter new experiences and new situations. God is also developing your children, and the opportunities of purpose he will create for them now and in the future will draw together their life experiences and interests.

For instance, my child is currently particularly sensitive to people who are feeling pain. When he is watching television, the thing that most disturbs him is people getting yelled at or falling down. He was profoundly hard of hearing for half his life, so he is very tuned into faces and emotions. When he is around adults, teens or children that I know to be fragile or having a hard time in life, I see him behave differently. Normally a boisterous child, he is very gentle around them and often will lightly touch their knees or shoulders or pat reassuringly. In most games that he plays, he will create accident scenarios and spend the majority of the play time rescuing and comforting the vehicles and stuffed animals involved in the extensive and traumatic accident. If there is a child crying in a room, Caleb will inevitably walk over to the child and try to help or sit next to him to give him some companionship while he is sad. When he is playing and another child grabs his toy, he will grab it back, but if the other child is upset about it, Caleb will instinctively share (or hide the toy and come back to comfort). Emotion currently trumps possessions with him.

Will this sensitivity continue for his whole life? I don't know. I do know that it is of particular importance to him now, so I am doing all I can to facilitate him growing in and learning skills based on this sensitivity. As it becomes part of his character, I want to do all I can to help it settle into his mind and spirit in a way that honours God. If this sensitivity were left undisciplined, he could learn to be powerless in the face of others' pain or to be afraid of it. I prefer to train him to respond with compassion and strength, to frame for him what God is doing in response to other people's pain, and to offer him opportunities to learn how to respond in those circumstances.

Who knows? Next month Caleb could be completely wrapped up in a passion for sport, and I would rejoice in that with him and help to shape his character through those circumstances as well.

Children's interests, passions and spiritual sensitivities will be constantly changing throughout their lives, and our job is to walk alongside them on their journeys, facilitating the development of characters that can bear and operate out of purpose well.

We are on a journey with our children, helping them to discover what fascinates them, what excites them, and what resonates with their personality and spiritual heart. The more we can expose our children to new situations and adventures, the more chances we have to spark their hearts and shape their characters.

Every experience in life informs our children and gives them memories to draw from and skills to use on the journey. David played the harp and God used it to minister to Saul. Moses lived in Pharaoh's palace, so he knew how to deal with the court. Peter was a fisherman, so he instinctively understood what it meant to be a fisher of people. Every part of our path can be used by God.

Children's breadth of experiences and skills helps them to understand the world, God's creation and other people better. It's okay to let our children flourish in their experiences, trusting that the God who weaves all together is shaping our children.

Keeping connected to God

In order for our children to live their purpose, they need to be God-connected. In the Bible, we see that God's promises to people were about his presence, his closeness and companionship and the power that comes with that. In fact, the promise God repeats most often in the Bible is 'I will be with you.'

Our children deserve to live in a two-way relationship with God, sharing their hearts, hearing his voice, knowing his touch in response. Purpose flows out of relationship, so it is essential that we help our children connect themselves to God in order to do confidently what he is inviting them to do in this world. Why not try highlighting God's presence and how to have a relationship with him, using the six-stage circle?

Spiritual gifts

Being connected to God isn't the only spiritual component to purpose. Scripture lists many spiritual gifts: serving, teaching, prophecy, faith, exhortation, giving, leadership, mercy, words of wisdom, words of knowledge, faith, healing, miracles, discerning between spirits, tongues and interpretation of tongues, apostleship, helping, administration, evangelism and pastoring (Romans 12:6–8; 1 Corinthians 12:8–10, 28; Ephesians 4:11; 1 Peter 4:11). Some people believe that there are more, and these are just examples the biblical authors highlighted, while others believe that this is the complete list. The purpose of these gifts is for the good of others (1 Corinthians 12:4–7). They are given to us to help us minister to others, not to give us identity and better self-knowledge.

We can often be confused about how much emphasis to place on spiritual gifts with our children. I would suggest that we don't give our children quizzes to help them find their gifts or show them lists of all the gifts that are out there. I think that it is important to remember that these gifts are not the end point but a facilitation of our purpose.

It can be helpful to discuss the idea of spiritual gifts with them, and how God's tools for changing people's lives are amazing and come from him. We can chat about how when God asks us to do things, he will equip us to do it, and that these gifts are a part of our equipping. If he wants us to use a gift, we will feel that it is right at the time. We can assure our children that our spiritual day bags will always contain what is needed for us to do what God is asking us to do.

Our children are growing and flexing their muscles and developing, and while we can see trends in their lives, it is most helpful to allow them the flexibility to grow into their uniqueness without the need to quantify and define it.

Spiritual gifts help them to live every day well, equipping them to be significant in the relationships, places and areas of influence that they are in. We can tell our children that the gifts exist and that they are to help them love powerfully in the places that touch their hearts.

We can tell them that God will lead, equip and help them to accomplish any task into which he draws them. We can also tell them that spiritual gifts are not to be focused on or planned from. They are powerful, equipping gifts that God freely gives us to live purposefully every day and to accomplish what he has set before us.

The six-stage circle

So how do we invest in our children so that they have a purposeful and unique journey, walking every day together with God? Here are a few practical suggestions for how to begin to explore these ideas with your children.

Model

Give your children a peek into your motivations when you do things. Modelling counts, whether it's small or large. My husband told my son this week, 'Mummy is feeling very tired and stressed, and so I'm cleaning the house because it helps her to feel loved and happy and not worried.' All week, my child has randomly jumped off the couch and picked something up off the floor and put it away, saying, 'Love Mummy.'

Tell your child when something hits your current sensitivity and how you are responding to it. For example: 'Lately, whenever I see a young teenage mum on our bus, my heart beats fast and I feel as if my stomach flips upside down. I just keep thinking about how important having friends and family to help me was when you and your brother were small, and how she may not have that. I don't know why my heart is so sensitive to people in her situation right now, but I definitely want to do something about it. I just feel that God's poking my heart about it, so I'm going to have a think about what to do next.'

Frame

Watching your children play is often a great way to get a feel for their sensitivities and to be able to frame those for them. In fantasy games, what is the plot? What role do they play? My child is all about the rescue. For over a year now, almost every game involves someone getting lost or stuck. He then becomes the rescuer, coming in to lift the car back on to the table, fixing the helicopter wings or opening the door for me when I'm 'stuck' in the bathroom. He doesn't want to fight bad guys, just rescue people who have accidents. I find it interesting that of all the scripts he could be playing out in his head, this is the one he loves doing right now. What does your children's play look like? Are they the policeman who protects everyone else? Or the host who welcomes in? Or the teacher who leads when you play school? Whatever it is, while they are playing, try framing how what they are doing is a powerful example of the purpose that God has for us and is part of God's story. To my child, who loves rescuing, I read the Bible story of the lost sheep and tell him how Jesus was sent to rescue all of us from our sin. To a child whose current sensitivity and play is about protecting people, you could read Bible stories about Gideon and Hezekiah and how they partnered with God to defend people. You could also tell stories of times when your child protected people, and how that is spiritually and physically important and part of what God asks us to do on earth. No matter what your child's current sensitivity or interest is, you can surround it with scriptural backing and practical everyday stories so that they can see how important it is to God and others.

Watch movies or television together, with the particular view of seeing how important character is to what the main person accomplishes in the story. If you are doing this with younger children, just watch and comment out loud, naming what you see. For instance: 'Doc McStuffins is so kind. She stops her whole day just to help heal one stuffed animal. Just like Jesus! Wow, she does help a lot!' For older children you can wonder together about what could have been: 'What would have happened if the main person let it all go to her head and thought she was better than other people? Do you think she would have done things differently? Do you think she would have been as effective in accomplishing her task?' You can also look at the bad guy in the show and ask, 'What makes him so different from the good guy?' Often the 'bad guy' has a character flaw, rather than being 'evil'.

Equip

Celebrate failure. Often in a grand failure there are a thousand tiny victories of character and achievement. Take your ten-year-old out for an ice cream for showing grace and honour in the face of losing a race (instead of to try to make him feel better for losing). I have a friend who has a particular value for seeing every situation as a chance to improve. She inspires her children to think that way too. When her six-year-old comes off the court after losing a tennis match, he flings his hands in the air with a big smile and yells, 'Hey, Mum, I'm *learning*!'

Give your children possible ways to respond to what is in their heart. If your child seems to have sensitivity for generosity and helping lift people's sadness, then feed that. Show your child television shows where people are overwhelmed with generosity, or video testimonies of God using people to bless someone with the generosity of a gift, financial or otherwise.

I once told my youth group a story of how, when I was much poorer than I am now, some of the youth from our church used to spend their pocket money to buy my family food and leave it on our front door and run away. I shared how blessed we were by that gift and how much it helped us. The next week some of the children were buzzing. Children who really had a passion for helping people in need with generosity came back to church giggling with stories of giving away toys, spending pocket money on a sandwich for a homeless man (with parental permission and supervision) and buying a new pen for their dad when his broke. A new pattern emerged in those specific children because their passion was fed with testimonies of the power of that sensitivity put into action.

Create opportunities

Expand your child's experiences of the world in order to open their eyes and hearts to new areas of sensitivity. Visit the children's ward at a local hospital and play with the children there. Volunteer to clean a homeless shelter. Read *National Geographic* together and discuss places around the world and what people's lives are like. Visit a church that is a different denomination to yours, and highlight the similarities of how people love God and how they express it in a different way. Take your child to an evening where a missionary is sharing about her work.

When you are out together and see something that spiritually stirs you, point it out to your children and tell them what is going on in your heart. Invite them to chat with God about it in their heads, just sharing what they are thinking and feeling.

Invite your children to minister in your family. So often we want to rush to release children into leadership in the world or in our church, but actually your family is a great place to begin. I would consider your family a key place to release your children's purpose and passions. Whatever sensitivities are being raised in your children, invite them to use those in your family. If they have a particular heart for art, ask them to paint a Bible verse picture for your hallway. If they have a sensitivity to people who are hurting physically, ask them to be the ones to get the first aid kit and help dress wounds, or to turn off lights and get your pillows when you have a headache. When you release your family to minister, you can train them how to view themselves and their usefulness in the world.

Establish boundaries

Be aware of your child's character development as well as their behaviour. When I was a child, I was involved in theatre. This particular company would go out after the performance to meet the audience and sign autographs (for some reason, children loved getting these). I was ten, and while my behaviour towards people was absolutely fine, there was something sneaking into my character, a superiority and pride, that my mother was not about to let stand. She sat me down and talked to me about my attitude and about the value of other people. I was told that my character was more important to her than my opportunities, and if I couldn't figure out how to bless other people and keep an appropriate view of myself, then I wasn't going to be allowed to go outside and sign autographs. She knew that no matter what God used me for, I couldn't afford to have arrogance or pride as part of my character.

Give feedback

Focus on character as well as accomplishments. When your children do something, praise the character they showed as well as acknowledging what they achieved. For example: 'Well done! That violin recital was fantastic! Beautiful! I have to say my favourite part, though, was when you were all walking on to the stage and the boy in front of you tripped. All the other children kept walking and some even laughed, but you helped him up, brushed him off and helped him pick up his music. You knew he would be embarrassed, and so you helped him. My heart just wanted to explode. I was so proud of you!'

Debrief with children particular moments when they touched one life well and how God equipped them to do it, even without their noticing. One dad I knew had this exchange with his nine-year-old son: 'I noticed how that girl got left behind by her other friends and you walked over. I expected that you would invite her to play, but you just sat next to her and read a book! She read over your shoulder for a while, and then you started talking. She seemed to feel so happy and not lonely any more. How did you know that reading a book was the best way to help?' 'I don't know,' he said. 'I was going to ask her to play, but then I just felt that would be wrong. I just felt that reading a book would make her feel less stressed.' The dad smiled. 'You know, buddy,' he replied. 'I think that God gave you that knowledge, so you could help that girl in the best way possible. Pretty cool that you did just what God was asking you to do, and he helped you do it by telling you something you couldn't have known.'

20

Poised to act

Ruth had determined that she was needed. There was a need in front of her, a big gaping hole that required filling, and she figured she could sort it out. She was seven. On a Sunday morning, the crèche set-up and take-down was laborious, and the adult leaders struggled to get it all done in time. She asked permission to take charge of it. Our leaders agreed, and Ruth leapt into action. On time every Sunday, she would show up and work with passion and excellence to get everything out and set up just right. After church, she press-ganged her friends into helping with take-down, delaying the post-church playing until it was all finished. Week in and week out, this seven-year-old girl led a team of five or six children in the set-up and take-down of the crèche, not because she was shoved there because of her age, or because it was the simplest task adults could think to give her, but because she saw a need and decided to use her power to change the situation. She wasn't a helper or an add-on. She was essential to the process of a Sunday morning, and she was counted on. Her ministry brought real blessing, not just a tolerant smile.

The inevitable outworking of purpose is action. When we love God and love others, our actions flow out of that genuine place of love, and we want to respond with action. This is why it is so important that we lay the spiritual, mental and emotional foundations of our children well, so that their daily lives, choices and actions will reflect an inner life of love and strength.

A common mistake for us as parents is to so want our children to live purposeful lives that we accidentally push them into doing good works. While doing good works may be a good trait to build in our children, it does not foster and grow children's faith or create a lasting and permanent sense of spiritual purpose. James, a disciple of Jesus, insisted that faith without deeds is useless, but that when faith and actions are working together, faith is made complete by the actions (James 2:14–26). So as we talk about how to encourage and equip children's actions of purpose, it is essential that we approach it with a view to cultivating the desires and actions that flow from the heart, and not from a position of how we can encourage children to do good things. We cannot stop at cultivating their spiritual centres; we also have the joy of discipling and empowering our children's acts of love and purpose.

When our children are poised to be proactively purposeful throughout the day, then we have the honour of empowering their responses to what their hearts are provoked by, and to God's prompting of direction.

In order to do this well, we as parents must position ourselves to empower and coach our children, rather than partner with them or drive the action. We must treat them as powerful people who are genuinely responding from a heart of purpose. If we can manage not to insert ourselves into the centre of our children's actions, then we ensure that their journey of purpose stays theirs. They will be able to own the fruit they will see, the achievements they will make, the connection to God and others they will experience, and the life lessons they will learn. By allowing them to be the motivators, inventors and main workers, we allow their character to be forged and enable them to learn how to respond to the joys and difficulties of purpose. I would rather a child raised £30 on his own than £500 because his parent jumped on board and made it happen. Our job in all of this is to cheer them on and facilitate them practically, spiritually and emotionally. We can help them see the changes they make in individual lives, their communities and the world.

Coaching their hearts' response

As our children go through life, they will naturally run across experiences that provoke their hearts or push on their current sensitivities. When we train our children to see power when they look in the mirror, they will begin to feel more and more confident to act when they run across something that disturbs them or plays on their mind.

When I was a child, I became paralysed in almost all situations that required physical response. I would knock a glass of milk over and my mother would leap up, but for me the world slowed down. I would watch the cup start to fall over, then hit the table and spill. I would sit perfectly still and watch the milk flow off the table and the glass roll off, smashing on the ground. I would sit and watch in shock, my mind completely blank. Then, inevitably, my mother, who by now had found a cloth and was sorting it out, would look up at me and say (in a blend of patience and exasperation), 'Don't just sit there. *Do* something. Move!'

I am happy to say that I am now super-fast at responding even before the scenario has fully played out – but this took some years of training, working against my natural reaction. I think many of our children share a similar response to spiritual opportunities that happen right in front of them. They are surprised by a need – a child crying, a sibling fight, a grandfather in pain, a famine in West Africa, a friend at school who is poor, or a special needs family at church – and they freeze, letting the opportunity go by; not for lack of willingness as often their hearts will feel compassion, but for lack of readiness to act.

There is a fantastic children's movie called *Robots*, in which one of the main characters is an inventor. He describes the process of inventing like this: 'So look around for a need, and start coming up with ideas to fill that need. One idea will lead to another and before you know it, you've done it. See a need. Fill a need.'

It is important for our children to know that sometimes a need appears in front of us and we have the ability to respond. Our foundational purpose is to love, and sometimes it's our job to respond to a need when it arises. Daily purpose is sometimes simply a process of seeing a need and filling it.

A much beloved children's television host in America, Mr Rodgers, described how he learned how to view the news. 'When I was a boy and I would see scary things in the news, my mother would say, "Look for the helpers. You will always find people who are helping."' These people didn't necessarily feel 'called' to help; they responded, and that is just as powerful. Some of the greatest stories in the Bible are of people responding to a need.

Peter and John were walking to the temple when a beggar interrupted them to ask for money. Seeing his need, they responded, healing him instantly (see Acts 3).

Nehemiah heard the news of the terrible state of his homeland, and his heart responded. He instantly wept and spent days praying and seeking God. He then determined to do something about it and approached the king for permission to act (see Nehemiah 1—2).

Abigail was a woman married to an unwise man who made a potentially catastrophic mistake. As soon as she heard about it, she reacted quickly, running into the fray and acting with so much love, wisdom and bravery that she was able to turn the hearts of a leader and his army on their way to bringing destruction to her people (see 1 Samuel 25:14–35).

A heart ready to respond is a heart that can live a courageous daily life of purpose.

Planned action

Through children's regular daily chatter, we tend to learn about what is going on with them spiritually. They tell stories of what happened at school, at playgroup, in their clubs or at church. They wonder about it while watching television, or they ask questions when they are reading books. It will come up as a topic of conversation in the car or while you are making dinner. As they share about life, you will begin to notice patterns of what is stirring your children's hearts.

Most parents I know have found that the most helpful way of encouraging their children to act when their hearts and sensitivities are being stirred is to listen carefully and ask questions about the situation to help them fully explore the issue. Parents then ask the simple question, 'What are you going to do about it?' This question communicates to all children that as parents we care, that we hear them, and that we believe they can do something about the situation. We can always follow it up with an offer of support if and when they feel it's right to do something.

Sarah spent a lot of time thinking about missionaries and how lonely and homesick they could become. She read missionary stories online and talked about them frequently. When an opportunity at school arose to create a project to help someone overseas, Sarah's discussions about missionaries increased. Her mother asked the question, 'What are you going to do about it?' Sarah decided that she wanted to send boxes of familiar food, toys and books to a missionary who was teaching English as a second language in China. After submitting her idea and leading the project, over 90 kilos of 'home' were sent to this man in China. The missionary was overwhelmed and was also able to host many 'English' parties at his house, opening up opportunities for the gospel to be shared with his students much more frequently.

Raj was furious that there was a group of boys at school who would physically intimidate the younger children. They wouldn't hurt them or yell at them, but just set out to scare them every day with their presence and attitude. Raj felt intensely that it was unjust that people should be allowed to create such fear in others, especially in those so small. Raj's dad listened carefully and then asked him, 'What are you going to do about it?' Raj decided that every day he would watch the group of boys on the playground. If they started to intimidate the small ones, he would stop whatever he was doing and move over to the younger children's game so that they weren't frightened off the equipment or made to feel vulnerable. He did this for a full year, and eventually all his friends came round to the idea and joined him. The need to enforce this evaporated after one year because he so influenced the playground culture that it didn't happen any more.

As children get into the pattern of responding to situations that press on their hearts, they will begin to internalise the process of asking themselves, 'What am I going to do about it?'

Keenan's family drove a neighbour's family to church each Sunday. This family had a son, Richard, who was a little younger than Keenan and had Down's Syndrome. The church loved Richard but struggled to know how to help him when the children were in their groups. Keenan had been building a deeper and deeper heart connection with God and began to want others to have one as well. He attended our New Wine Kids' Leadership Academy event during the summer. As he signed up, he wrote on the back of his form a suggestion that 'special needs' was a seminar we should put on for children to learn how to help children with additional needs connect with God. We were so struck by the suggestion that we hunted him down and had a chat with him. Out of the 650 forms, he was the only one who had written down 'special needs'. He told us the story of Richard, and when we asked if he would like us to put something on especially for him, he paused and then said yes. When I asked him why he paused, he smiled a bit and said, 'I wouldn't say that I'm really interested in helping people with special needs, but I am interested in helping Richard. No one else is, and I think he needs to know how to connect with God because it's awesome. So I'll do it.' We trained him up during the week and sent him back home equipped to help Richard. The following year we remembered Keenan, and so we made a special needs seminar available for children who had a heart passion or sensitivity for helping people with special needs connect with God – and 85 children signed up.

Prayer is a practical response

Sometimes we forget that prayer is also a practical action response to our children's hearts being stirred or their sensitivities being provoked. Being poised to act is not just being ready to do physical things to help, but also being ready to respond emotionally and spiritually, taking the situation to God in prayer and intercession. Prayer is potent, but often our children don't understand the potential of it. As we cultivate our children's hearts for love and action, it is helpful to give them the strength that comes from understanding how prayer can affect the world in partnership with God.

The Bible is clear about how powerful prayer is. God moves in response to our prayers, and in prayer we ourselves are transformed. We aren't meant to be carrying burdens of the heart alone. Children need to know that our loving God responds to our human desires. James declares, 'The prayer of a righteous person is powerful and effective. Elijah was a human being, even as we are. He prayed earnestly that it would not rain, and it did not rain on the land for three and a half years. Again he prayed, and the heavens gave rain, and the earth produced its crops' (James 5:16–18).

Children can know that there is nothing too small or too large for God's attention, and it is our privilege to pray anytime, anywhere, about anything that is being stirred in our hearts.

The apostle Paul's letter to the Ephesians encourages us to 'pray in the Spirit on all occasions with all kinds of prayers and requests. With this in mind, be alert and always keep on praying for all the Lord's people' (Ephesians 6:18).

Our children can establish a pattern of bringing concerns to God in a way that brings peace and connection with the Father whose heart shares their same concerns. Paul's letter to the Philippians lays this out: 'Do not be anxious about anything, but in every situation, by prayer and petition, with thanksgiving, present your requests to God. And the peace of God, which transcends all understanding, will guard your hearts and your minds in Christ Jesus' (Philippians 4:6–7).

When our children grasp this, they begin to feel the importance of prayer as an action. One afternoon at a camp, a children's leader approached us looking upset and told us that his sister had just been taken to hospital for an abscess on her ovary. She was in such extreme pain that the maximum dosage of morphine was not working. The doctors were taking her into surgery the next day, and she was likely to lose her last ovary in the operation and, therefore, her ability to have children.

The next day, the day of the operation, nine children came to the prayer tent to pray for their leader, as they were concerned about him and his sister. These boys, between the ages of seven and ten, sat with their leader, thanked God for who he was, and asked him for his healing and peace to come on the leader's sister. The next day we got news. At the same time as the boys had been praying, the sister's pain instantly stopped. The doctors were so surprised that they did another scan. The abscess had completely disappeared, and all dead tissue had been restored. Surgery was cancelled and she was discharged. The doctors acknowledged that it was a miracle.

The children were ecstatic, as well as the leader. They prayed for other things over the next couple of days. Sometimes they saw the fulfilment of their prayers, other times they didn't. But they kept praying.

Prayer is powerful, and we are told that prayer is key to our purpose on earth. If we truly love people, we will naturally want to bring them and their situations to our Father God. It is our job not only to empower our children to act physically in response to their hearts, but also to react spiritually. If we focus on cultivating their hearts, then the big question of whether or not we see our requests fulfilled is less important than the genuine heart response of living in connection with God and bringing our requests to him.

Empowering God-directed opportunities

We can go through life completely focused on ourselves and on what we need to accomplish in the day. I'm always struck by the oddity of it when I'm on a train. Here we all are, crammed into a tin can speeding down a track centimetres away from each other, yet we are all trying to exist in our own little worlds. We prize having that privacy, that space. It is so easy to switch that isolation on as we walk down the road, go shopping, sit in church or while we are working.

That switch, though, often isolates us from God's promptings as well. Part of living out our purpose every day means lowering those barriers more and more, and making ourselves aware of what opportunities God may be opening up, what he may be whispering to our hearts, and what he may be asking us to do for people and situations around us.

For every one of us, each day is a new opportunity to live full of purpose, ready to impact the world. Our children need to know that they have a choice: to go through the day focused only on themselves, or to be aware of their own heart, of the needs of people around them and of what God may ask them to do. We can create a culture and understanding in our home so that every day we wake up and think, 'What shall we do today, God? I am ready.'

Our children need to learn what that prompting looks and feels like in everyday life. As parents, we are in the position to be able to create windows into how we hear and respond to God's promptings daily. They will watch us go through our day and look for how we respond to other people. They will notice when we stop along the road or change our plans because of something we feel pressing on our heart. We can frame for them what is happening inside us when we hear God.

I was walking in the rain with a friend's ten-year-old child, Molly. We were huddled under my umbrella, trying to walk quickly to a shop to get some drinks. We passed by a homeless man who had set up a little temporary place of warmth in a doorway. He wasn't getting wet and he looked warm enough. As soon as I walked past him, I felt a check in my heart. I felt that I needed to go back and give that man our umbrella. I fought with God and told him that this was an expensive umbrella, and that I couldn't let my friend's child get soaked. I highlighted that he'd never asked me to give away my umbrella before, and so why was now so important? After about 20 steps, God was unconvinced by my arguments, and I knew I had a choice to take the opportunity or pass it by. I turned my head around, and I repositioned my selfish heart to love this man for whom God had asked me to sacrifice so little.

'Hold on, sweetie. Stay here, I'll be right back,' I said, pulling her into a doorway and interrupting what she was telling me about her day. I dashed back in the pouring rain and offered the man my umbrella. He looked confused, and I quickly said, 'Sorry to bother you, sir, but God told me to come back and give this to you.' The man looked at me and said, 'But you're getting wet.' I smiled as water soaked through my shirt, then replied, 'I guess God was less concerned about me getting wet than about you having this! He really likes you a lot, you know.' I laughed and he laughed and I ran back to Molly. We fashioned our bags into coverings and dashed to the next coffee shop we could find.

'What was that all about?' she asked as we sat down. I told her the whole story and her eyes got wider and wider. We talked for half an hour about how God speaks, about his love for people, and why my heart got selfish. We talked about her experiences with God, and his purposes for both of us.

The more we debrief our experiences with children, the more we can ask our children about theirs. We can create the space in our errands to ensure that as we go about together, they have the opportunity to respond to what they feel God is prompting their hearts about. We can surround them with stories and opportunities to act in response to God.

God is already stirring our children's hearts, even at an early age. If we listen, we can help to shape their understanding of it quite early on. Isaac was two and ran up to Sally, his mum, during the worship at church, insisting that she leave her seat and come to the back of church to hug a woman she barely knew. Isaac's mum resisted for a while, but Isaac was so insistent that she began to think something beyond Isaac's playfulness was at work. She stood up, followed him to the back and stood quietly, watching the woman for any signs of distress or any indication that a random hug would be helpful. She didn't see any, so she started to head back to her seat, but then Isaac stamped and repeated, 'Hug the lady, please.'

Sally tiptoed up to the end of the aisle, slipped her arm around the woman and said, 'Good to see you. How are you doing?' The woman turned her head, looked at Sally and tears filled her eyes. Sally gently pulled the woman to a side room, and they talked for an hour. Sally was later able to tell Isaac how good it was that he and God asked her to hug the woman, and he glowed with pride, exclaiming, 'Isaac helped the lady!'

When we begin to coach our children towards responding to what provokes their hearts and sensitivities, to the needs that are in front of them and to God's prompting of direction, then we can empower our children to match their action with their hearts. We can show them how, in the process of responding, God has equipped them with his voice and his gifts. We can highlight how the power he gave them as individuals has impacted people and the world around them.

21

Part of the body

Two boys joined our church around the same time, and they were in the same school year. One was outgoing, and one seemed very shy. Both were going through all the insecurities of joining a new church and establishing who they were in a new community. They floated for a couple of months, and their parents and I were becoming concerned. These children had heart-to-heart connections with God; their parents had discipled them in that. They were also very confident in who they were, both in how God made them and in what that meant in the wider community. But that wasn't enough for them to feel that they belonged in our church. They needed purpose in the body of Christ.

As I came alongside these families and matched the boys up with other adults and teens in the church who saw their passions and skills, these boys began to flourish. One of the boys, Asher, loved praying and listening to God. One day as we were all worshipping, he was suddenly reminded of a verse in the Bible, a promise of God's presence in struggle. As he pondered the verse, he felt that it would be helpful to share it with the senior pastor during worship. Asher came to me, and I walked with him to the front row so that he could chat with the pastor. Our pastor listened to Asher and thought that the congregation would be encouraged by what he had to say. He asked Asher to come up to the front and share the verse with the church himself. Asher was shaking when he shared it with the congregation, but he was able to see with his own eyes how people responded to the encouragement that God shared with him. He came back to his seat glowing, and throughout the next weeks and months he grew in confidence in his connection with God and in his usefulness to the church body. He joined the prayer team and served faithfully. He worshipped more intensely and for longer. He talked to people more before and after church. He began to call it 'our church' instead of 'the church I go to'.

It's a well-known strategy to give children 'jobs' in order to engage them in a programme. Getting children involved can indeed gain their engagement, but the change in Asher wasn't because we gave him a job. He changed because God spoke to his heart and gave him an authentic purpose in his community.

I keep coming back to the apostle Paul's analogy of how a church is like a body:

> A person's body is one thing, but it has many parts. Though there are many parts to a body, all those parts make only one body. Christ is like that also. Some of us are Jews, and some are Greeks. Some of us are slaves, and some are free. [I would add in here, 'Some are adults, some are children.'] But we were all baptised into one body through one Spirit. And we were all made to share in the one Spirit.
>
> The human body has many parts. The foot might say, 'Because I am not a hand, I am not part of the body.' But saying this would not stop the foot from being a part of the body. The ear might say, 'Because I am not an eye, I am not part of the body.' But saying this would not stop the ear from being a part of the body. If the whole body were an eye, it would not be able to hear. If the whole body were an ear, it would not be able to smell. If each part of the body were the same part, there would be no body. But truly God put all the parts, each one of them, in the body as he wanted them…
>
> So then there are many parts, but only one body. The eye cannot say to the hand, 'I don't need you!' And the head cannot say to the foot, 'I don't need you!' No! Those parts of the body that seem to be the weaker are really necessary. And the parts of the body we think are less deserving are the parts to which we give the most honour. We give special respect to the parts we want to hide. The more respectable parts of our body need no special care. But God put the body together and gave more honour to the parts that need it so our body would not be divided. God wanted the different parts to care the same for each other. If one part of the body suffers, all the other parts suffer with it. Or if one part of our body is honoured, all the other parts share its honour. Together you are the body of Christ, and each one of you is a part of that body.
>
> 1 CORINTHIANS 12:12–18, 20–27 (NCV)

Too long we have stood apart as adults in church and looked at children and teens and said, 'We love you, we value you, but we don't need you.' For too long children have been able to look at the adult church and say the same. Often they are so disengaged from the service and the church community that their children's group or youth group culture can function without the rest of the church. We were not designed like this. Our churches were not meant to function like this. If we continue to be fragmented, then we will never experience the joy of what was promised. Have a look in Ephesians:

> So Christ himself gave the apostles, the prophets, the evangelists, the pastors and teachers, to equip his people for works of service, so that the body of Christ may be built up until we all reach unity in the faith and in the knowledge of the Son of God and become mature, attaining to the whole measure of the fullness of Christ.
>
> EPHESIANS 4:11–13

The reason we need to be a full body, empowering children and youth and adults all together, is so that we can achieve the full measure of Christ. I can't experience the fullness of life in Christ unless I'm living life alongside and ministering alongside purposeful people from all parts of the body, including children and youth, and that's really challenging to me, because I'm not. I'm trying. I think there is a greater amount of God's presence, a greater amount of the Spirit, a greater amount of power and a greater amount of worship when we begin to have each member of the body empowered.

We are called to love and serve each other and this world, so that together we can 'grow up in every way into Christ' (v. 15, NCV). Another translation says that we can have the 'whole measure of the fullness of Christ' (v. 13). In order for us to experience and achieve what is possible as a church, we need to enable our children's purposes in our communities. We can't act as if we don't need them. We can't make them nice add-ons or cheerful extras. We need to begin to empower every member of the body of Christ to be an essential member. Then we will together experience a fuller and more accurate representation of what we have been called to be here on earth: the powerful body of Christ.

We have been missing what life as a church would be like with all our members ministering. We have allowed ourselves to be cheated out of something wonderful. We have cheated our children and teens out of something wonderful too: the experience of being a powerful part of a wonderful and diverse group of people who love and minister to each other. Our churches have the power to establish a community of purpose in which all people participate. We can be the place where children feel most powerful, most seen, most discipled and most released. We can be the church that God designed.

Helping our children be part of the body of Christ

We explored a bit about helping our children engage with church as a whole in Chapter 11. How can we as parents empower our children to not just be purposeful in their daily lives, but also serve as part of the body of Christ within the church?

1 Have the expectation that they will serve within church. My parents always expected that I would be a consistent member of a church community (whether it was in a Sunday service or mid-week group) and that I would serve in the church in someway. That was the boundary of expectation that was communicated to me. It was up to me as an older child and teen to decide where I wanted to serve in the church. Most of us don't have that expectation of our children, and so they sometimes float around church on the outside. Our children need to know that they are needed by the church body, and are powerful within it. Decide as a parent how often you are willing for them to serve on teams, or how much time they are allowed to pour into a bigger leadership role, then set that expectation for them to step into. Often we dance around the edges, waiting for our child to be invited in, rather than telling our children how vital they already are.

2 Help them discover where they want to invest. Many times children aren't sure what they want to do within church. Ask them questions to discover what they are passionate about within church. Questions like, 'If I could give you £50,000 to spend on something at the church, what would it be or why?' or 'If you could change one thing about the church to help people, what would it be?' may help the whole family begin to see the child's passions.

3 Facilitate your children to try it. Many times we wait until an official policy can be changed to allow children on a team. Don't wait. Have a conversation with the team leader and see if they would be open to your child coming officially into the team. I have known so many children who have managed to get on a team only open to adults because they asked. Help facilitate doors opening to enable your children to step into the areas where they feel called to serve at church.

Part III

Parenting children for a life of confidence

22

Core of confidence

Scripture is full of people who just ooze confidence. Moses and Aaron strolled into Pharaoh's palace to declare God's purpose and said, 'Let my people go!' Jeremiah delivered God's words to kings and rulers with not an eyebrow flicker of doubt. Jesus challenged smug religious leaders and calmly dealt with violent mobs. Young Mary stood boldly under the judgement of her community because she had a deep knowledge of her call. Paul weathered imprisonment and shipwrecks without fear or worry.

If you have ever been around someone who is truly confident, you will find it strangely compelling. The blend of openness, genuineness and freedom is so appealing. In our society, confidence is not just a quality to be prized; it is a commodity to be greatly treasured. Confidence roots us in who we are and enables us to deal with anything and everything with strength and peace. It is the essence of a 'can-do' approach. We want it for ourselves and we want it for our children.

The world has a formula for confidence. It goes like this:

> You are amazing and perfect, just the way you are. People should love and accept you for who you are, and, if they don't, well, that's their problem. Be proud of yourself! Change for no one! Love yourself wholeheartedly! Figure out who you are, and then shout it from the rooftops: 'My name is Rachel Turner and I AM AWESOME!'

Some of the Christian community goes along with this formula. We can be told in church:

> God made you perfect and precious. You are unique and wonderful, like a gemstone in his eyes, worthy of so much. To criticise yourself is to criticise your creator, so stand up tall, look in the mirror and say, 'I am perfect just the way I am! I have distinctive talents and spiritual gifts that only I can bring to the world. I can do all things through Christ who gives me strength. Bring it on! I am special, important, and I AM AWESOME!'

We think that if our children could just believe those statements deep in their hearts, then they would be confident. If they could discover who they are and express it well, then they would have joy. If only they could live those beliefs, they would be able to weather the storms in the world.

The problem is that the formula doesn't work. Our children are still swayed by the latest trends at school, and they want the toys that everybody else wants. They are still self-conscious about their voices or their clothes or their bodies. They still get random fears, and they still buckle under performance pressure. We see their confidence being slowly torn away and self-doubt creeping in, so we repeat the mantra again and again to them: 'You are perfect just the way you are. You are unique. You are special. You are awesome.' But what we long for most for our children – the inner strength of true long-lasting confidence – rarely, if ever, emerges in them.

The reason, I believe, is that we have a wrong view of confidence.

I don't think Moses successfully led a nation because he strongly believed in his unique talents. I don't think Samuel was confident because he looked in the mirror and truly believed, 'I am special. I am unique. I am perfect just the way I am.' I don't think Paul sang in prison with joy because he loved expressing his true inner self and had a great singing voice. I don't think Mary was bold, after hearing from the angel that she was to be the mother of the Son of God, because she daily reminded herself, 'I am awesome!'

Do you think their confidence came from their own opinions of themselves? Of course not. So, since we hold up these people in scripture as some of the most confident, effective, peaceful champions of faith and life, we need to ask ourselves: what was their secret?

Their core of confidence was different. Their core of confidence was in God, and not in themselves. When people in the Bible speak of confidence, they are almost universally referring to a confidence in God, not a confidence in themselves. As one of the psalmists says, 'For you have been my hope, Sovereign Lord, my confidence since my youth' (Psalm 71:5; for other examples, see Jeremiah 17:7; 2 Corinthians 3:1–6; Ephesians 3:12).

Look at people in the Bible. What if King Hezekiah and the judge Deborah were so confident because they were aware that their success really wasn't about their capability at all? What if the apostle John was so confident because he knew he was fully and totally loved by a faithful God, imperfect as he was? What if Peter was so confident because he knew that God's grace was perfect in all his weaknesses, and that God wasn't finished with him yet? What if Elizabeth's joy and confidence were rooted in the humble knowledge that God was inviting her, as the mother of John the Baptist, to be a small part of his mind-blowing salvation plan?

What would our children's confidence look like if they truly knew how good and perfect and wonderful God is, and if they knew in every part of themselves that his love is very real and he is deeply faithful? What would our children do and how much joy would they have if they were content with being imperfect and were unimpressed by the world's expectations? What would their days be like if they could walk into school thinking, 'God, what shall we do together today?' instead of 'Please, God, I just want people to like me'?

I think that confidence, essentially, is about freedom – freedom to just be in the place where I am, unafraid, totally loved by God, doing what he is asking me to do, and enjoying loving him and the community I am in. In this part we are going to explore how to develop this core of confidence in our children's lives.

I believe that a healthy core of confidence consists of these three beliefs, which underpin all the tools and skills that we will be building through this final part:

- God is awesome and holy, and he loves me totally and unreasonably.
- God is daily shaping me to be more like him, and I am not finished yet.
- I am invited to be a small part of God's wonderful plans.

But, before we continue, I want to remind you of a few things.

First, God is awesome and holy and he loves you beyond anything you could ever imagine. He is daily shaping you, as an individual and as a parent, to be more like him, and he isn't finished with you yet. He is calling you to be a small part of his body to accomplish his wonderful plans and purposes on this earth, and that includes his marvellous plans for your child to be solidly confident, free, loved and rooted in him. You are not alone. Parenting is a journey. It is a dance. It's a constant adjustment to ever-changing human beings and a daily process of learning and failing and succeeding. It's a joy and a worry, a delight and an agony. It's a lifetime calling that doesn't end when our children move out. Parenting continues.

Second, we are all on a journey of developing confidence. You don't need to have it all sorted. Our goal isn't to say, 'Look at me, kids. I'm super-confident and sorted.

Be like me!' Our goal is to position our hearts so that we say, 'God has a great life planned for us and has given us a way to be confident every day, everywhere. I want that for myself and I want it for you, so let's go on the journey together of discovering God's best way for us.'

Third, as with the previous two parts of this book, in this final section I share many stories from people I am working with or have worked with in the past. You will soon add your own stories to the mix. Join me as we explore together how to raise our children to face the broken world clear-eyed and full of confidence, joyfully living in the freedom that Jesus has purchased for them.

May God fill you with peace and hope as you read these pages. May he speak to you and guide your thoughts with clarity. May he give you fantastic sleep and wonderful, precious times with him. And most of all, may you see the fruit of your heart and your parenting as your children grow in their personal confidence in God and in their love for him.

23

It's not about me

For you have been my hope, Sovereign Lord, my confidence since my youth.
PSALM 71:5

God is awesome and holy,
and he loves me totally and unreasonably.

We are not the first ones to go on this journey of confidence. We may think that self-esteem is a fairly modern preoccupation, but self-centredness is timeless. Over and over again in scripture, we find people confronting situations with the same questions that we have. In today's culture, we may read these stories with our own filters, so it is helpful to go back and look at solid examples, from different times and circumstances, of how God shaped those people like us who asked the very same questions.

Moses

I have spoken about Moses already, but I will again mention him a lot in this section, as he must have had a lot of confidence (and he is also one of my favourite people in the Bible). He was raised in a palace as a member of the Egyptian royal family, ran away and spent years as a shepherd in the desert, and then God gave him the biggest and most nerve-racking job ever. His job was 1) to say incredibly unpopular things to the king of his empire, whom he had known since he was a child; 2) to demand, in essence, the economic collapse of his childhood nation by calling for its slaves to be released; 3) to speak God's words consistently while the country he had lived in for half his life was being devastated by plagues; and 4) to lead a huge number of people into a desert and deal with their whining, complaining and rebellion for the next 40 years. This was not an easy gig, and definitely not in Moses' skill set.

Take a look at how it begins. God calls to Moses from a burning bush and tells him that he is God, and Moses responds with deep reverence. God then pours out his purpose and calls Moses to take part in it.

The Lord said, 'I have seen the troubles my people have suffered in Egypt, and I have heard their cries when the Egyptian slave masters hurt them. I am concerned about their pain, and I have come down to save them from the Egyptians. I will bring them out of that land and lead them to a good land with lots of room – a fertile land. It is the land of the Canaanites, Hittites, Amorites, Perizzites, Hivites, and Jebusites. I have heard the cries of the people of Israel, and I have seen the way the Egyptians have made life hard for them. So now I am sending you to the king of Egypt. Go! Bring my people, the Israelites, out of Egypt!'

EXODUS 3:7–10 (NCV)

God himself talks to Moses through the miracle of a constantly burning bush and reveals his plan to rescue the Israelites supernaturally, but where is Moses' focus? How does he instantly respond? Does he say, 'Oh, God, you are powerful and mighty. Thank you for hearing your people's cry. Thank you for preparing a land of wonder and provision. You are faithful and I trust you'? No. Moses' first response to hearing this amazing news is to take a good hard look at himself and reply with a question that we will all understand: 'I am not a great man! How can I go to the king and lead the Israelites out of Egypt?' (3:11, NCV).

This is not a surprising question for Moses to ask. Numbers 12:3 tells us that he was 'a very humble man, more humble than anyone else on the face of the earth'. God loves humility. Moses' humility was one of the reasons why God chose him. When faced with such a monumental task, Moses saw his own smallness and asked the question, 'Who am I to do this?'

From our perspective, we might expect God to respond, 'Moses, you know royal court etiquette. You know about shepherding, which is just like leading people. You know the desert. You have all the experiences and skills you need to do this job well. You're not such a crazy choice. Be confident in who you are. You will be great!' But that isn't where God wants Moses to focus. I absolutely love God's response. He simply ignores Moses' question and gives him the only answer he really needs: 'I will be with you' (3:12).

I believe that God's answer to us when we ask, 'Who am I?' is the same as the one he gave to Moses. He tells us who he is and where he will be, because that's the only permanent truth in which we can have confidence.

God goes on, in Exodus 3:14—4:9, to tell Moses how to answer the people's questions, giving him clear instructions, along with displays of his own power and might.

Then something very familiar happens. For me, this is one of those passages of scripture that play in my mind and make me fully aware of my weaknesses and the dangers that lie within them. After God has revealed so much of himself – his heart, his power, his plans and his will – Moses brings the conversation back to himself. You see, he still doesn't feel confident enough. He's still not ready to say, 'It's not about me. It's about you.'

> But Moses said to the Lord, 'Please, Lord, I have never been a skilled speaker. Even now, after talking to you, I cannot speak well. I speak slowly and can't find the best words.' Then the Lord said to him, 'Who made a person's mouth? And who makes someone deaf or not able to speak? Or who gives a person sight or blindness? It is I, the Lord. Now go! I will help you speak, and I will teach you what to say.'
> EXODUS 4:10–12 (NCV)

Moses looks at himself and decides that the God of the universe's plan to use him is a terrible idea, because his own view of himself is in the way. Again, though, God does not respond to shore up Moses' belief in himself; God highlights his own absolute ability to make up for any and all weaknesses that Moses may have. For many of us, that would be the end of the discussion, but Moses is a stubborn man. Even after God's assurance that he himself made all mouths, that he shapes the ability to speak or not to speak, to see or not to see, and that he will teach Moses all he needs to know, Moses still can't do it. He says, 'Please, Lord, send someone else' (4:13, NCV).

Moses' inability to put God's ability and character at the centre of his confidence causes him to reject outright the opportunity that God has for him. Just think about that. How many opportunities has God placed before us, which we didn't take because our view of ourselves was more important than our trust and belief in God? I never, ever want my child to turn down God when he calls because my child thinks he is not suitable for the task. The answer isn't to bolster my son's view of himself so that he says, 'Yes, I am worthy to be used.' The answer is to shape his confidence so that when God says, 'I will do this and I want you to do it with me,' my son will say, 'That seems totally impossible, God, but I'm excited to be a part of what you are doing. I trust that you will teach me what I need to know and that you will pour your grace on everything I think I'm unable to do.' When Moses rejects God's choice and says, 'Please, Lord, send somebody else,' he is essentially saying, 'I don't trust you to work in me,' and God responds with deep emotion:

> The Lord became angry with Moses and said, 'Your brother Aaron, from the family of Levi, is a skilled speaker. He is already coming to meet you, and he

will be happy when he sees you. You will speak to Aaron and tell him what to say. I will help both of you to speak and will teach you what to do. Aaron will speak to the people for you. You will tell him what God says, and he will speak for you. Take your walking stick with you, and use it to do the miracles.'
EXODUS 4:14–17 (NCV)

God is faithful to his choice of Moses because he is a faithful God, so he works with Moses and his fears by sending Moses' brother to help him. A small part of me, though, always wonders what it would have looked like had Moses said from the start, 'It's not about me. It's about you, Lord.'

Jesus

We can see this God-centred focus most clearly in Jesus' ministry. Jesus talks to a Samaritan woman at a well, on his way home from a ministry trip (John 4:1–42), and he recognises that she has great needs. She has had a series of five husbands and she is willing to be in a relationship with a man who is not her husband, in a time and place where that arrangement wasn't acceptable. Having a series of husbands could create insecurity in anybody, as it apparently had done in her. Many scholars point to the fact that she came alone to the well at noon, instead of coming during the cool of the morning or evening when the rest of the women of the community would have been there. This subtle detail indicates how lonely and isolated she probably was.[8]

Jesus sees the Samaritan woman's need and responds. Nowadays, many of us would leap into this situation with words of encouragement to bolster her confidence: 'You are worth so much more than this. You deserve a happy life in a committed relationship. You are beautiful and clever and funny, and you are just as good as the other women around. God thinks you are amazing.' Jesus doesn't do this, though. He doesn't flatter her. He doesn't try to convince her of her good qualities or tell her how perfect she is, just the way God made her. He doesn't respond to her insecurity by trying to shore up her self-image. His response to her need is simple.

He tells her about himself. He tells her that he is the Messiah and that he can give her 'a spring of water welling up to eternal life' (v. 14). His response to her life situation is to show her more of God, not more of herself.

Examples throughout scripture

Over and over again in scripture we see God talking with people in this way. Gideon was a farmer whom God commanded to lead an army to save Israel. When Gideon asked, 'Lord, how can I save Israel? My family group is the weakest in Manasseh, and I am the least important member of my family,' God answered, 'I will be with you. It will seem as if the Midianites you are fighting are only one man' (Judges 6:15–16, NCV). To take another example, Job was a wealthy man whose world collapsed. When he questioned God about it, God responded by highlighting the breadth of his almighty power and glory: 'Where were you when I laid the earth's foundations?' (Job 38:4).

God makes it very clear that our confidence should not be in ourselves or our capabilities. Confidence is not a denying of ourselves; it is a recentring of what is important. When we place ourselves aside and put God in the centre, then something wonderful happens: we get to dream bigger. Moses adjusted his core of confidence and saw the end of 400 years of slavery in Egypt and the establishment of a nation. Mary was a teenager going about her daily life when the angel appeared to her and told her she would give birth to the Saviour of the world. She responded not with the question 'Why me?' but with a heart of amazement and gratitude toward God. Mary, then, had the joy of raising Jesus, the Son of God. The Samaritan woman placed her confidence in God and had her hope renewed. As a result, her entire town responded to her words and ran out to meet Jesus.

While Jesus was praying in Gethsemane, he told God the Father, 'Not my will, but yours be done' (Luke 22:42). Jesus' confidence in his Father's will was such that he was able to endure the unimaginable horrors of the cross and redeem us and all humanity.

Paul faced down venomous snakes, shipwrecks, a stoning, kings and imprisonment because he knew, 'We worship God through his Spirit, and our pride is in Christ Jesus. We do not put trust in ourselves or anything we can do' (Philippians 3:3, NCV). By keeping his confidence in God, Paul was able to play a part in spreading the gospel across the entire Roman empire.

Again and again in scripture we see that those who put their confidence in who God is, and not in who they are, are the ones who carry the peace, love, joy, and power of God with them. When we focus on ourselves, our frailty and imperfections become huge, and our view shrinks so that we see only our weaknesses. But when we truly believe that God is awesomely wonderful, and we put our confidence in him, then we can live freely. We can catch God's heart for the world, and we can believe that we might be a small part of his grand plans. When our children take on this belief, they will look at school and see God's heart for their friends and communities. They will see injustice and want to do something about it. They will see pain and want to respond.

They will no longer limit their dreams and hopes to what they feel they are capable of doing, but they will broaden their dreams to what God is able to do and will recognise when he wants to do it.

**God is awesome and holy,
and he loves me totally and unreasonably.**

I am loved

When Moses asked who God was, and God revealed himself, God said two things, not one:

> God said to Moses, 'I am who I am. This is what you are to say to the Israelites: 'I am has sent me to you.'' God also said to Moses, 'Say to the Israelites, "The Lord, the God of your fathers – the God of Abraham, the God of Isaac and the God of Jacob – has sent me to you." This is my name forever, the name you shall call me from generation to generation.'
> EXODUS 3:14–15

We always focus on the big, booming 'I am who I am' part of this passage, but I find it interesting that 'I am who I am' isn't the complete picture. In the other half of the statement, God declares his ongoing relationship with people. He says, essentially, 'I am God, and for a very long time I have been in relationship with you and your family.' Relationship is very much a part of God, and we need to train our children to see God through the lens of relationship, through the lens of his love.

Paul's prayer was 'that you… may have power, together with all the Lord's holy people, to grasp how wide and long and high and deep is the love of Christ' (Ephesians 3:17–18). God's love is complete and unconditional. We cannot earn it, lose it or deserve it, and we definitely aren't worthy of it. We are loved because he chooses to love us. He made us, and his love for us is the foundation of our confidence.

Throughout scripture, we are assured of God's deep love for us. It is undeserved and unreasonable; he simply loves us. In order for the impact of his love to hit home for our children, two things need to happen: they need to understand his love in context, and they need to be trained to see and feel God's love.

Who loves me?

Our children are loved by many people, including parents, grandparents, aunts, uncles, siblingsand friends. Some people can communicate deep love well, while others mention love only casually in cards for birthdays or Christmas. Children care about who loves them, and the more important a person is to their lives, the more that person's love matters.

If a stranger walks up to you and declares her permanent friendship for you, you won't instantly celebrate and invite her round to your house for cake and tea. No matter how much she insists on her feelings of friendship for you, the encounter will feel weird because you are strangers. But if you and she spend lots of time together, and you discover that she is kind and funny and generous and humble, something might begin to shift in your thinking. Your respect for her will grow. You will admire her, celebrate her and find her amazing and delightful. Then, when she turns to you and says, 'I so love being your friend, just as you are right now. I cherish our friendship. There is nothing you could do to make me love you more as my friend, and there is nothing you can do that would ever change my feelings,' you will feel deeply loved.

The first key concept in the core of confidence is crucial for children to understand: God is awesome and holy, and he loves me totally and unreasonably.

When we talk with children, we often talk about God's love, separate from who he is, focusing more on love than on the one doing the loving. The more children get to know God and how wonderful he is, the more they can be lifted up by the knowledge of his faithful and gigantic love for them.

How do I know?

In order to help our children access God's love, we need to teach them how to see God's love, how to understand God's love, and how to encounter God's love personally, so that their connection with him will last a lifetime.

One summer I met a ten-year-old boy at an event I was running. He had a stutter and was desperately shy. All of us workers had spent a whole week with the children, exploring the character of God – who he is, and how awesome and holy he is. The boy told me that he was tired of being scared all the time and that he wanted to talk with God about it. I sat down next to him, placed my hand on his shoulder and asked God to meet with him, speak to him and give him everything he needed. As we sat side by side in silence, the boy engaged with God in his mind and heart, chatting back and forth. Eventually, a smile slowly spread across his face. We were both quiet for about five minutes while he sat with his eyes closed, quietly smiling and praying. At one point he gently raised his hand and put it on his own chest.

After a while, I asked him what God was doing. He opened his eyes and glowed as he told me that God had put his hand on his chest 'right here', patting his hand over his heart. He continued, 'God told me he has spent every day with me, and that I make him laugh with happiness, and that he is my real dad. My biological father left when I was tiny, and my mum is a single mum, but God wants to be my dad! I can still feel his hand!' Not once did the boy stutter while he told me about his encounter with God, and I had the privilege of watching him walk tall and laugh loudly and look freer than I had ever seen him before.

When we train our children to know powerfully that 'God is awesome and holy and he loves me totally and unreasonably', it roots them in a relationship with God that lasts a lifetime. I think that when Jesus said he had come to give us life, and life to the full (John 10:10), this was part of what he meant. Confidence comes from knowing and experiencing the fact that it isn't about us; it's about him. In his glory and wonder, he turns his heart and his face towards us and loves us completely and totally.

24

I'm not finished yet

Blessed is the one who trusts in the Lord, whose confidence is in him. They will be like a tree planted by the water that sends out its roots by the stream. It does not fear when heat comes; its leaves are always green. It has no worries in a year of drought and never fails to bear fruit.

JEREMIAH 17:7–8

**God is awesome and holy,
and he loves me totally and unreasonably.**

**God is daily shaping me to be more like him,
and I am not finished yet.**

I am invited to be a small part of God's wonderful plans.

Perfection

We live in a world where perfection is king. We describe our ultimate ideal as 'perfect', whether it be a person we love, an experience on holiday, or the way a meal is cooked. Perfection is something to be prized and achieved, and we expect it to be the goal of leaders, colleagues and spouses alike. Many people seek to appear 'perfect' to others, in terms of their happiness, job satisfaction, achievements and family life. We can sometimes hide our flaws so people will think we are closer to the ideal than we actually are. Everyday life is warped on television and in movies, presenting a more 'perfect' reality than the one around us. We can spend a lot of spiritual and emotional energy in trying to appear as personally perfect as possible and working to perfection in our home life and work. Unfortunately, our children are not spared from the scrutiny.

This value of perfection is damaging our children. They feel their imperfections and they begin to look at themselves through new eyes as they learn that anything less than perfection is failure. Consequently, we try to make them feel better by assuring them of their perfection. We insist that they are perfect 'just the way they are'. We assure them that God sees them as perfect. We try to redefine 'perfection' for them so that it is achievable today. Perfection isn't seen as a journey; it's seen as an expectation for *now*, and one in which our children will constantly fail.

Objectively, we know that perfection is not attainable. None of us is without flaws; none of us has achieved perfection. So why do we allow our children to think that perfection is the ultimate goal and that they have achieved it 'just by being them'?

The truth is much more liberating. Paul tells us, 'All have sinned and fall short of the glory of God' (Romans 3:23). Jesus lived on earth and died and rose again in order to pay the price for our imperfection and provide the grace and mercy required to give us a close relationship with God and freedom from sin. It is impossible for us to generate our own perfection, which is why God became perfection for us.

The truth is that each of us, child and adult alike, is on a journey with God, a journey of transformation to become more and more like our Father. We are on a lifelong journey of being shaped by God to reflect his glory and to be effective and purposeful wherever he plants us. What that truth means for us is that, at any one point in our lives, we are only partially through our journey of transformation.

I see it like this. Picture a baker who is creating a beautiful wedding cake. The design is already complete and the cake has been paid for. All the components for a masterpiece are in place. The baker then takes the ingredients and begins to shape the mix into a batter. How foolish we would be if we popped our heads into the bakery and scoffed at the bowl of cake mix, dismissing it because it didn't look like a wedding cake! It will be a cake one day, but this is only the first step. The baker has plans for the mix: he wants it to go through more processing and finessing. It will undergo many stages before it is unveiled as the perfect wedding cake, but the baker already sees what the finished product will look like.

We would be foolish, too, to look in on the baker with his mixing bowl in hand and announce that the cake he's stirring is absolutely complete and perfect just as it is, and that no more work needs to be done. We can't celebrate it as a finished cake, because it isn't finished yet. However, we can sample the mix and cherish the stage that it's in, appreciating it for the potential it holds. We can appreciate the hints of the final design in its current state, and we can help in the kitchen, acting as partners with the baker in his work.

Unlike a cake mix, though, our children can be active partners with God in their own growth. Our delight as parents is to empower our children to embrace the stage they are in, instead of judging themselves for not being complete. We can train our children to be in proactive partnership with God and us as they embrace their current stage of transformation and boldly move toward the next.

Personality versus character

We can often forget that there is a difference between personality and character. For the purposes of this discussion, I mean that personality, broadly, is the set of predispositions we were born with, the way we are genetically wired to encounter the world. It includes our openness to new experiences and ideas, our drive for stimulation, how comfortable we are with others, and our responses to negative emotions such as stress and anxiety.[9] Some psychologists assert that babies come into the world with these things hardwired into them and, even before their births, we can begin to notice the differences in their personalities. Personality rarely, if ever, changes.

Character, on the other hand, is constantly growing and changing. It is the way we apply our personalities, faith, values and beliefs and engage with the world. It governs our choices and, eventually, our behaviour. Character is about sacrifice and perseverance, integrity and forgiveness, generosity in the face of need, choosing joy in adversity, and more.

We are called as parents to celebrate our children's personalities and disciple their characters. A child's personality may mean that he naturally dislikes new experiences, for example, but the way we encourage that child to wrestle with his fear and develop an appreciation for bravely adventuring into the unknown is all part of parenting his character.

God's journey with us

This is what God does with us. God seeks to draw us into relationship with him through the freedom he provided for us on the cross, and he desires to take us on a lifelong journey of transformation to be more like him.

> The Lord is the Spirit, and where the Spirit of the Lord is, there is freedom. Our faces, then, are not covered. We all show the Lord's glory, and we are being

changed to be like him. This change in us brings ever greater glory, which comes from the Lord, who is the Spirit.
2 CORINTHIANS 3:17–18 (NCV)

Throughout our lives, we know that we are not complete yet: we are on a journey of transformation. When we embrace that knowledge, it will bring freedom and joy into our lives. We won't expect ourselves to be perfect, because we'll recognise that it is an impossible goal. All we can do is humble our hearts to be content in all things, and engage fully with God as he transforms our hearts and minds. God is faithful to take us on a glorious journey, and we can trust in his faithfulness to take our children on a glorious journey, too.

Paul once wrote that he was 'confident of this, that he who began a good work in you will carry it on to completion until the day of Christ Jesus' (Philippians 1:6). God loves our children; he is faithful each day to lead them gently and wisely on a journey of transformation, and we are partners with him and our children in that lifelong process. What would our children's lives be like if they were perfectly content to be who they are in all their imperfections? What would their lives be like if they were perfectly content to be where they are on their journey, with hope and joyful anticipation for the future?

We don't have to be perfect to be useful

**God is awesome and holy,
and he loves me totally and unreasonably.**

**God is daily shaping me to be more like him,
and I am not finished yet.**

I am invited to be a small part of God's wonderful plans.

The wonderful thing about God is that he doesn't wait for us to be complete or perfect before using us in powerful and purposeful ways in this world. God is already in the world rescuing people, awakening their hearts and ministering to their minds, and, no matter where we are on our journey of transformation, he invites us to act as partners with him.

To be partners with God is an undeserved honour, as well as a key part of our own transformation process. While we are on our muddled journeys of transformation, we get to see God work. We can be a small part of his wonderful plans on this earth, all because of his grace and faithfulness. Whether we are mature in Christ or brand new to God, whether we are old or young, our relationship with God invites us into purpose.

Our weakness and incompleteness create space for God's power. The default setting in our heads screams that confidence comes from within, from feeling calm and secure in ourselves. When we believe this, though, we miss out on one of the great truths of God: it is precisely in our weakness, our brokenness and our inability that God moves in power.

Paul was a man who hated Jesus' followers and persecuted them fiercely until Jesus appeared to him on the road to Damascus and turned his life upside down. Paul then began a long journey of personal transformation, slowly becoming one of our greatest heroes of faith. It took time. In one of his letters to the church in Corinth, Paul described himself as a weak jar of clay that held the treasure of God's light, God's truth: 'But we have this treasure in jars of clay to show that this all-surpassing power is from God and not from us' (2 Corinthians 4:7).

For Paul, his human weakness and incompleteness enabled him to live with the obvious power of God in his life. Once, Paul wrote that he had pleaded with God three times to solve a personal problem.

> But [God] said to me, 'My grace is sufficient for you, for my power is made perfect in weakness.' Therefore I will boast all the more gladly about my weaknesses, so that Christ's power may rest on me. That is why, for Christ's sake, I delight in weaknesses, in insults, in hardships, in persecutions, in difficulties. For when I am weak, then I am strong.
> 2 CORINTHIANS 12:9–10

For our children

Our children are not perfect, nor should they be. Because God loves them, he is daily transforming them to be more like him. Our children will learn that throughout their journeys, God's power will be strong, even in their weaknesses. He invites them to do wonderful things with him, to be a small part of his great plans for this earth.

When our children know deep down the freedom that comes from being on this journey with a God who pours his grace around their weaknesses, then an unshakeable confidence will begin to grow within them.

25

Hearts and minds

For this people's heart has become calloused; they hardly hear with their ears, and they have closed their eyes. Otherwise they might see with their eyes, hear with their ears, understand with their hearts and turn, and I would heal them.

MATTHEW 13:15

Blessed are the pure in heart, for they will see God.

MATTHEW 5:8

You will keep in perfect peace those whose minds are steadfast, because they trust in you.

ISAIAH 26:3

Confidence is a tricky thing, and it can seem an intangible and slippery idea for children. How do we approach the task of building a deep and positive core of confidence within our children? What tools can we use?

Throughout scripture God seems very concerned with our hearts and our minds, because he often refers to them. Sometimes he just talks about our hearts and sometimes he just talks about our minds, but often he talks about the two together. For example, God tells Jeremiah, 'I the Lord search the heart and examine the mind' (Jeremiah 17:10). Then, when a Pharisee questions Jesus about the greatest commandment, Jesus answers by quoting an Old Testament verse: 'Love the Lord your God with all your heart and with all your soul and with all your mind' (Matthew 22:37; compare Deuteronomy 6:5).

The apostle Paul writes that people's 'thinking became futile and their foolish hearts were darkened' (Romans 1:21). In his letter to the Philippians, Paul encourages believers by writing that when they pray, 'the peace of God, which transcends all understanding, will guard your hearts and your minds in Christ Jesus' (Philippians 4:7).

As we begin to train our children in confidence, we can use the idea of 'the heart and the mind' as a useful focus, because the heart and the mind are often our battlegrounds in the fight for confidence in our children.

What do we mean by 'heart' and 'mind'? Each one of us might describe these concepts differently, but, for the purposes of this book, I have defined them broadly as follows. The heart involves:

- Feelings
- Spiritual concepts (for example, purity, sin)
- Pain and suffering
- Instincts, reactions, responses born of experience
- Relationships
- Personality

The mind involves:

- Thinking
- Perception
- Decisions and choices
- Attention
- Wonderings and ponderings
- Judgements
- Character

True confidence is rooted in both the heart and the mind. For example, we want our children to feel deeply confident (the heart) and we want them to choose confidently (the mind). We also want them not to be afraid, but to be able to respond freely and confidently to people and situations (the heart), while we also desire them to look at themselves and other people with humble confidence and clarity (the mind).

These are by no means perfect definitions. You may not even feel that they are good ones, so feel free to disagree and swap things around. In essence, I want us to understand that God is concerned with both the heart and the mind, and we as parents are called to give our attention to both of them in our children. Different tools are needed to nurture and develop our children's hearts and to train and shape their minds. In this chapter we will look at the tools we can use to draw close to our children's hearts and minds, in order to build a life of confidence in them.

Hearts

My husband and I once owned two tiny yucca trees, George and Malachi (yes, we name our plants). We bought them for our wedding with the oh-so-grand and romantic intention of growing them through our entire lives and then having them planted on our graves when we died. After about three months they began to look... wrong. Not wilted. Not dead. Just... off. The trunks were a bit too squidgy and the leaves were a bit too sticky. The colour was inconsistent. Nothing was catastrophic; things were just wrong. After six months we knew something bad was happening, but we couldn't figure it out. We had followed all the advice on the little card. We couldn't make sense of it.

One day George and Malachi just fell over. Then we discovered that their roots had completely rotted. The main source of their health, of their life, had rotted away, and we hadn't even noticed. What happens to a plant's roots is crucial to its overall health and well-being. Those roots may be buried deep underground and may spread so far and wide that it is impossible to know all the areas from which the plant draws its nutrients. We notice something is wrong with the root system only when the effects finally begin to show up on the plant.

I feel that something similar often happens to our children, particularly in terms of their hearts. We see the effect of hidden influences in their lives, whether it is fear, shame, anger, hesitance, unreasonable desire or stubborn refusal. Sometimes we instinctively sense that there is something underneath their behaviour, something happening in their hearts, but we feel ill-equipped to find out what it is. This perception arises especially in areas of confidence because confidence touches upon such deep feelings and experiences in our children.

There are key tools that we can use to access our children's hearts, so that we can monitor the health of their roots. Root issues can only be sorted at the root level. For something like confidence, we need to have a good handle on how to nurture our children's hearts at the root level.

Exploring together

Our children often can't understand what they are feeling, much less why they are feeling it. In the course of everyday life, our job is to help them negotiate that emotional path, and, if we are particularly intent on developing our children's confidence, it is even more important that we do so.

When we can understand what they are feeling, when we can truly get alongside their hearts and see what is happening underneath their behaviour, then we can help them grow healthy roots, emotionally and spiritually. Time constraints can trap us into disciplining outward behaviour instead of disciplining hearts, but confidence is nearly impossible to correct from the outside. We need to get into their hearts.

No matter how much pruning, music playing and encouraging talk you give a plant, if the roots are damaged or are drawing from a poisoned source, then the plant will suffer. If we never learn to address our children's hearts, we miss our opportunity to be as effective as we might be.

Four tools for drawing close to children's hearts

Understand through curiosity
Children can smell an agenda a mile away. In your relationship with your children, develop a regular pattern of asking them questions just to understand them better. This can be a helpful tool in getting snapshots of your children's hearts without any of you feeling the pressure to do something. So often we look at our children's hearts with a clumsy surgeon's approach: we want to fix the damage quickly, so we ask questions with an obvious agenda to fix something right then and there. As a result, some of our children shut down emotionally before we can make any progress. However, if we begin having conversations just to develop a culture of understanding, like taking a temperature or testing the level of chemicals in water, our children will feel more comfortable with the questions and much less threatened by the process.

As parents, we may stop long enough to understand the problem but not take time to drill down into how our child actually sees the problem. This approach goes beyond just having good listening skills. It's about working in partnership with God and your child to understand your child's heart, not just to understand the presented problem. It means keeping the conversation going until you can accurately say, 'Ah, I see. To you it looks like this and feels like this. I understand!' and your child can say in return, 'Yes. That's it!' This kind of interaction stirs your compassion: you understand not just what the child's mind is thinking, but also how her heart feels, which is what we are aiming to shape. Our first achievement is not to fix the problem, but to understand it.

Good conversations often start with something that makes you ponder. It may be the huge fight you had with your child or a tiny inflection in your child's voice. God will poke you as you notice a hesitation in a sentence or a reaction that doesn't seem quite right – a little thing, revealing that there may be a part of your child's roots that is not in the best condition.

Be genuinely curious and willing to go down the rabbit hole for the pure sake of understanding. We all long to be understood. When we genuinely set our hearts to want to understand our child and to see through his eyes, then we are on the path to building true heart connections with our child. It doesn't take much more time than a regular conversation. It just means continuing a little to see how far it goes. Most of these conversations take five minutes, and they can be done while in the car, walking to school, cuddling in bed or making dinner. Just set your heart to be curious, and start asking. As your child is talking, ask open-ended questions or make statements that follow what your child is saying, with no real direction or end goal. Here are a few examples:

- Tell me more about… That sounds interesting!
- What would happen if…?
- Does it feel more like this, or like this?
- Why? Why not?
- What are you afraid might happen?
- How did that make you feel?
- You seem to be feeling… Is that true?
- What happened to make you feel that way? When did it start?
- We can decide that later. Now I just want to understand better. So tell me more about…

When you think you understand – when you think you can see the situation from the child's eyes – summarise it for them in the way that you think they would put it. 'I see. This is what you think and feel? This is how it looks to you? Wow!' Affirm their emotions while they're at the bottom of the hole. Once you understand and can say, 'I see!' then it's important that you meet them with empathy and compassion, no matter how crazy the problem looks to you. Of course they are feeling what they are feeling. Look at how they see it.

When my son had just turned four, he went through a time of hiding his wounds. He would instantly show his little cuts or bruises to whichever parent was around, and we would comfort him and treat them. After the initial treatment, though, we noticed that he would try to hide the wound. He would cry if we wanted to look at it, and he would become deeply embarrassed and uncomfortable. If he got knocked at the swimming pool, he would be incredibly self-conscious and not want anyone to look at his bumps.

We, of course, began to be concerned about this. It was affecting his confidence with friends and other adults. We knew his wounds weren't caused by anything very serious because we were with him when he got them. We thought maybe he was afraid of being judged or mocked. When we asked him about it, he said he didn't want people to feel bad. We assumed that meant he didn't want people to comment or ask about it. We thought he was embarrassed, and we became very concerned about what this meant for his future in terms of his body image.

One day I decided to find out more. I wanted to ask questions until I could really and truly see the issue from his view, without judging or worrying. I just wanted to understand. The next time it happened, I asked him why he didn't want me to see the tiny scratch on his knee. 'I don't want you to feel bad,' he replied. 'Why would I feel bad?' I asked. 'You would say, "Oooo, that looks like it would hurt!" and then it would hurt you.' He placed his hand over the tiny scratch. I was confused. 'It would hurt me because I say, "Ooooooo," as if it hurts me?' I echoed. 'Yes!' he said, and then he started crying.

I moved in closer. 'Oh, babe, it doesn't hurt my body when I see your owies. Is that why you hide them?' I asked gently. 'Yes... no. I don't want you to be hurt,' he replied, struggling to explain himself. 'Tell me more. What else are you worried about?' I enquired. 'I'm afraid you'll be... disappointed!' he exclaimed. And with that he started sobbing.

Now I have never, ever used the word 'disappointed' in our relationship, but for some reason he was worried about it. I rubbed his hand gently and asked, 'Oh, honey, you are worried about disappointing me? What are you afraid of? What do you think would happen if I were disappointed?' The sobs continued in earnest. 'I'm scared you will throw me away!' he cried. 'Oh, my son! That sounds very scary!' I acknowledged. 'Yesssss,' he wailed.

Respond with empathy and bring truth
Once we get to the bottom of the issue, it is important that we respond with empathy and understanding. Too many times, after we have uncovered something in our children's hearts, we respond with our emotions: we laugh at the silliness of the fear; we become angry that they have never told us their fear before; we are shocked at their behaviour or thoughts, or we are visibly relieved. When we allow that to happen, we can lose the influence of the moment because our children then respond to our emotion instead of staying focused on their issue and on what we want to say.

202 PARENTING CHILDREN FOR A LIFE OF CONFIDENCE

I encourage you to find that place of compassion and understanding within yourself from which you can respond to your children's hearts in the moment with genuine concern, peace and love.

The next question to consider is this: what is the truth that needs to be spoken here?

At this vulnerable moment in the conversation, we often try to bring in our oh-so-wise judgement, either positive or negative. What is needed, though, is not our judgement; what is needed is the truth. Our children don't need us to say, 'Don't think that!' or 'What a silly thing to feel!' What they feel is what they feel, and that's okay. In this moment we need to ask ourselves and God what truth would restore health to our child's roots, and then decide if now is the moment when that truth can be sown.

'Oh, my son, look into my eyes,' I said. I lifted up his chin and then I began to place truth into his heart: 'I will never, ever, ever throw you away. I love you. There is nothing you can do that will make me stop loving you. There is no part of your body, inside or out, that can be broken bad enough to make me want to throw you away. My love is so big for you, as big as my whole body, and Daddy God's love is even stronger because his heart is gi-normous! Do I love you when you are sweet?' 'Yes,' his little voice came back. He gave a smile. 'Do I love you when you yell, when you are angry?' 'No,' he said. His chin started to wobble. '*Yes!*' I said. 'I love you bigger than the whole world, even when you are angry. There is nothing that can make me stop loving you.' His eyes widened. 'Do I love you when you laugh?' I asked. 'Yes,' he replied. 'Do I love you when you don't listen to me?' 'No...' he answered. '*Yes!*' I exclaimed. I love you so much, even when you don't listen to me. There is nothing that can make me stop loving you.'

A smile broke across his face. 'Do I love you when you cuddle with me?' I continued. 'Yes!' he shouted. 'Do I love you when you throw things?' I asked. He paused for a long moment and then he shouted, 'Yes!' 'Yes, I do!' I shouted back in agreement. 'I love you more than Christmas, even when you throw things. There is nothing that can make me stop loving you. I love you when you are sweet. I love you when you are angry. I love you when you laugh and when you don't listen, when we cuddle and when you throw things. There is nothing that can make me or God or Daddy stop loving you or ever want to throw you away. Nothing!'

He jumped up and flung his arms around my neck.

Connect children to yourself and God

Our heart connection with our children is incredibly important. It's what allows us to wade into the deep parts of their heart, so we need to set aside a time for them to connect with us, even if it's only a brief moment. God is the only one who can truly mend hearts and transform minds, so to give our children the opportunity to meet with him is very important.

As my son hugged me, I whispered, 'Oh, Daddy God, thank you for making Caleb and me family. Thank you that you love us more than we can even think of and that you will never throw us away! My heart is so happy right now, God.' 'Me too, God,' Caleb whispered.

Help children to be powerful for the next time

We want children to remember the truth they have learned and to remember how they dealt with the situation, so that if the problem arises again, they will be able to handle it powerfully. They need a plan, and we can help them make one.

'Hey, wait a minute,' I said to Caleb. 'Daddy has some cuts on his legs. Let's look! Do you want to throw Daddy away because he has those cuts?' *'Noooo!'* Caleb exclaimed. 'I love Daddy forever!' 'That's right!' I said. 'How are our hearts? Are they far away from each other or together again?' 'Together,' he replied. He smiled and then let out a sigh. 'Okay,' I said. 'So what do you do the next time you have a cut on your body?' 'Don't be scared. Just show it,' he answered. He popped up and pointed at each of us. 'We don't hide from each other. We love each other.' 'Absolutely,' I said. 'Now, I'm going to make dinner. What are you going to do?'

Each tool on its own is useful and, sometimes, using one of them in isolation is the most powerful thing you can do. In combination, they allow you to delve quickly and easily into the heart issues affecting your children.

- Understand through curiosity.
- Respond with empathy and bring truth.
- Connect children to yourself and God.
- Help children to be powerful for the next time.

It is so easy to get into the groove of dealing with behaviour that we can miss the opportunity to dig down to the roots of our children's actions. As we look to build children who are spiritually and emotionally confident, our ease and skill in calmly ministering to their hearts will grow, and we will have the joy of shaping confidence from its deepest roots.

When we teach our children's hearts, the lessons stick for a long time. Even now, years later, in the midst of other behaviour discussions, my son will glance up at me or look over his shoulder as he heads to his room and call, 'You still love me a lot, though. That doesn't change!' One good conversation can last a lifetime, because heart lessons produce fruit.

Minds

'Are you excited about your new school?' Sonia asked, bending down and helping Ben slip his jumper over his shoulders. She wondered if he could adapt to a new home and a new school so quickly.

Ben nodded. 'God chose my school!' he exclaimed. 'There were no places there so we had to wait and wait. God moved all the people around so I could be at this school.' 'That's wonderful, Ben!' Sonia replied. She checked his hair one more time, then asked, 'Are you worried about making new friends?' 'No.' Ben assured her. He grinned, then added, 'God chose my school, so it's perfect for me. I will find my friends and be kind to them and it will be just right. We fit each other, me and my school.'

What are we talking about when we say 'confidence'? For me, confidence is the combined freedom, peace, strength and joy that come from seeing ourselves, others and the world with a godly mindset. When we parent our children for a life of confidence, we are essentially building and focusing the way our children think. The world is as it is: it is broken and wonderful and sad and heavenly and everything in between. How we perceive it and respond to it all depends on how our mind sees it. Our mind defines reality for us. It is the filter for our lives, the operating system for our choices and relationships and for the way we view ourselves and others. It's the essence of how we approach living.

Have you ever met someone who thought radically differently from you? I have. I was once very ill with ME, bedbound and unable to work. One day my husband came home from work with a big smile on his face. He greeted me with a kiss and announced, 'Guess what, honey? We get to live by faith!' I sat up, very confused, as he went on: 'I had my six-month review, and they feel that I am not cut out for this type of work, so they aren't going to renew the contract. I'm fired! We get to live by faith. Isn't that cool?' He took his shoes off and hummed to himself as he went to the kitchen to grab a drink.

My brain started freaking out as I saw 100 million horrible things cascading towards us: no electricity, no place to live, no food and no future. My husband, all the while, happily drank his water and smiled confidently.

At that moment, my mind allowed me to see only money problems and hopelessness, but my husband had trained his mind to see something else entirely. My mind defined the situation as a widening chasm of fear and worry, but my husband's mind enabled him to see a situation where the faithful God who works all things together for the good of those who love him was going to do something wonderful. My husband quickly got another job that worked out much better for our family, and I had to recognise that perhaps my mindset wasn't the best.

Scripture talks a lot about the mind. It often mentions the blessing of a mind rightly aligned. For example, 'If people's thinking is controlled by the sinful self, there is death. But if their thinking is controlled by the Spirit, there is life and peace' (Romans 8:6, NCV).

'Life and peace'. Oh, if we could raise children who truly had fullness of life and a steady and deep daily peace. What a goal!

Various biblical authors give us suggestions for how to set our minds, but I believe Paul sums it up well when he writes, 'Do not be shaped by this world; instead be changed within by a new way of thinking. Then you will be able to decide what God wants for you; you will know what is good and pleasing to him and what is perfect' (Romans 12:2, NCV). Many of us, including our children, don't realise what we are missing by living with the world's mindset.

The day I got glasses, my life changed forever. I was ten years old and I remember sitting in the car wearing my new glasses and being absolutely fascinated by trees. Did you know that it was possible to see the leaves on trees? I didn't, until that day. The trees weren't just big green blobs any more. I could see the leaves on all the trees *at the same time, from the car*! Until that day, nature had not been a big deal to me because it was just large swathes of colour, but all of a sudden I was amazed by everything. I could read signs. I could see nature. I could recognise friends from across the classroom. I could volunteer to answer problems on the chalkboard. I could play sports and react to the ball before it was within two metres of me. I felt like a superhero with amazing vision. My headaches even went away. It was wonderful! My glasses enabled me to walk and read and write and sightsee and play sports and engage with life confidently because they had been finely tuned to enable me to see the world with clarity. My glasses made all the difference.

I believe that we have this same type of perception problem spiritually. The way we see the world is different from the way we were meant to see it. Over the years, our mind builds a perception of the world. Our parents, family, friends, music, magazines, books, schools and the internet all shape us. We walk through life perceiving ourselves and others through this filter and responding from that perspective. The problem is that those perceptions may not be the ones that God designed for us. The world declares that beauty, money and success are important, that self-worth is based on others' approval, and that happiness should be pursued and won. The fruit of the way the world works is fear, worry, insecurity, fragility and striving.

The life God has for us brings restoration, wholeness, purpose, security and true confidence. The mindset God designs shows us that he is awesome and wonderful and that he is everywhere and active. A godly mindset helps us to live in the knowledge that God loves us totally and completely, imperfect as we are, and that he is daily shaping us to be more and more like him. It enables us to see that God's purposes on earth are mighty and that he has called us to be partners with him to bring beauty from ashes and his rightness on earth.

If our children's view of the world and themselves is of that godly mindset, it will affect every area of their lives – how they look in the mirror, how they feel walking down the street, what they think the moment they walk into school, and even how they react when someone shoves them into a wall or calls them a name. It will shape their boldness in compassion and in trying new things. It will be the fuel for the kind of friends or husbands or wives they will be and, eventually, it will affect the way our grandchildren face the world. A godly mindset empowers children to have a confidence that lasts.

How can we begin to build a godly mindset? How can we teach our children to think and to see themselves, others and the world at large from God's perspective?

An optician's approach

Only you can see through your own eyes. An optician can't see the world exactly as you see it. When she is working with you, her job is to diagnose and treat your eyes primarily by using your feedback, your words and your judgements. Her job is to try to understand what you see as well as she can, but she is unable to know it exactly. Her physical examination helps her make a general guess, and then she knows where to start. She asks you to put on a set of glasses that can be adjusted or she asks you to look through a big machine, and a very subjective process begins.

The optician shows you wall charts of letters or numbers, and she begins to put lenses in front of your eyes. 'Is this one better, or this one?' she asks. 'Number one, or number two?' You answer her questions the best you can. Together, through a series of choices, the two of you narrow down the lenses that are right for you, the ones that give you the sharpest eyesight for your life. It's a partnership. The optician's job is to trust you to answer correctly and to understand how you are seeing now, in order to make the necessary adjustments so that you can see better in the future.

If we are going to position our children's minds well, then we need to have an element of the optician in us. It's not just about deciding what to do and doing it. It's about setting ourselves to walk along a life journey with our children, constantly adjusting the way we parent, to help them develop a godly mindset, which will produce the fruit of true confidence, peace and the knowledge of God's will for them and others.

Five tools for shaping children's minds

Direct children's attention and values
One way of shaping the way our children perceive and think is by looking at what we draw their attention to and what we give our attention to. Most of the ways we operate in everyday life are almost unconscious. Years of habit have drawn us into behaving and speaking in a certain manner, and our children pick up on our speech and behaviour. It's the little things that shape their perceptions.

For instance, when your child walks into the room, what do you look at first and what do you say? I have a friend whose mum would almost immediately look her up and down and comment on her appearance. Often it was a positive comment, but it created a way of thinking within my friend. She grew up considering personal appearance to be a central part of the way she viewed herself and others, and, therefore, her confidence became rooted in appearances.

When you are out and about with your children, what do you point out to them? Where do you draw their attention? What do you comment on? What do you talk about? What values do you think you are communicating to your children through the topics of conversation that pop up along the road and at home, through what you laugh at and what you roll your eyes at?

Use foundational phrases
Language is one of the key tools for how we think. What we say lays down a framework for understanding. Throughout our children's lives, we will be establishing this

skeleton of thinking, this framework, from which all other understanding will hang. Foundational truths lie at the base of everything we do. Every family tends to have favourite phrases or sayings. Some of these are clichés, and some are not. If you think back to your childhood, you may remember some of them, for example: 'If you can't say anything nice, don't say anything at all'; 'Hug a tree if you get lost'; 'Life's not fair'; 'Blessed to be a blessing'. In the movie *Meet the Robinsons*, the characters often repeat, 'Keep moving forward,' and 'See a need. Fill a need.' All of these phrases and sayings give children easy-access language for developing helpful values.

But there are also deeper things that parents say, which stick with children – key phrases and ways of responding that embed themselves into our children's brains. I'm sure you have had the experience of hearing your own parents' words accidentally leaping out of your mouth when you're talking to your children. Some phrases just stick in our minds. We as parents have an opportunity to deliberately craft foundational messages that will become part of a framework for our children's thinking.

Verbally frame what children are seeing
Children's brains are constantly trying to make sense of the world – trying to understand, for instance, cause and effect, power in relationships, how culture works and where God is in all of it. One of the most powerful tools you can use is the ability to 'frame' the world for your children. In essence, we help our children to see the world around them, and then we provide understanding so that they can make sense of what they are seeing. We teach them what they are looking at. When our children are under five years old, we do this almost all the time because at this stage of life they are constantly asking 'why?' They draw us into framing the world for them. They ask 'why?' about people and relationships and nature and machines. Unfortunately, as they get older, they often stop asking 'why?' and we forget that the need for framing is still there.

Our children still need us to frame the world for them, to train them how to see and understand it. If we don't give them that framework, then books or television will, or their friends, or the internet. Throughout their lives, it is our blessing to answer the questions they may be thinking but are not openly asking yet. It's our job to get ahead of them and frame for them the questions and issues that may be coming next in their lives, instead of desperately trying to chase and chip into the perceptions that the world has already put in. We want our children to see the world through the framework we have helped them to shape in their minds.

Encounter God and his truth

While we may only be able to take an optician's approach, coaching our children from the outside, God himself can work with them from the inside. He created them and he is with them always. He knows what they are thinking. He knows what is in their hearts and he is daily developing them to be more like him. He is also speaking to them and acting in partnership with them in their spiritual and mental transformation. It is important for us, as parents, to keep that truth at the forefront of this process.

Another key tool is for us continually to coach our children to connect with God through scripture and through a heart-to-heart relationship with him. So much in our world shifts. When we help our children to ground themselves in the Bible, then they will have unshakeable access to truth. When we encourage and equip them to ground themselves in a vibrant, joy-filled relationship with God, then they will have unshakeable access to the love, healing and blessing of the Almighty.

Equip children to be powerful in shaping their own minds

Ultimately, each of us is responsible for the way we think and perceive, and we have a lifetime of opportunities in which we can continue to adjust our minds. After all, we are on a lifelong journey of personal transformation. While our children are in our homes, we can create tools for them to use, to help them adjust their thinking and perceptions on their own. Over time and with use, some of these tools will become a natural part of our children's own tool set. By the time they leave to live on their own, we want them to be fully equipped with a powerful arsenal of practised strategies that they can employ when life presents challenges. We want them to be able to assess themselves effectively and make changes, keep a God-centred mindset, adjust their plans when necessary, and continue to learn along their journey of personal transformation.

When I first had my glasses, I was not in the habit of wearing them. I began to discover that the cost of amazing vision was to remember my glasses, to take care of my glasses, and to actually wear my glasses. It was inconvenient at first, but after a while I didn't even think about it. I wouldn't even consider not wearing my glasses or my contact lenses now. It is one of the healthiest, most wonderful daily blessings I have. Once our children learn to see the fruit of a God-centred mindset in their lives, they will learn to value and embrace the cost of choosing to go on the journey of partnership with God in transforming their minds.

26

Everyday applications

**God is daily shaping me to be more like him,
and I am not finished yet.**

I am invited to be a small part of God's wonderful plans.

When I was young, I thought that parenting was instinctive, that it would naturally flow out of me just the way I wanted. As I grew older I began to realise that rarely does anything good come out of me by pure instinct. The instinctive me is clunky and inconsistent and variable and selfish and, often, inflexible. Anything good I do has come out of a deliberate choice to make what is on my heart and mind bear fruit in my life and be reflected in my decisions and relationships. From pursuing health to trying to be a more gracious and loving boss, to giving my husband my best instead of my emotional leftovers, I must look at my life and the way I operate and I must choose to be the person I want to be.

Parenting for confidence is a choice. It requires us to step back for a moment, to look at our parenting and ask ourselves, 'Is this the way I want to do it? Is this producing the spiritual fruit in my children's lives that my heart longs for? Am I being who God has called me to be here? What do I need to change in myself and in my approach, so that my children can be truly confident?'

I can't tell you how many times I have read a parenting book and tried to pick up the suggestions, only to be annoyed that they didn't 'work' with my child or frustrated with myself when I couldn't remember the programme or stick with it. Chasing formulas is exhausting and disappointing, and it somehow feels disconnected from what's happening in our hearts. My goal is for you to feel that parenting for confidence can flow naturally from your heart.

The remaining chapters of Part III will:

- focus on a specific parenting moment and address its key questions;
- take a deeper look at the issue;
- put the tools of hearts and minds into action.

Before we continue, here is a quick reminder of the tools we've covered in the previous chapter. Don't worry about remembering them. Throughout the following chapters, I will specifically list the tools when they are put into action, so that you can see when they are used.

We will use these *tools for the heart* to help us draw close to our children's hearts.

- Understand through curiosity.
- Respond with empathy and bring truth.
- Connect children to yourself and God.
- Help children to be powerful for the next time.

We will use these *tools for the mind* to help us adjust our children's thinking.

- Direct children's attention and values.
- Use foundational phrases.
- Verbally frame what children are seeing.
- Encounter God and his truth.
- Equip children to be powerful in shaping their own minds.

When we begin to parent out of our deep beliefs, then the pressure of doing everything 'just right' can fall away. We will become more bold and proactive as we choose to parent from our hearts, and the fruits of confidence will begin to grow in our children.

27

Who am I?

Key question: What do we do when our children concern themselves with asking, 'Who am I?'

One day I was walking across the park with Joseph, one of the young people from my church. He wanted to talk.

'Secondary school is different from what I thought it would be,' he said. 'People aren't mean. It's just…' He paused and nervously swept his hair across his forehead. 'Well… it's just that Mum keeps telling me to be myself. She says that if I'd just be myself, then people would like me for who I am. I feel like I'm supposed to know what that is. But I really don't. How can I be myself if I don't know who I'm supposed to be? Is that wrong?'

When our core of confidence centres on the belief that 'I must be confident, proud and bold in who I am,' then the question 'But who am I?' becomes a huge one. Never before has there been such pressure on children and young people to be able to define themselves, to be able to describe and summarise who they are. The belief that we are all special and unique and should be able to express ourselves in a way that reflects our individuality thunders in their ears. The pressure on our children to prove their uniqueness can be stifling.

A deeper look at the issue

Society has rushed in to help us discover our uniqueness so that we can categorise ourselves and define ourselves clearly. There are countless personality tests, colour profiles, quizzes and categories for our children to discover themselves in. We see our children quickly jumping into these 'tests', seeking to understand who they are and to define themselves, because the demand of the world has fuelled their curiosity to dis cover and define who they are and who they are not.

Personality versus character

As we discussed before, there is a difference between personality and character. Personality is a hardwired instinct in our brains. For instance, when children are faced with something new, each child will react differently. One child may be naturally cautious, waiting for someone else to try the activity first, while another may be reckless, rushing right in before she has even looked at it properly. Broadly speaking, current research studies show that the personality we have in preschool is, essentially, the personality we will have for the rest of our lives. Personality can be changed, but it requires much conscious and deliberate effort on our parts.

While personality may affect how we initially feel in a scenario, character determines how we will respond to it. Character is something that we can shape. Character is about who we are in the moment, the combination of our past and our present, our hopes for the future, and the way we make decisions. We can teach our children to be brave in the face of something new, even if bravery is not their initial reaction. We can teach them skills to reduce their anxiety. We can teach them how to see a new situation so that it is no longer either terrifying or unreasonably attractive. We can teach them restraint, so that they assess the dangers before they jump. Character is constantly being moulded as we go through life because our life lessons and experiences constantly shape the way we choose to respond to situations and scenarios.

Too often we begin to muddle personality and character in our heads, and then our children become confused about them, too. They begin to view everything about themselves as permanent. They begin to believe that when they were born, they were born complete, and that their lives are simply a journey of understanding themselves better and better and learning to be confident in who they are. This confusion is damaging our children and stopping them from experiencing the freedom that God designed for them, because the truth is far different.

Limits within the box

By placing an increasing value on individuality, society has replaced the value of personal transformation with an emphasis on personally expressing what already exists. Inevitably, then, our children begin to see themselves as fixed, locked into who they are. They can begin to think, 'I was created in one way, and now that's it. I have to live within that realm of my personality.' Their journey becomes about expressing themselves where they are, as opposed to anticipating, with hope and joy and freedom of choice, the person they will be tomorrow. When our children view themselves as fixed, they accept both character flaws and weaknesses as part of their identity, and they don't see that these flaws can possibly be changed.

Our children often learn to see themselves in a box. They believe that in order to succeed in this world, they must define that box as quickly and as comprehensively as possible, and then they must defend the box vigorously.

- I am good at maths. I am not good at reading or writing.
- I am sporty and funny. I am not clever.
- I hate being in charge. I love serving.
- I say it like it is, and that's just me.

They then conclude, 'I must be a pastoral, sporty, fun-loving girl who could get only these types of jobs and serve in these areas of church,' and they reject everything that doesn't fit in their boxes: 'Oh no, I couldn't do that. It's just not "me"'; 'I couldn't speak at the front. It's just not "me"'; 'I couldn't write a book. I have dyslexia. It's not "me".'

But when we think in terms of possibilities for change, there are no limits on how God can use us. There is nothing for us to argue with God about. We will be able to respond to him like this: 'I am me, and God loves me. If he's asking me to do this, then I will do it, because he knows me way better than I know myself.'

When you ask your child to do something you know he is capable of, do you want to stop and have a debate with him about whether or not it fits with his personality? Do you want your requests to be restricted, based on what he thinks his limitations are? You know your children well, and you want them to be living in the fullness of who they are. You may know better than they do what that is.

How much more does our Father know the depths of the personality, skills and giftings he's put in each of us, and how our character is being developed at any given moment.

Freedom outside the box

If it's not important for our children to know what 'boxes' they fit in, to be able to answer God's call, why push them to pursue that knowledge? Of what benefit are the boxes? If we never focus our children's attention on the boxes, but instead encourage them to focus on the fact that they are loved totally by a great God who is asking them to do powerful things today and tomorrow, then our children can begin to respond to their heart and to God's heart without the walls of a box blocking them in.

If we refuse to accept our children's boxes, we prevent our children from placing their confidence in themselves, in their own definitions of who they are. If God asks me to speak at a conference, I could respond, 'Yes, I can do that. I'm good at it. I am a teacher and a preacher. I am funny and people really enjoy laughing at my talks. Not a problem. Yes, God, I will do that.' Or I could respond, 'Thank you, God, for choosing me to do this thing with you. Thank you for what you want to say to these people and for the joy I will get in doing this with you. Absolutely, yes!' In both cases, I accept the speaking engagement, but where I place my confidence is radically different in each case.

I love the way God declared himself to Moses. Moses stood before the burning bush and asked, 'What is your name?' God answered, 'I Am Who I Am' (Exodus 3:13–14). He didn't rattle off a list of traits showing who he was. At that moment he didn't hyper-define himself. His initial response to Moses was to say that his name was 'I Am'. You see, God is the ultimate everything, and so the most powerful, most complete description he could use was simply 'I Am'.

Wouldn't it be great for our children to be so comfortable and confident that it is enough for them to wake up every day and think 'I am just me'? No limits; no boxes; secure in the knowledge that they are totally and completely loved by an amazing God, by the great 'I Am'. Then they would be free to laugh and be silly, to like what they like and be good at what they're good at. They can hope in the future and not be limited by their self-imposed boxes. They can embrace the journey of letting God develop and transform them, and they can experience the joy and freedom that comes with being in the middle of it all. They can acknowledge their weaknesses and failings and be aware that they are not yet all they want to be. They can feel unashamed to get help and to grow. They can delight in the everyday incompleteness of themselves, knowing that their 'now' is good and their future is glorious because their God is faithful.

The danger of labels

If we want our children to live free from a box, we must be careful not to attempt to create one for them. When we tell our children who they are, we may want them to take our words on as part of their identity: 'You are wonderful, beautiful, funny and clever.' We want them to define themselves by the labels we create for them. We want them to believe those things about themselves and to be confident in them.

We believe that our job as parents is to help our children define themselves in a positive way. What happens, though, is that when we construct an identity like this for our children – a box for them to cling to and live in – that identity becomes a fragile core that they must contain. If we tell them, 'You are unique; you are perfect; you are funny and beautiful and clever', then we are setting them up for a battle. What happens to their confidence when they find that someone else doesn't think that way about them – when someone criticises them or says hurtful things? What happens to their confidence when we have told them they are unique and special, and then someone else comes along with the same traits or skills? What happens when their 'uniqueness' isn't unique any more? It shatters them. It makes them question everything about themselves because their trust was in their labels.

In our effort to help our children form a good self-image, we essentially judge them and then ask them to adopt our judgements. We have watched and assessed them, and then we declare, 'Yes, according to me and the world, you can be classed as clever. Here you go – accept this label. Put it in your box.' So our child does as we say. Later on, though, someone else comes along and says, 'I disagree. You are stupid. Here you go – accept this label. Put it in your box.' So our child puts that one in his box, too. Eventually it becomes a battle of the labels, a battle between the influences that shout ever louder, 'You are this! You are that!' Sadly, we often lose the battle.

God's approach is different. Remember what God said to Moses when Moses wanted an affirmation of his own identity (Exodus 4:11–12)? Remember what Jesus said to the woman at the well? He spoke about himself (John 4:14). When we connect our children to God, he shows them who he is and he whispers his love for them. He connects with them heart to heart and draws them to his heart, instead of shouting one more label into the cacophony of labels bombarding them.

How can we lay a foundation in God so that our children can develop their core of confidence in him and not in themselves?

Putting the hearts and minds tools into action

Here are a few suggestions to get you started in building a core of confidence.

**God is awesome and holy,
and he loves me totally and unreasonably.**

**God is daily shaping me to be more like him,
and I am not finished yet.**

I am invited to be a small part of God's wonderful plans.

Affirm children through relationship, not through labels

Hearts: Connect children to yourself and God
Minds: Use foundational phrases; verbally frame what children are seeing

Truth is in the relationship. I believe I'm funny because people laugh, not because people tell me I'm funny. I believe my mum loves me because I see it in her actions, her eyes and her hugs, so when she says that she loves me, I believe it. If we change our language, so that we are affirming our children through relationship, we will build in them a freedom to be loved and to be 'I am' in our presence. We will build in our children a relationship where they can see who they are, reflected in how others react to their character. Today they may love playing the trombone, and tomorrow they may love bowling. Through it all, as they tell us stories of their lives and the worries of their hearts, we can affirm them on their journey.

Try communicating encouragement, love and approval to your children in ways that emphasise your relationship with them and their effect on you, instead of pushing them to accept the label you want them to embrace. For instance, avoid using sentences starting with 'You are…' or 'You look…', such as 'You are so smart. You are so clever. You are so funny. You look so beautiful. You are so creative.'

Instead, describe how you are affected by who they are or what they do – for example, 'I love watching how you do…'; 'I love… about you'; 'When we are together, I feel…'; 'When you do… I feel…'

There is such a difference between 'You are loved' and 'I love you with all my heart.' There is such a difference between 'You are funny' and 'I love laughing with you. Days with you are filled with fun.' There is such a difference between 'You are beautiful' and 'I feel such joy when I am with you. I admire you so much.' There is such a difference between 'You are clever' and 'I love the way your mind works.'

If we do this well, our daughter won't agonise about whether random strangers think her body is beautiful or not, because she will know that her family and friends cherish her heart and delight in her presence. She will be better able to decide whom she wants to be with and what relationships are healthy for her, because she already sees how she positively affects those close to her and how others have a positive effect on her. She can wisely choose to be in relationships where people deeply value, protect and cherish her.

If we do it well, our son won't be desperately focused on trying to live out labels, because he will know that we love everything about him. We delight in his company. He brings us joy and laughter. He makes our hearts feel full with love. Our favourite parts of the day are when we get to hear his thoughts and play with him, and when we get to share our hearts about things we feel and think. Not everyone is going to feel that way about our sons – but we do, and God does.

Talk about transformation and share your stories

Hearts: **Connect children to yourself and God**
Minds: **Direct children's attention and values; equip children to be powerful in shaping their own minds; encounter God and his truth**

When we make our core of confidence about God, then we begin to grasp that we have not finished growing yet and that God invites us, every day, to be a small part of his great plan. We begin to realise that who I am today isn't who I am going to be tomorrow, because God is shaping me and I'm helping him to do so. Labels don't fit because we are constantly changing.

Create a culture in your home where changing, learning and improving are regularly celebrated, discussed and expected. Talk about what you are learning at school or work. Share stories of how you are changing in response to scripture or circumstances. Share what you and God have been talking about. Apologise when you need to, and discuss what it's like to be on your own journey of transformation. In this way, as I've mentioned before, you create windows into your own life with God. Invite people over for dinner who have great stories of meeting God and can explain how having him in their lives has made a radical difference.

Talk about labels that you have believed about yourself, and how you are on a journey of realising that your core of confidence has been misplaced. Have conversations about characters in movies and on television who constantly talk about themselves and about 'being themselves'. Wonder why they say that, and invite your child into a conversation about it.

Read Bible stories with your child, focusing on people who had a good core of confidence and whom God took on a journey of transformation. Discuss the changes in the disciples and in characters such as Esther and Joseph, and notice how God continued to develop them throughout their lives.

At night, spend time with your child chatting with God about your days and what you have been thinking. Invite God to shape your characters and hearts to be more like him. The more we can make our home a place where we can all delight in the middle stages of our process of transformation, the more our children will learn to embrace each stage of their growth in God.

28

Encouraging for confidence

Key question: How do we encourage our children if we no longer use labels?

Our children believe that we value the things we praise. They hear how we praise them, and they think that what we praise most, we value most. I would suggest that most of us haven't thought much about what qualities we praise.

A deeper look at the issue

We often praise what is before our eyes – the most obvious thing. Often we encourage our children without thinking. They come down for church dressed well and we praise the way they look: 'You are beautiful'; 'What a handsome little man.' They win a competition and we praise their achievement: 'Well done! You won!' We praise their obedience: 'Good boy!'

I would suggest that we have been taught to praise these things, maybe by the world or maybe by our own parents. We praise children because we want them to feel confident; we want to build their self-esteem. The problem is that our praise isn't always an accurate reflection of our parenting values. For me, the three most important traits I would want to see in my child are not the ones above – looking good, winning and being obedient – but they are the qualities we unconsciously end up praising. Think about it. What do you praise the most in your home?

The world says we must 'be' many things, so we strive to meet those standards, but our insecurity and pain illuminate our wounds when we feel that we don't measure up. We end up defeated and say, 'I guess I'm ugly' or 'I'm not that funny.' Then, as Christians, we hear these words and rush in to fill the hole. 'Yes, it's important to be beautiful and funny!' we say to ourselves. 'In God's eyes you *are* those things. Ignore what those mean people say. Ignore what you say to yourself. To God you *are* beautiful and funny. Feel confident! You *are* all those things, just by being you.'

Actually, though, when we look closely at what the world says is important, all those things don't amount to much. They are just worldly judgements and worldly values. In the end, most of them don't matter – at all.

What matters to God? What traits are the core of the way he sees us? Our heart. Our holiness and righteousness in him. Our decisions. Our humility. Our love.

Instead of praising according to the world's measuring sticks, what if we encouraged and praised in accordance with what God has called us to? What would it look like if we deliberately praised our children for the traits we really want to see growing in them? What if we praised our children not for the things we see on the surface but for the deeper values we want to see in their lives?

The following is not a comprehensive list; it just happens to be my list. It's a sampling of the character traits I see valued in scripture, so I often talk about these traits when I'm with children. Each of us will have different values we cherish from the Bible, so your list may not look the same as mine. That's okay!

These are the traits I want to see in my child:

- Love of learning
- Ability to see opportunity in failure and to bounce back easily
- Curiosity
- Deep compassion
- Love
- Joy
- Peace
- Patience
- Kindness
- Mercy
- Grace
- Humility
- Goodness
- Gentleness
- Faithfulness
- Self-control
- Courage
- Sacrifice
- Generosity
- Love of being on a team and ability to value others' contributions

- Wisdom
- Boldness
- Bravery
- Justice
- Perseverance
- Problem-solving ability
- Ability to be a good friend
- Honesty

Note that this isn't a gendered list. It is a list of character traits that God calls us all to develop, no matter what our gender. It is important that we praise our boys for their kindness and self-control as much as we praise our girls for those same traits. Similarly, we should praise our girls for bravery and sacrifice as much as we praise our boys. All of these character traits reflect Christ, and we are each called to be like him.

When we stop or greatly reduce our praise of the superficial, such as cleverness, beauty, physical strength, politeness or being good at something, and start praising the biblical character traits and truths we see in our children, then those traits will begin to develop and blossom.

I want my child to be confident that he can control himself and his emotions, that he can be powerfully courageous and filled with joy each day. I want him to flourish in progressing with his maths, even if he isn't at the top of his set. I want him to see the power of his gentleness with others each day. If I want all of this, I have to start showing him that these things are important to me and to him.

For some of us, this will take a huge mind shift and, most of all, a change in our habits. When I started, I was amazed at how many platitudes I was throwing at my child, how many superficial things I was praising. I had to learn to look for and praise a different set of qualities.

Putting the hearts and minds tools into action

Here are a few suggestions to get you started in building a core of confidence.

**God is awesome and holy,
and he loves me totally and unreasonably.**

**God is daily shaping me to be more like him,
and I am not finished yet.**

I am invited to be a small part of God's wonderful plans.

Pause to reflect

Minds: Use foundational phrases

Take some time to listen to yourself. If you do nothing else this week, just pay attention to what you are saying when you praise your children. Some of us are effusive parents, praising everything all the time. Some of us have fallen into the trap of praising with the phrases we've always used. Perhaps we don't actually praise our children very often at all, and we may need to look at ways we can increase our praise.

If it would help, jot down the phrases you say most when you encourage and praise your children. Circle the phrases you like, and put a big X through the ones you want to replace. Do you agree with the phrases still on your list? Are those your values? Could you be any more specific about the ones you like? Could you tell stories about them? Maybe you could ask your children more questions to push further into those areas of encouragement that you have already identified as important.

Brainstorm your own list of key character traits you want to develop in your child. Use your Bible and your knowledge of God's character as the basis for your list, or you are likely to end up using the world's values instead. Keep in mind that your list will change as your child grows and matures. Once you have created your list, pick out a few traits you would like to start working on right away.

Give specific praise

Minds: Verbally frame what children are seeing

Create some affirming phrases and try them out, so that you will have them ready to use when the opportunity arises. Here are a few examples.

- Great effort! That is so kind!
- Wonderful perseverance. You never gave up!
- I saw you were getting angry, and then you kept control of your body and words and didn't hurt anyone, even though you were angry.
- You were so courageous today. When you went up on to that stage, you looked even braver than David from the story of David and Goliath!

Try to stay away from labels. Instead of saying, 'What a kind boy', try saying, 'That was so kind.' Instead of saying, 'You are so good', try 'I love seeing how you keep choosing goodness every day.' The fewer labels children have to carry, the more confident they can be in their capacity to change and to become better tomorrow than they are today.

Give feedback

Hearts: Connect children to yourself and God; respond with empathy and bring truth
Minds: Direct children's attention and values

Our children are doing great work all the time, and they are powerful people who have an impact on others. Don't just praise them when an event happens. Notice when your children are exhibiting character traits that make you proud, and feed back to them how their actions affect you and others:

- Thank you so much for telling me you love me. When you do that, it makes me feel so warm and happy inside.
- You are always so quick to share your treats. It makes me want to share, too. Thank you for being generous.
- I know I can count on you to have your seatbelt buckled before I start the car. I really appreciate your faithfulness. It makes me feel as if we are a team.

Ask questions

Hearts: Understand through curiosity; respond with empathy and bring truth

The questions we ask our children reveal what we consider to be important. Of course we want to find out what happened at school today, but we can ask other questions, too:

- What made you really happy today?
- Was there anyone lonely or lost who you managed to help?
- What was the worst part of your day? What was the best?
- Did anything worry you?
- How is your best friend feeling?
- Can you tell me a story of someone who needed your kindness today?

Tell stories

Hearts: Connect children to yourself and God
Minds: Verbally frame what children are seeing

Often our children only hear us tell stories of their misdeeds or the funny things they have done. Hero stories are a feast for children, whether they come from the Bible, books or TV programmes. Our children aspire to be heroes, so begin to tell stories in which your child is the hero. I've found that the car is a great place to do this.

> Once upon a time, there was Sophia, and she was at gymnastics class working really hard. Up she jumped to the balance beam, and then – ooops – she fell off! Sophia fell off over and over again, but did she give up? No, she did not. She kept trying. Up she went again, and this time she went a bit farther, but then – oh, no! Off again. What should she do? Should she scream and cry? Should she get angry? Should she stomp away? Did she give up? No, she did not! She kept trying and learning and getting better and better! Woo-hoo! Go, Sophie!

> Honey, did I tell you about what Sakib did today? I was feeling tired when we got home so I flopped on the couch. Then my son, who I love, said, 'Mummy, you look tired. Do you want to read a book?' and he brought me a book before he went to play in his room. I felt so taken care of. I was so blessed by Sakib's kind and caring heart.

Our children need to know that we see the deep character that is growing inside them and that we celebrate and care about it.

29

Media and the world's messages

Key questions: Our children live in a broken world, which has values and standards very far from God's design. How do I as a parent build healthy, powerful foundations for my children so that they can face the world's assaults with confidence? How do I train my children to engage with the wrongness of the world's messages? What skills and tools do I need to give them so that they can recentre their core of confidence by themselves?

A deeper look at the issue

When we talk about this topic, we often use the phrase 'in the world but not of the world'. It's a summary of Jesus' words in the gospel of John, when he prayed for his followers before he died on the cross (see John 17:14–19). It has come to mean something quite specific to us: we are to live in this world, which holds ideals so different from ours, and yet we are not to own those ideals or to let those standards rule us.

When we look at an issue such as how the world is influencing our children, we feel stressed partly because we see the destructive nature of the world and we want to protect our children from it. We don't want them to be growing up with body-image issues or shame about their lack of skill in one area or another. We don't want them to feel alone or the odd one out.

I think we have to remember God's goal for us – a deep relationship with him that brings us love and joy, personal transformation and a daily purpose with him. God does not guarantee us an easy and perfect life on earth.

Jesus spoke clearly to his followers about what life would be like for them on earth. He taught them that 'in this world you will have trouble' (John 16:33) and he explained to them why 'the world hates you' (15:18). He was preparing his followers for difficulty because life would not be easy for them. Over the decades after Jesus' resurrection, many of his followers were imprisoned, beaten, attacked, shipwrecked, yelled at and chased out of town, and some were even martyred. Others stayed in their own villages, raising families under oppression and abuse. I would propose that even through all these hardships, many of them persevered and committed themselves to living lives full of God's love, peace, purpose and joy. They established deep, supportive communities and they saw their numbers increase as more people were healed and transformed, even while facing persecution. These early Christians didn't have easy lives, isolated from the world, yet they lived in fullness of life in the midst of their fearful and evil world for the purposes of God's glory. We want that kind of fullness of life for our children today.

Isolation from the world isn't God's goal for our children. God wants them to experience the freedom and goodness that come from having him at the core of their confidence while living in the midst of a broken world that needs him.

So how do we train our children to be purposeful in the world and operate boldly from a God-centred core of confidence? How do we raise our children to be 'in the world but not of it'?

I would suggest that:

- We *empower* them with the skills and wisdom to look at the world and see the unhealthy and warped messages and standards that are being sold to them.
- We *equip* them to monitor and feed their own hearts and minds so they can continue to adjust themselves and stay close to God throughout a lifetime of being bombarded by media and the world's standards.

Let's look at how we can do all of this by using the hearts and minds tools.

Putting the hearts and minds tools into action

Here are a few suggestions to get you started in building a core of confidence in your children.

Serpents and doves

How do we train our children to engage with the wrongness of the world's messages? We empower them with the skills and wisdom necessary to see the unhealthy, warped values that the world tries to sell to them.

When Jesus sent out his twelve disciples to start ministering, he said to them, 'I am sending you out like sheep among wolves. Therefore be as shrewd as snakes and as innocent as doves' (Matthew 10:16). He was sending his disciples into a hostile and hurting world, and his advice to them was to be both wise and innocent. He wanted his disciples to walk in love and accomplish the purpose he sent them for, but to do so gently and wisely. It was Jesus' strategy for them to be in the world but not of it.

Let's explore some of the hearts and minds tools that our children need in order to be wise about the world and yet to respond to it well.

Spot the lie
Hearts: Understand through curiosity
Minds: Direct children's attention and values; verbally frame what children are seeing; equip children to be powerful in shaping their own minds

The world's messages are subtle, creeping into our children's minds and hearts through advertising, television, casual con versation and games. The power of subtlety is that the message slides in without our knowledge. One of the significant things we can do to counter it is to shine a light on the strategies the world uses to send lies our way. We can make our home a place of glaring truth and equip our children to see the lies for themselves.

For instance, you can expose the techniques that the world uses to promote its destructive values, from product placement (where companies pay to have characters on TV and movies using their products, so that we think they're cool) to computer retouching of photos in magazines. Ask 'Did you know?' questions and drop titbits of useful information into your conversations as the facts pop into your head, when you watch TV or when you see an advert on the side of the bus. Watch YouTube videos that show how models are made to look more muscular or thin than they really are. Question the plot lines in movies.

You can also laugh at the lies. Make a game out of it, declaring them not to be true. So many times, the world's messages go unchallenged as they enter our homes. Don't just let them slide in; instead, highlight what is wrong and laugh at messages that are lies or make no sense. Play a game of how many untrue things you can find on adverts as you walk down the high street. Challenge the logos and photos, saying, 'What? That's crazy!'

One afternoon, my husband Mark and I were at a restaurant with our then three-year-old son. Mark leaned across the table and picked up the kids' entertainment pack that my son had been given to colour. 'Caleb, look at this!' he said. 'There's something very silly on this paper. What is the difference between the boy picture and the girl picture?' Caleb scrunched up his face and analysed the pictures hard, but he couldn't find any difference. My husband pointed to the drawing of a girl. 'Look,' he said. 'They drew her body super-small, much smaller than the boy's! How silly is that?'

I looked at the pictures and was surprised to see how different they were. The girl's body was half the width of the boy's, even though their heads and feet were the same size. Caleb's eyes widened. 'Girls don't look like that! How silly!' he exclaimed. Then he started to giggle, adding, 'She would break like that!' 'Hmm… well, what could we do?' Mark asked, sittingt back in his chair and watching Caleb think. 'I can make her right,' Caleb said, and then he added width and muscles to the girl's picture. 'Silly draw-ers,' he concluded.

From adverts to television to books and toy packaging, there are so many lies that we can expose, debunk and laugh at. There is even a Twitter hashtag, #notbuyingit, dedicated to enabling people all over the world to voice their disagreement with the dangerous expectations outlined in movies and advertising. What would it look like if our children grew up identifying the unhealthy values portrayed around them and simply dismissing them?

Try shining a light on destructive values in the media. Sometimes our children need to see how to apply God's love to something that seems innocuous, like a television show. What if they heard you say something like this: 'I really don't like this programme, because it wants us to laugh at other people. Look at those contestants! They have hoped and dreamed for years for an opportunity like this, and then they've practised for days and waited in a queue for hours. I think they are brave and should be given respect and honour for their efforts. I don't think I want to laugh at them, and I don't like it when they're treated like that.'

Your words could open up a significant conversation with your family, and together you can decide how to move forward. So many television shows portray all sorts of assumptions that are not the truth – for example, that muscular men are the only ones who are attractive to women, that children are expected to be rude to their parents, or that siblings will inevitably hate each other. Television shows give us assumptions about life and values and ask us to accept them. Some of them are true, but, with those assumptions that are false, we have a marvellous opportunity to shine a light on the lies.

Engage with fiction, keeping God's love and values in mind
Hearts: Understand through curiosity; respond with empathy and bring truth
Minds: Verbally frame what children are seeing; encounter God and his truth

The question we have to ask ourselves is this: what stories surround our children and what are these stories telling them? There are very few stories in the world that fully embrace all of our values, and that is okay. Most stories present a combination of values that we agree and disagree with. As parents, we need to decide which stories we allow into our home and how we are going to engage with their content.

An example of this is the 'Harry Potter' series, which centres on a child who lives in a world of magic and attends a school that teaches him magic. An evil wizard arises and the seven books outline the story of a battle against this wizard and his terrible army. Many Christian parents came out quite strongly against the series, not allowing their children to read the books or watch the films that came later. Other Christian parents read the books with their children, discussing them along the way. Others saw nothing wrong with the stories and allowed their children to read and watch them freely, discussing them as plot points came up in conversation. I have my opinion, and I'm sure you have yours, but I mention it because things like this happen all the time. From old Disney movies to the most modern Pixar films, stories are flooding towards our children, and we must choose how we want to engage with those stories.

Choosing not to let your children watch or read something is absolutely fine, and it gives you a good opportunity to explain why. When I was a child, my mum refused to let me see the musical *Grease* until I was a teenager. She told me repeatedly that she didn't like the way the leading girl character changed her values at the end, and that it wasn't worth the money or the time to watch the film. Eventually, when I was a teenager, we did go to see a performance of *Grease* at a local theatre. By then, I definitely understood what my mum had been talking about, and I agreed with her that it was not a happy ending for the girl, because she had compromised her values and her integrity for a guy.

Please don't misunderstand me: stories are to be enjoyed and delighted in. Read books for fun; watch movies to laugh. Please don't turn into the parent who has to have a conversation about everything, before, during and after every story or movie. You know which stories will make for interesting conversations about values and choices, so open up conversations about them.

Ask questions. What is the character thinking? Would you do that? Why? Is that the way the world works? Why? Should it? What would you do in that situation? Who are you most like? Is that right? Wait a minute, a good character just did a bad thing; is that okay? Wait, a bad character did a good thing; does that mean he's not bad? Are people either good or bad? If this story were real, what would God be doing? Stories unlock our hearts and allow our children to find similarities between their own journeys and a character's, and to find differences between them, too. They can be powerful tools for exploring actions, choices and consequences.

It isn't just controversial stories that can give us interesting discussion opportunities. Even our most basic stories can open up some wonderful heart conversations with our children. The plot line of 'Goldilocks and the Three Bears' brings up an interesting thought: basically, the story is about a crime of breaking and entering. How did the bears feel? Why did Goldilocks feel it was okay to go in? Why wasn't she ever just content and grateful?

Look at some traditional Disney movies. How are leaders and royalty often portrayed? How do they use their powers? Take, for instance, the movie *Aladdin*. The sultan is an idiot and his chancellor is power-hungry. The basis for the plot is that there is an unjust law requiring a woman to marry before her 21st birthday. When the sultan's daughter rejects marriage, instead of changing the crazy law he allows her to become a pawn in a power game. What would your child do in that situation if they were the sultan? What is God's plan for bringing justice through leaders? These conversations are great for those bored-in-the-car moments when you can explore all angles of a well-known story or movie. The car is also a great place to discuss songs: 'Hey, I was thinking about that song we were singing and the words are kind of funny! What do they mean?'

Empowering children to recentre on their own

What skills and tools do we need to give our children so that they can recentre their core of confidence by themselves? We can equip them with tools to monitor and feed their own hearts and minds, so that they can continue to adjust themselves and stay close to God through a lifetime of bombardment by media and the world's standards.

Give children windows into your life in the world
Hearts: Connect children to yourself and God; help children to be powerful for the next time
You are perfectly positioned to show your children not only who God is but also who he is in relationship with a person – with you – which is so important. You can give them a peek into your own life with God. After all, you are the greatest resource your

children will ever have. Daily, you model for them what is funny, what is terrifying, how to behave in a restaurant or on the beach, how to cope with anger or hurt. They are watching you. Unfortunately, we most often process our life with God silently, in our hearts and minds; our children are left guessing about how to do life with God, because we don't show them. One really powerful thing we can do is to create windows into our lives so that our children can see how we live with God. You don't need to share everything with them; this isn't a full disclosure policy. Just get into the pattern of regularly letting your children hear what is going on in your head and heart.

Life with God is about relationship with him and our purpose on earth. As our children grow, it is helpful for them to see that there is a difference between what we choose when we are close to God and what the world chooses. It is helpful for them to see how we negotiate being 'in the world but not of the world', and where God is in the process.

Create windows to allow your children to see a little of your journey of faith and decision-making when you are faced with a conflict of values. For example: 'Today I was at work, and my boss publicly said some really rude stuff about one of my colleagues. Everyone laughed really nervously, but I just froze. I felt that it was hurtful to my colleague, and not right. I thought I could either stay quiet, say something there, or confront my boss about it later. I ended up respectfully defending the man, and my boss wasn't pleased at all. I just couldn't let my boss's cruel words stand. Everyone needs someone to stand by them.'

Share stories with them of how the media affect you and what you do about it. For example: 'I just can't watch *Britain's Next Top Model* any more. I spent so much time looking at myself in the mirror after that. How ridiculous! No more *Top Model* for me.' Explain the choices you make and how they help you live with integrity according to what you feel God is asking you to do. Invite your children to watch how you choose to be 'in the world', to hear how God speaks to you, guides you and encourages you, and to understand why you do what you do.

Help children monitor their own roots
Hearts: Understand through curiosity; respond with empathy and bring truth; connect children to yourself and God; help children to be powerful for the next time

Minds: Equip children to be powerful in shaping their own minds

Each of us is responsible for our core, for what is in our hearts. As our children grow, one of our goals is to help them learn to reflect on what is going on in their own hearts so that they can adjust themselves with God and can keep their hearts right.

In Chapter 25, we looked at tools to help us draw out our children through questions and through speaking truth into deep places. As our children grow, it's also helpful to teach them to do this for themselves. How can they notice what is going on in their heart's root system? How do they fix it? Jesus once said:

> 'Each tree is known by its own fruit… Good people bring good things out of the good they stored in their hearts. But evil people bring evil things out of the evil they stored in their hearts. People speak the things that are in their hearts.'
> LUKE 6:44–45 (NCV)

I often tell children that one of their best clues to what is going on in their hearts is to listen to their own words. Are you complaining or whining a lot? Are you saying that you are scared or annoyed, or that you are fat, or that you want to be like someone else? Take a second to ponder what you are feeling underneath, that makes you so angry or worried, and start to bring some truth into your feelings. What does God's word say about your need or situation? Remind yourself of God's words. Remind yourself of his truth.

As parents, we can begin this process by reflecting our children's words back to them and coaching them through the reflective process. We might say, 'I noticed that every day this week you have used the word "stupid" about school. What's going on in your heart, that the word "stupid" keeps coming out? Just wondering'; or, 'You keep saying that you can't do this maths. You know that's not true about you, right? What is true?'

Sometimes the hurts that these words reveal need to be brought to God. We can also coach our children through the process of chatting with God about our hearts and of inviting him to come and heal, love, and fill our broken places and to communicate his wisdom and words to us.

Remain in God
Hearts: Connect children to yourself and God; help children to be powerful for the next time

Jesus said:

> 'If the world hates you, remember that it hated me first. If you belonged to the world, it would love you as it loves its own. But I have chosen you out of the world, so you don't belong to it. That is why the world hates you... They will do all this to you on account of me, because they do not know the One who sent me.'
>
> JOHN 15:18–19, 21 (NCV)

We can often get wrapped up in defending ourselves against a world that hates us, and we worry about how to protect our children from that sting of hatred. When we pull back and take a wider look at John 15, we can see that right before Jesus talks about the world's hatred, he gives his disciples a strategy, a way for them to sustain themselves in him. He tells them this:

> 'I am the vine, and you are the branches. If any remain in me and I remain in them, they produce much fruit. But without me they can do nothing... I loved you as the Father loved me. Now remain in my love. I have obeyed my Father's commands, and I remain in his love. In the same way, if you obey my commands, you will remain in my love. I have told you these things so that you can have the same joy I have and so that your joy will be the fullest possible joy. This is my command: Love each other as I have loved you. The greatest love a person can show is to die for his friends.'
>
> JOHN 15:5, 9–13 (NCV)

Love is the centre of our confidence – being loved by God and loving him and remaining in his love. Throughout our children's lives, they will continue to grow in knowing God's love and in loving him. They will also grow in using tools, skills and disciplines that enable them to remain in his love, to reposition themselves in God and to connect with him whenever they want.

My son began to struggle with being afraid in his room at night. We encouraged him to chat to God and he did, but he still wasn't really able to settle. We knew that the key was for him to meet with God about it, as 'perfect love drives out fear' (1 John 4:18). We were reminded of the verse 'Whatever is true, whatever is noble, whatever is right, whatever is pure, whatever is lovely, whatever is admirable – if anything is excellent or praiseworthy – think about such things' (Philippians 4:8), so I went and got a notebook, a pencil and a torch. My son couldn't write at the time, but he could draw, so I gave him the supplies and told him to draw pictures with God of all the wonderful things in his life – some beautiful thoughts, adventures he's gone on with God, and things and people he loves. I told him to draw lovely and excellent things with God until he fell asleep. He fell asleep easily that night. Even now, he keeps a pack filled with supplies in his bed because this is a tool he continues to use on his own when he is afraid at night.

As your children grow, think about gradually giving them tools to use that will enable them to express their love for God and to connect with his love in return so that they can 'remain in him' well.

Connect to community
Hearts: Understand through curiosity; help children to be powerful for the next time
Let's look again at those verses from John 15. After Jesus has encouraged us to remain in him, see what follows (highlighted in bold):

> 'I am the vine, and you are the branches. If any remain in me and I remain in them, they produce much fruit. But without me they can do nothing... I loved you as the Father loved me. Now remain in my love. I have obeyed my Father's commands, and I remain in his love. In the same way, if you obey my commands, you will remain in my love. I have told you these things so that you can have the same joy I have and so that your joy will be the fullest possible joy. This is my command: Love each other as I have loved you. The greatest love a person can show is to die for his friends.'
> JOHN 15:5, 9–13 (NCV)

It appears that one of the other techniques for remaining in him and for existing in a world that hates us is to be rooted in a loving community, one that loves us and empowers us to love others. For some of us, this community is made up of good Christian friendships, but I would suggest that a church community can also challenge us to go deeper with God and equip us to live boldly in the world.

- Invest in your church; invest in those relationships. Invite people around for dinner when your children are awake so that they can participate in the conversations and play games with your friends. The more you can give them a multigenerational community of people who love God and love them, the more they will be able to live in a community of love, where people continually help them and encourage them to remain in God's love.

- Invest in your church; invest in those areas of service. Empower your children to join a ministry team and to serve on it faithfully and well. Release them to learn from others and to love God through service.
- Invest in your church; invest in learning. Help your children to engage with the service and the teaching. Encourage them to expect to be challenged and to grow deeper in their knowledge of God's word and in their encounter with him.

When your children are raised to invest in deep relation ships with other Christians and with God himself, they will experience what Jesus promised – the fullest possible joy.

Ask your children curious questions to enable you to understand more of their experiences in church, with other Christian children and adults, at home and in their daily lives. The more you understand their hearts, the more you will be able to speak truth to their hearts and build a structure for relationships that will support them when they face the world. As they grow, they will begin to hold this value closely. When they leave our homes, their investment in relationships with God, his people and a church community will help them stay resilient against the world's pull.

30

Comparison and contentment

Key question: My children are constantly talking about how they want to be different, how they dislike bits of themselves and want to be like other people, to live like other people. How can I help my children to be content simply with who they are and where they are?

I think one of the moments that really tears at our hearts as parents is when we see our joyful, free children begin to shrivel and hide as they compare themselves with others and start to feel inadequate. When our children are pulled into comparisons, we often feel powerless to help because it has to do with what is going on inside them, and we feel locked outside.

The desire to compare is not new: 'I wish I were smarter/prettier/skinnier/taller/richer… If only I had… then I could be happy.' With today's technology, our children aren't limited to comparing themselves with those in their immediate community; now they can compare themselves with people all around the world!

Comparison steals contentment because it pulls our children completely out of a God-centred core of confidence.

A God-centred core says this:

**God is awesome and holy,
and he loves me totally and unreasonably.**

**God is daily shaping me to be more like him,
and I am not finished yet.**

I am invited to be a small part of God's wonderful plans.

But comparison breeds a core of confidence that says this:

Some people are cool and competent and possess the right things, and they will be loved by all.
If I can become one of them, I will be loved and I will have confidence in who I am.
If I can prove to God that I'm worthy enough, maybe he will use me to do great things.

Comparison makes our children focus on themselves. It causes them to believe that their worthiness to be loved and be powerful rests in the eyes of others. They will always lose that battle: it will bring fear and isolation and will steal from them the blessing and peace of community and the belief that 'we are better together than we are apart'. Comparison robs our children of the joy of being loved by a powerful God.

A deeper look at the issue

Envy is one of the roots of comparison, one of the deep motivations that drive it. One definition of envy is 'the painful or resentful awareness of an advantage enjoyed by another joined with a desire to possess the same advantage'.[10]

God speaks a lot about envy in the Bible. Envy is even in one of the ten commandments: 'You shall not covet your neighbour's house. You shall not covet your neighbour's wife, or his male or female servant, his ox or donkey, or anything that belongs to your neighbour' (Exodus 20:17). One of Solomon's proverbs speaks to the centre of the matter: 'A heart at peace gives life to the body, but envy rots the bones' (Proverbs 14:30).

When we allow ourselves to look at other people and want what they have, be it material things, natural qualities, relationships or ways of life, we instantly begin the destructive cycle of comparison. When we allow ourselves to say, 'What they have is better than what I have,' we also begin to think, 'Who they are is better than who I am.'

I don't think desire is unhealthy. We all have needs and hopes and desires. Scripture makes it clear that we are to bring them directly to God and lay them before him with trust and love. Envy develops when we take those desires and focus our attention on what we think the solution should be. 'I desire a job where I am making an impact' can quickly become 'I want his job. If I could only have that job, I would be happy.' Our children are no different. 'I desire good friends' can quickly become 'I want shoes and clothes and toys like hers. I want to be like her so that people will like me.' God's design is not for us to chase after wants, but for us to live in contentment and peace.

We often think that the path to contentment and peace is about creating a life with no wants, where there is enough of everything – but that is not true. Look at Paul. He was in prison in Rome when he wrote to his friends in Philippi:

> I am not saying this because I am in need, for I have learned to be content whatever the circumstances. I know what it is to be in need, and I know what it is to have plenty. I have learned the secret of being content in any and every situation, whether well fed or hungry, whether living in plenty or in want. I can do all this through him who gives me strength.
> PHILIPPIANS 4:11–13

Paul had managed to find a way to be content in circumstances that were incomplete and scary. Scripture repeatedly tells us that the key to peace is to have a grateful heart, being humbly conscious of who God is and what he has done (see Philippians 4:6–7). Contentment, at its core, is a combination of peace and gratitude in every situation.

The writer of Hebrews tells us:

> Keep your lives free from the love of money and be content with what you have, because God has said, 'Never will I leave you; never will I forsake you.' So we say with confidence, 'The Lord is my helper; I will not be afraid. What can mere mortals do to me?'
> HEBREWS 13:5–6

I believe that contentment is inextricably linked to a God-centred core of confidence. So how do we raise our children to be content, positioned away from envy?

Putting the hearts and minds tools into action

Here are a few suggestions to get you started in building a core of confidence.

Managing materialistic wants

Hearts: Respond with empathy and bring truth
Minds: Verbally frame what children are seeing; use foundational phrases

Our world bombards children with advertisements to feed their wants and desires. Our culture is constantly telling them, 'You need this. You need that. Look at what you don't have but really want!' When this happens, it instantly draws their eyes into a comparison: 'I have this, but I could have that. I am not content with what I have. I want more.' Envy seeps in.

Let's look at some of the main battlegrounds where we can help our children fight against envy.

Advertisements on television

In the UK we have several channels that don't show adverts, but many do. Adverts are designed specifically to push messages into your children's heads to make them feel discontented and envious. It's worth exposing this manipulation to your children so that they can see it for what it is. Have a chat about why adverts exist and how they are designed to make us want things. Highlight how ridiculous it is to think that owning a thing would make us happy, pretty, popular or cool. I would suggest that you regularly mute the adverts and, instead, use the time to talk or do other things. You can also watch programmes on a catch-up system so that you can fast-forward past the adverts. Picture a life at home with no adverts, with nothing speaking, 'You need, you need…' into our children's heads.

Shopping with children

Walk into any supermarket or toyshop and you will join hundreds of other parents trying to wrestle with the 'But-I-really-want-you-to-buy-this-for-me-now' dance. Many families have found that having boundaries can be very helpful not just for managing behaviour but also for managing hearts. For instance, try offering your children as much choice as possible, so that they have some freedom in choosing cereal, types of apples or other everyday products. Also try setting a policy about heart attitude. In our family, saying, 'I want this,' or 'I need this,' or 'Please will you buy this for me' is off-limits. What we can say is, 'Oooo, look at this. Isn't this interesting?' There is no expectation that anyone will purchase the thing that's been pointed out. We are just enjoying a trip and looking at interesting things along the way. I have, on occasion, made an impulse purchase for my family, but it was never in response to a demand, a request or an envious heart.

Gift giving and receiving

Hearts: **Understand through curiosity; help children to be powerful for the next time**

Minds: **Direct children's attention and values; equip children to be powerful in shaping their own minds**

I have worked with many children and families over many years, and I have noticed that families with contented children tend to handle gift giving and receiving in similar ways. For most of us, gift giving is expected at birthdays and Christmas. Because gift givers want to ensure they are giving efficiently, they ask the person what they would like (or ask the parents what they think the child would like). Whether through the guise of writing letters to Santa or informing family and friends before a birthday or holiday, children are encouraged to ponder long and hard about what they want to receive. If they receive it, they are very happy. If they don't receive it, or if they receive something similar but not quite the same, then they might feel disappointed. In these cases, gratitude is dependent on receiving what they wanted.

The problem with this approach is that it deliberately encourages children to envy, to look around and think, 'What do I want? What do I want you to get for me?' When that happens, they judge the gift giver according to whether he gave a 'good gift' or a 'bad gift' – whether the request was filled correctly or incorrectly. It also creates a culture of expectation – the idea that they deserve a gift because it is their birthday or because it is Christmas. The expectation removes the joy of the unexpected and not-demanded gift, and replaces it with a focus on the fulfilment of children's wants through relational obligations.

So what do we do? Every year our children go on a cycle of desiring things and expecting their desires to be met. I would suggest that we need to re-examine the way we do gift giving.

What would it look like if no one were allowed to ask for anything? What if birthdays were about celebrating the person, and gifts were a minor byproduct, or if Christmas was about cultivating our hearts towards blessing each other instead of focusing on what we were going to get?

I would suggest telling our children that gifts are just that – gifts. They are undeserved, unasked for, and come from the heart of the other person to you. They are not to be expected or hoped for, quantified or judged. A gift is about someone saying, 'I thought this might bring you joy.'

When we receive gifts, it is from a position of seeing the heart behind the gift. If Grandma gives you an old weird toy, it's because she loves you very much and she thought you might enjoy it. Be grateful that you have a grandma who loves you that much. Enjoy it! Teach your children to embrace what has been given instead of what could have been given. Raise children to pay attention to the hearts of the gift givers and to understand that gift giving is about relationship.

One day, when Jesus was watching people drop gifts into the temple treasury, he saw many rich people give extravagant 'good' gifts, but he also saw one poor woman give just two small coins, which were all she had. Jesus was touched and told his disciples that this woman 'gave more than all those rich people' (Mark 12:43, NCV). He saw the heart behind the gift – the sacrifice and the love that went into it. We can equip our children to look for that, too, so their eyes will not be on the 'good gifts' they desire but on the heartfelt relationships behind the gifts.

This also works the other way in gift giving. When we train our children to give gifts from their hearts, everything changes. Christmas provides the perfect opportunity to shift to giving gifts from the heart. You can coach your children through this by first asking questions:

- What does... love thinking about or playing with right now?
- What would make her laugh?
- What do you think he would love but hasn't seen yet?
- Is there anything she enjoys that would really help her in her work or with her hobbies?
- What gift expresses the way you feel about him?

When our children begin to understand that gifts are an expression of relationship, undeserved and not demanded, they can begin to access God's gifts with a greater freedom and a right heart as well. God gives us so many gifts – salvation, hope and comfort, to name a few. When our children have hearts of contentment, they can begin to be grateful for all the gifts God has freely given them, instead of being annoyed or disappointed when he hasn't given them exactly what they wanted. Learning how to live in gratitude for God's blessings and gifts is core to living free of comparison and envy. When children focus on who God is and the undeserved blessings and gifts they receive from him, their eyes won't be so focused on what people are demanding and receiving from others.

Deeper questions and heart connections

Hearts: Understand through curiosity; respond with empathy and bring truth; connect children to yourself and God
Minds: Equip children to be powerful in shaping their own minds

As we explore these ideas with our children, it is worth remembering that envy has deep roots within the heart. Envy and discontentment are not really about objects we want, but about the deeper roots of want and need. A great question to ask your children when they begin to react out of envy, wishing they were like someone else or wanting what others have, is this: 'How would your life be different if you had that thing? Why?'

As you ask deeper and deeper questions by following your curiosity, seek to understand what is going on in your child's heart. Affirm their feelings and bring in any truth you feel they need to understand. Share your journey. Empower them to take their needs and wants to God. Suggest that they tell God exactly what is on their heart, what they are thinking and feeling right now. They can do it in their head or out loud, but it's between them and God. Allow some quiet time for them and God to meet about it. Spend some time thanking God for who he is and how he is faithful to meet our needs, even our deep ones. When we do this, then something great comes – God's peace.

> Do not worry about anything, but pray and ask God for everything you need, always giving thanks. And God's peace, which is so great we cannot understand it, will keep your hearts and minds in Christ Jesus.
> PHILIPPIANS 4:6–7 (NCV)

As we encourage our children to engage with God, it is also essential that we help them to look for his provision, his movement, and his shaping in their lives. God is an active God, living and speaking and working among his people. After our children have brought their desires to God and his peace has come, we must also shape their hearts to expect him to be moving in response. Chat about how you can enable your eyes to stay on God, trusting in his plans and purposes.

Create some next steps to help your children combat envy in the future. Help them to make plans for the next time they feel envious of a friend in school, or embarrassed on the playground. They can quote scripture to themselves, sing a song, take themselves for a walk or write in their notebook. Help them to create their own plan to disciple their hearts in difficult circumstances.

31

Manliness and beauty

Key question: My son is really self-conscious about being one of the smallest boys in his class, and he keeps asking about how to get muscles. I caught my daughter looking in the mirror, and she asked me if she was fat. I feel as if I'm watching my children really struggle with how they look, and I'm getting worried. How do I help my children negotiate the storm of images that tell them what boys and girls are supposed to look like?

Throughout history, cultures have defined what the ideal male and female forms look like. With the rise of multimedia outlets, we are experiencing an unprecedented level of communication targeted at us and our children, insisting that there is a deep value attached to what our bodies look like. They display ideal beauty or manliness and tell us what we should do in order to achieve it.

Fad diets, plastic surgery, corrective undergarments, fancy creams, dressing right for your shape, gym memberships and magazine articles all promise ways to correct our naturally unacceptable bodies into something that people will admire. Our children are growing up to be deeply dissatisfied with what they see in the mirror, and they are slowly getting sucked into a desire to pursue this ethereal, ultimate goal of beauty or manliness. They begin to judge themselves and they expect to be judged by others. At a younger and younger age, they become self-conscious and self-judging, wishing to be like someone else. It is affecting not only their confidence but also their participation in opportunities. A government study from 2012 showed that a significant majority of teenage girls who don't participate in activities like after-school clubs and sports choose to avoid them because of anxiety over their body image.[11] Eating disorders are increasing among children and teenagers of both genders, and we as parents are doing everything we can to try to bolster our children's confidence enough to stem the tide of negative messages.

There are excellent resources online and in books to help children understand the media's messages that stream towards them. But what does this topic look like from a spiritual point of view? If we are parenting our children with a biblical core of confidence, how does it help them in this world of physical obsession?

A deeper look at the issue

Beauty

At the very core of the body image issue, I believe, is the fact that the debate robs our children of their fullness. The primacy attached to an ideal body tells our children that their character, their heart, their mind, their passions, dreams, skills and giftings are all secondary to what is really important – the way they look. Beauty becomes the key to everything, from friends and romance to joy and confidence. It's not just about how they look; it's about what their physical appearance opens up for them – love, acceptance, praise and approval.

The reason why body image is a major battleground is that it forces children's eyes, hearts and minds to focus on the way they look and how they feel about the way they look. Body image demands that our children place themselves firmly at the centre of their confidence. This is why the issue is problematic for them.

On one side, the media and society bombard our children with images and values about what they should look like and feel like. Children are told that beauty (both male and female) looks like *this* and makes you feel powerful, free, fun, confident and irresistibly attractive.

The other side rises up and says, 'Yes, beauty *does* make you feel powerful, free, fun, confident and irresistibly attractive. But how dare you tell me it can only look like *that*! It can look like *this* too! Everyone is beautiful, and it is important that everybody knows it and believes it, so that they can feel all those things too.'

Both sides of the debate accept that 'beauty' is the key for all of us. They just disagree on what is classified as beautiful. We are encouraged to love ourselves and love our bodies, and we are told to believe that we are all truly beautiful so that we can all experience the rush of feeling powerful, free, fun, confident and irresistibly attractive.

The problem is that none of that reflects the Bible's view of beauty. Interestingly, beauty doesn't rank as anything important to God. The idea that our bodies are beautiful 'just the way we are', no matter what their shape, simply isn't in the Bible. God doesn't want our eyes focused on beauty. In fact, God tends towards the opposite. If he is enabling us to grow more like him, then our view of human beauty is to be the same as his:

Charm is deceptive, and beauty is fleeting; but a woman who fears the Lord is to be praised. Honour her for all that her hands have done, and let her works bring her praise at the city gate.
PROVERBS 31:30–31

But the Lord said to Samuel, 'Do not consider his appearance or his height, for I have rejected him. The Lord does not look at the things people look at. People look at the outward appearance, but the Lord looks at the heart.'
1 SAMUEL 16:7

Your beauty should not come from outward adornment, such as elaborate hairstyles and the wearing of gold jewellery or fine clothes. Rather, it should be that of your inner self, the unfading beauty of a gentle and quiet spirit, which is of great worth in God's sight.
1 PETER 3:3–4

In scripture, it appears that considering our own physical beauty isn't part of God's plan for our lives. What is important is the development of our hearts and minds, the inner beauty of a transformed life. That's not to say we are to deny any physical beauty that people ascribe to us, or to think ourselves ugly. Our job is not to convince ourselves that we are not beautiful according to the world's standards.

It is just that we are called to value other things far above worldly beauty, and to let our hearts and minds draw strength and confidence from those things. Remember our core of confidence:

**God is awesome and holy,
and he loves me totally and unreasonably.**

**God is daily shaping me to be more like him,
and I am not finished yet.**

I am invited to be a small part of God's wonderful plans.

Personally, I know I am not beautiful according to the current standards. I don't say that to many people as they tend to get concerned that something is seriously wrong with my self-esteem and confidence, so they kindly try to rush in and assure me of my natural and unique beauty. The truth is, though, I don't seek or want to be beautiful by the world's standards. I don't worry about wrinkles or fat or what is in style or how my body looks. I want to pursue holiness and goodness and health; I want to love God fully, love others sacrificially and enjoy my friends and family and the world. I would much rather that people found me funny, loving, engaging, powerful and encouraging than that they found me beautiful. For someone to stop and praise the outside of me seems odd. It's as if someone was given a gift and spent most of her time focusing on the wrapping paper. The gift isn't about the wrapping! It's about what's inside. Our children are gifts to us and others, deep and multifaceted. Let's not allow them to think they are all about their wrapping.

When we as parents accept that beauty is valuable, we unwittingly make it a focus for our children. For both our boys and our girls, we need to shift our focus away from physical appearance and instead concentrate on their character and passions, because those are the issues on God's heart, and those are what will last an eternity.

In Part III we have already explored some of the skills that will help us go on this journey with our children. Let's see how a few of them can apply specifically to this issue.

In Chapter 25 we talked about conversations that open up our children's hearts, to enable us to find the root of what is growing in them. We need to explore what the key of beauty would unlock. For instance, we could start by asking these questions: 'You said that you would love to look like... Why? What would change if you looked like him/her?'

In the same chapter we discussed the power of transforming our minds. One of the tools for shaping minds is to frame verbally what our children are seeing. My dad often stuck Post-It notes on my mirror and door, filled with little messages like these. 'I'm so proud of your bravery. I love seeing how hard you work – keep going! You are so precious to me. I'm so grateful you are my daughter.' I used to keep them on my mirror so that, as I got ready in the morning, I would be reminded of how my dad saw me. I learned to see that person in the mirror.

We also discussed, again in Chapter 25, the tool of directing our children's attention to things. Explore how you describe other people. Do you comment on their appearance at all, or just the content of their character? How do you talk about yourself in front of your children? Consider having bold conversations with your children in which you tell them that you might have been focusing on the wrong thing, and invite them to see a little window into your journey of transforming your core of confidence.

In Chapter 27 we discussed how we can affirm our children within relationships instead of by using labels. In Chapter 28 we looked at how we can move away from labelling our children to praising the character traits we want to see growing in them. Have a think. What would it look like if you took the words 'beauty/beautiful' or 'handsome/ manly' out of your vocabulary? How would you affirm your child? What godly traits in your children shine out of them from their core?

In a similar vein, when you greet children outside your family, how do you normally say hello? Often we comment on their outward appearance: 'My, what a beautiful coat!' 'You are looking fantastic today!' 'Don't you look nice?' 'What a beautiful baby!' 'Look at those muscles. What a strong little man!' 'He's just perfect!' Take time to ponder some new phrases to use and new questions to ask. Consider these: 'Good to see you! What book are you reading nowadays?' 'Well, hello, your face tells me you are happy today. What's made today so good?' 'My goodness, you were so kind when you helped your mummy open the door.'

Have a look back at chapters 29 and 30, on media, and ponder specifically how your children engage with the messages of the media. What education do you need to give your children about how the media lie to us about beauty? Can you play 'Spot the lie' with advertisements that tie beauty to happiness or fun or friendship?

Romance and the future

I was recently watching a television programme in which some of the dialogue between a mother and teenage daughter struck me:

Daughter: I want to be pretty.
Mother: You are pretty.
Daughter: You are my mum. You have to say that. I want to be pretty to other people.

As our children grow, it is helpful to notice that, in our society, messages about beauty and attractiveness are linked to the possibilities of romance and future relational happiness. Sometimes the motivation behind our children's desire to embrace the beauty ideal is that they see it as the main way to finding future happiness in relationships. Think about all the movies, music, television programmes and books that communicate this message to our children. The idea of 'love at first sight' is a prevalent one, in which there's a beautiful woman who meets a devastatingly handsome and musclebound man, and instantly they're physically attracted to each other.

Children watch these storylines over and over again, and then they crave to be seen as beautiful or handsome because they want what that beauty will bring them – an instant admirer who sees them as worthy straight away and chooses them above all others. As they enter the preteen and teen years, children become focused on how they rank in attractiveness, and they want to learn how to become more beautiful or attractive. They can get involved in bad relationships because what they are seeking, based on the stories and messages they have been taught, is a partner who chooses them initially for their looks. They learn to seek out someone who will respond to the shallow value of beauty.

In order for our children to put aside this central value of beauty, they may need a broadening of the romance story they've been told. Most couple's love stories don't begin with 'I saw her across the room; I was overwhelmed by physical attraction, and I knew I wanted to marry her.' Most love stories are sweet and long and involve a slow-growing understanding of each other's character. Our children need to hear these stories. I would suggest that you invite friends around and invite them to tell their romance stories. Look for movies and books that tell the story of real love, deep love. Watch anniversary videos of elderly couples on YouTube, and read about disabled people who have found deep and powerful love.[12] Highlight stories about how God brings people together, so that children can continue to grow in their trust and hope in the Lord as he weaves their futures. May our children fully embrace a core of confidence that will bear much fruit in their lives.

32

Comparison and humility

Key questions: God tells us that we are to be humble. Are we really supposed to encourage our children to think that other people are better than them? Won't they get trampled on? Or are we supposed to know how wonderful we are and then choose to treat other people as if they are better than us, even though we know they're not? Isn't it damaging for our children to go around thinking that other people are better than them?

When we talk about confidence, often the question of humility comes up. Many people find the balance hard to achieve. We are familiar with scripture verses that say 'In humility value others above yourselves' (Philippians 2:3) and that we are to 'take the lowest place' (Luke 14:10). Our conclusions fuel some big questions for us about how we are to raise confident children who are also humble.

I believe that we have a warped view of what scripture means by humility. Our idea of humility becomes damaging when we allow the world to infect the idea. The world says that hierarchies are important. Who is the best, the one on top? Who is the worst? Who is worthy and who isn't? Sometimes, when we hear the word 'humility', we think we need to enter into those judgements about hierarchy, putting ourselves at the bottom, thinking that everyone else is better than us and considering ourselves less important than others. We can begin to believe that humility is about comparing ourselves with others and judging ourselves to be not as good. Rightly, something in us chafes against that idea, particularly when it comes to teaching it to our children.

The humility that we are called into by God has nothing to do with hierarchy, nothing to do with being 'better' or 'less' than others. It has nothing to do with comparisons. It has to do with two things – understanding who we are to God and understanding who we are to others.

A deeper look at the issue

Scripture tells us often that God wants us to be humble before him.

> What does the Lord require of you? To act justly and to love mercy and to walk humbly with your God.
> MICAH 6:8

> Humble yourselves, therefore, under God's mighty hand, that he may lift you up in due time.
> 1 PETER 5:6

> For the Lord takes delight in his people; he crowns the humble with victory.
> PSALM 149:4

Humbling ourselves before God means simply living out the first sentence of our core of confidence: 'God is awesome and holy, and he loves me totally and undeservedly.' It means understanding who God is and who we are, imperfect and small in the face of such a mighty and wonderful God. When we enable our children to understand that 'it's not about me but about him', then their hearts can have the right sort of humility – seeing their own fragility and smallness compared with a mighty, powerful and loving God – and they can have the joy of being loved by him.

Most of us, as parents, feel comfortable with this aspect of humility. It feels right. What causes us more concern, though, is the way in which our children are called to walk humbly with their peers. It's easy to know that we are nothing compared with God, but what if we are comparing ourselves with other people?

As we have seen, true humility isn't about hierarchy. It isn't about thinking that we are rubbish and others are much better than us. It isn't about comparison or competition. It's simply about loving and serving others well. It's about making others a priority in our decision-making processes. It's about delighting in being a small part of a community that, together, is a greater representation of the essence of Jesus than we are as individuals, apart from each other.

I have already mentioned the need to 'value others above yourselves', but look at this verse in its context. Paul was writing to a new church and encouraging its members to live like Jesus, loving each other in unity and service.

Therefore if you have any encouragement from being united with Christ, if any comfort from his love, if any common sharing in the Spirit, if any tenderness and compassion, then make my joy complete by being like-minded, having the same love, being one in spirit and of one mind. Do nothing out of selfish ambition or vain conceit. Rather, in humility value others above yourselves, not looking to your own interests but each of you to the interests of the others.
PHILIPPIANS 2:1–4

When Paul says, 'Value others above yourselves,' he is talking about where we allow our hearts to rest, and how we make decisions. For Paul, humility is about removing selfishness as the main force behind our decisions and, instead, putting our desire to love, serve and lift up others as the main force. It isn't about tearing ourselves down, a process of making ourselves feel inadequate or 'less than' others. It's about repositioning our hearts. Humility is a way of feeling and thinking that insists on love and service to God and others staying central, so that we can truly 'love the Lord your God with all your heart and with all your soul and with all your mind' and 'love your neighbour as yourself' (Matthew 22:37, 39).

How do we parent for this outcome? How do we empower our children to walk confidently with strength and humility, without giving in to the world's view of comparison and hierarchy?

Putting the hearts and minds tools into action

Here are a few suggestions to get you started in building a core of confidence.

Seeing others and judging

Minds: All tools

We start with shaping the way our children perceive other people when they see and encounter them. The way our culture is set up, it is easy to see others as rivals in the competition of life – rivals for friends, for status and for success.

As Christians, though, we are called simply to see others as people whom God loves and sacrificed himself for. We are called to see people who are loved by God, who aren't finished yet but are still a small part of his wonderful plans. Some are far from him and haven't met him yet; some are connected to him and are on their journey to becoming more like him; but all are loved by him, with God-designed plans and purposes for their life. Our role is to be humble, and serve and love.

I believe that this is why Jesus was so outspoken about judging others. I love the way Jesus explains it here:

> 'Do not judge, or you too will be judged. For in the same way as you judge others, you will be judged, and with the measure you use, it will be measured to you. Why do you look at the speck of sawdust in your brother's eye and pay no attention to the plank in your own eye? How can you say to your brother, "Let me take the speck out of your eye," when all the time there is a plank in your own eye? You hypocrite, first take the plank out of your own eye, and then you will see clearly to remove the speck from your brother's eye.'
>
> MATTHEW 7:1–5

Let's look closer at these verses. First of all, Jesus indicates that my sin, my faults and weaknesses, my incompleteness, can be greater than the other person's and yet I can still see their faults as the primary problem. So often, our children spot the wrongs in others and yet feel totally justified in their own experience of sin and wrong choices. As we parent for confidence, it is helpful to train our children to reflect more on what God is doing in them than on what God is doing in others. When a conflict arises, children may want to blame others and discuss the wrongness of others. They may want to gossip about others' failings and rejoice in others' downfalls. This contributes to their desire to be better than others, to see others' weaknesses and faults as larger than their own – and, as a consequence, they can feel superior to others.

As these moments arise, take time to reinforce the idea that everyone is on a journey and no one is perfect yet. Discuss the children's experience of the event or issue, and coach them through what is going on in their own hearts and minds. It is not their place to judge other people, but, instead, to grow as much as they can on their own journey in each circumstance.

The second thing that strikes me is in the first two verses: 'Do not judge, or you too will be judged. For in the same way as you judge others, you will be judged, and with the measure you use, it will be measured to you.' I believe this is a really poignant truth. The way our family judges other people is the way our children will learn to judge others, and, through that, they learn how to judge themselves. Judging others is often a part of everyday conversation.

'Did you see what she was wearing? I just don't get it.'

'Whoa, look how much weight he's lost. He looks amazing!'

'I was so bored talking to Joe. Why didn't you rescue me? He is so annoying.'

'Did you hear about John's new job? He just keeps getting promoted.'

From the way other people structure their family life to what they eat and where they go, little judgements can seep into everyday life. We even train our children how to judge us as their parents: 'Ugh, I'm so lazy today,' or 'I'm so hopeless with bills.' Quickly we can create a life pattern for children that encourages their natural sinful propensity to judge others according to the world's standards. Then they begin to get a hardened heart towards others, and they begin to feel superior. Ultimately, their compassion lessens.

When we judge, our sinful desire to be better than someone else emerges. Our broken world sets up standards for us to achieve and then celebrates or ridicules us, according to how well we have achieved those standards. Whether it's about success at school, a high-paying job, a good standard of living, a popular personality, or the way we look and behave, we are all surrounded with 'ideals' to achieve, and how we are doing at achieving those ideals becomes a competition. Who is better? Who can be the best?

What is also scary is that our children take all of those judgement criteria and apply them to themselves. When we look at other people and call them fat, and then we look at ourselves and complain about our bodies, we have communicated effectively to our children that their bodies are supposed to look a certain way and that people will judge them if their bodies aren't perfect. When we comment on other people's jobs or successes or failures, children learn that they should be judged by that measure, too.

The way we train our children to see others is the way they will see themselves. The way we train our children to see *us* is the way they will see themselves.

Think about these questions. What do you say about others when you are watching television or walking down the road? How do you speak about the people at church on your way home or about your colleagues and friends? How do you speak about yourself? What judgements are you encouraging in your family, and what are you training your children to see in you?

Now ponder these. How do we *want* our children to see others? How do we *want* them to see themselves?

Scripture says that we are not to compare ourselves with other people or to judge others. Our measuring stick is Jesus (Ephesians 4:13). We know that 'everyone has sinned and fallen short of God's glorious standard' (Romans 3:23, NCV), so we simply walk the path of knowing the core of confidence in our own lives:

God is awesome and holy,
and he loves me totally and unreasonably.

God is daily shaping me to be more like him,
and I am not finished yet.

I am invited to be a small part of God's wonderful plans.

We are also called to believe the same of other people. We are called to believe that God loves *them* totally and unreasonably; he is daily shaping *them* to be like him, and *they* are not finished yet; but *they* are still invited to be a small part of his wonderful plans on earth. It isn't our place to judge them for where they are on their journey with God. What we can do, instead, is to expect to see God at work in each person's life.

When our children have this viewpoint, they can begin to look for the good in others instead of the sin and incompleteness. They can see each person as loved and valuable, knowing that God is growing and being refined in each one.

Think back to Chapter 28, where we talked about praising what we want to see growing in our children. We discussed considering all the biblical character traits that God is developing in our children and how we could encourage our children within that context. I would suggest that the list you use to encourage your children can also be used when you discuss others. When you tell stories from work or see people you know at church or notice random people on the street, what are you going to draw your children's attention to? Try noticing others' perseverance, love or connection with God. Invite your children to tell stories of their friends, highlighting their good points. When you leave someone's house, ask each family member these questions: 'What did you really like about them? How did we see them being a bit like God?' Discuss how you learn about God through other people, or how you are challenged by their circumstances and how they are coping.

In speaking about others, what would it look like if we as families truly considered living by Paul's encouragement in Ephesians?

Do not let any unwholesome talk come out of your mouths, but only what is helpful for building others up according to their needs, that it may benefit those who listen. And do not grieve the Holy Spirit of God, with whom you were sealed for the day of redemption. Get rid of all bitterness, rage and anger, brawling and slander, along with every form of malice. Be kind and compassionate to one another, forgiving each other, just as in Christ God forgave you.

EPHESIANS 4:29–32

When we do this, our children will begin to see others as loved, imperfect people whom we can value and learn from, and they can consider themselves to be the same.

Not designed to be alone

Minds: All tools

One of the reasons that true humility is about loving and serving God and other people, as a central position of our heart, is that Christians are not designed to be alone. We are designed to be together as the body of Jesus Christ.

Do not think of yourself more highly than you ought, but rather think of yourself with sober judgment, in accordance with the faith God has distributed to each of you. For just as each of us has one body with many members, and these members do not all have the same function, so in Christ we, though many, form one body, and each member belongs to all the others. We have different gifts, according to the grace given to each of us. If your gift is prophesying, then prophesy in accordance with your faith; if it is serving, then serve; if it is teaching, then teach; if it is to encourage, then give encouragement; if it is giving, then give generously; if it is to lead, do it diligently; if it is to show mercy, do it cheerfully.

Love must be sincere. Hate what is evil; cling to what is good. Be devoted to one another in love. Honour one another above yourselves. Never be lacking in zeal, but keep your spiritual fervour, serving the Lord. Be joyful in hope, patient in affliction, faithful in prayer. Share with the Lord's people who are in need. Practise hospitality.

ROMANS 12:3–13

As individuals, we were never designed to be the whole package. We weren't made to be the best at everything, comprehensively better than other people. We were deliberately shaped to be puzzle pieces, incomplete in and of ourselves, but fitting together as the body of Christ. If we train our children to think that life is about a hierarchy, we are robbing them of the delight of being a part of the body of Christ. When they see themselves as pieces of God's great plan, they are not surprised or hurt by others, and they are not competitive with them; they genuinely delight in and are grateful for people who are shaped differently from them.

When we teach our children that together we are stronger than when we are apart, and that having weaknesses is not only okay but necessary, then they can relax. When the stress of having to be it all and do it all goes away, all that is left is to trust our magnificent God to guide us, and to be faithful in playing our parts as he asks us to. As small parts of his body and his big plan, we can trust that God is weaving things together for good, and we can develop a deep sense of value in working as a team.

Here are a few suggestions for how we can begin to develop this value with our children.

Make sure your child knows that God is active and doing things in the world, and that he invites us, individually and together, to follow him and see lives and communities transformed. Talk about what God is doing in the world and what his activity looks like. When you read the Bible with your children, highlight God's plans and purposes for people's lives and for their towns and cities, and highlight the way God worked with people to bring about wonderful change and to put his love and himself at the centre again. Jesus said that he only did what he saw the Father doing (John 5:19). Help your children to understand what the Father is doing and to know how you, in particular, have learned to do what he is doing.

Watch movies, YouTube or Upworthy clips about what God is doing around the world in and through people. Note that the stories often focus on one individual as the 'hero', but that the individual actually has many people around him or her, with different skills and personalities, who together form a great team.

For example, South Korean pastor Lee Jong-rak saw a desperate need in his community: women were abandoning their babies on the streets. When he felt God's heart for these little ones, God raised up a team around him. They made a box in which women could place their babies safely; when the women did so, Lee Jong-rak and others committed themselves to raising these children by opening an orphanage. Today they are raising children in South Korea to know that they are loved by God and others. The project needed teams of all kinds, from people who loved cooking to those who loved rocking babies, to those who could handle the politics and paperwork to get money and attention. Teams of all ages and shapes and sizes were needed, and together they continue to save children's lives.

Watch videos that focus on one person, and point out the helpers in the background, the teams around the individual. Highlight the fact that one person can never achieve as much as the team together.

Train your children to take genuine delight in other people and their accomplishments. Talk about what is wonderful about everyone you meet, even the difficult people. Share your stories of how you choose to look at the good things in people, instead of focusing on the bad. Model how to think through the different skills and gifts you need on your team for a project, and brainstorm together who would be perfect to invite into the team with you. Ask your children questions and help them process how to genuinely love and serve other people. Ask regularly, 'What can we do to help lift this person up, so that others can see those great things about them?'

Create a deep value for teamwork within your family. Build foundational phrases that encourage teamwork: 'Go, Team Turner. Let's team it! We are much more powerful together. Let's make it happen as a team!' Reward team thinking. Create challenges that your children can complete only if they work together. Praise creative thinking and the use of each other's skills and gifts. Praise children for submitting to each other's strengths and delighting in them, instead of fighting about who can do things best. The more our children learn to think as a team and to prefer teams, the more comfortable they will feel in not having to do everything alone.

Developing a healthy view of competition

Hearts: All tools
Minds: Direct children's attention and values

When we begin to look at humility, we might wonder about the nature of competition. Some of our children are naturally competitive, and the way this quality plays out in their lives is an important question.

There are many aspects of competition – personal, professional, relational, and formal competition in terms of sports and the like. I find it helpful to consider the heart behind it all. As we discussed at the beginning of this chapter, the world categorises people according to success, according to who is best. We have award shows for theatre, movies and sporting competitions. We have popular music chart winners, restaurant stars and online rankings of the most popular or attractive people. The world ingrains in our children, at a very early age, that being the best at something is essential to happiness and success. So, at its worst, a drive to be competitive is a symptom of the desire to be better than others, to succeed and feel proud of oneself for being the best. It's about comparing ourselves with others and proving ourselves to be at the top. If this is at the core of what drives our children, it will always be damaging to their integrity and their heart.

There is a way, though, of humbly engaging with competition without being competitive. It just takes a heart shift – a different path of progression.

If we can channel our children into keeping their eyes on themselves instead of on others, then competition takes on a new aspect. If we train them to have a heart that says, 'I am not finished yet, and God is daily shaping me to be more like him', then we can empower them to embrace and work in partnership with the journey of personal transformation. What if competitiveness wasn't about being better than someone else, but about an internal drive for excellence? What if it was about wanting to be better tomorrow than we were today – achieving more, improving more and pushing our bodies and minds to greater and greater possibilities? What if it was about giving our best, in heart, soul and mind? A heart of humility in competition delights in challenge and also delights in competitors. A sportsman can be a shining light of God's love, generosity and service while he is still competing. What happens in our hearts defines a right or wrong engagement with competition.

It's about the difference between saying, 'I want to be the best actor/singer/tennis player/leader in the world and crush my opponents' and saying, 'I want to be the best actor/singer/tennis player/leader that I can be, and serve others in love and humility while I try.' As parents, we are called to disciple our child's character as they develop their ambitions. Yes, let's encourage and empower our children to pursue excellence; let's release our children into the activities that they passionately want to pursue; but let's also remember to disciple their hearts and minds while they do it.

Use curious questions to monitor children's motivations. When you see children becoming stressed or overcompetitive in a negative way, begin to open up conversations using the tools from Chapter 25. Help them uncover what is going on in their root system that is causing the stress, and minister into it. This approach applies to all types of competition, from students' test results to children's video games. Say, 'You seemed so… Why were you feeling that? What do you wish had gone differently? How did you want it to go? Which part did you enjoy? If I could give you a magic clock to erase one minute, which minute would it be?'

Playing games gives us plenty of opportunities to equip children with healthy views of competition. When you play games at home, set some boundaries around attitude as well as behaviour. For instance, what sort of language do you allow, and what body language? I would suggest that much gloating and superiority can be seen during game playing at home, from board games to football, which trains our children's beliefs about what is acceptable in competition. Have a look at the way children treat each other while playing a board game, and how some adults gloat over being the best, and you will see much in common between them. Do we allow gloating or celebrating others' failures or faults? Do we laugh at each other's mistakes? Do we allow each other to call people 'loser' or to celebrate a win too enthusiastically? Or do we insist on encouraging and generous attitudes while playing, so that everyone feels valued?

I'm not saying that children should not play to win, because I think we should allow them to push themselves to excellence in all areas of their lives, but we need to disciple them to do it generously and with consideration for others. They can strive for their best, but they should not strive to be better than others.

Invite to your house Christians who excel in the fields your children are interested in, and who walk humbly and well in their professions. Ask them questions about integrity and competition. Invite them to tell stories of their journey and how they manage to serve and love others while also pursuing their best with all their strength.

Enable your children to describe themselves in terms of their passions and character, not according to what they are best at. We often describe children by picking out one or two main characteristics, to make it easier to talk about them, and we base our description on what they are best at, compared with the other children. For example, we might say, 'This is Alice, and she's our intellectual. This is George. He's our sporty one. This is Katherine, our drama queen extraordinaire.' These labels can cause our children to make connections between their personal identity and the things they are better at doing than others. This is part of the reason we see children being mean to each other or trying to prevent others from improving their own abilities. If a child's identity is wrapped up in an attitude of superiority, seeing anyone else's success causes fear, hurt and instability. Instead, try saying something like, 'This is Alice, our oldest. Alice, what have you been really interested in investigating lately? This is George. He has recently taken up leading his team and is doing a great job of ensuring that all members feel really valued. And this is Katherine. Whenever she is with us, she brings us great joy.'

Our tendency to describe children according to what they can do better than others also prevents them from embracing the fact they are multifaceted and ever changing. It is okay for a child to love the flute, even though his sister loves it too and is better at playing it. If the flute brings him joy, he should keep playing the flute. It is all right to be a mediocre football player if the sport brings joy. A child might be sporty and dramatic today, and tomorrow the same child might decide she loves science and maths. It doesn't matter if your children are the best at any of it, because God is awesome and holy, and he loves them totally and unreasonably. He is daily shaping them to be like him, and they are not finished yet. They are invited to be a small part of his wonderful plans.

We need to be careful how we encourage our children when they are struggling over comparisons with others. Our language can accidentally set up a hierarchy in their minds. I have heard many parents say to their children, 'The others are just jealous, and that's why they are mean to you.' Parents often say this because they want their children to believe that because they are so clearly better than others, people are unable to handle their own envy. The children then distance themselves from anyone mean or hostile because of their condescending belief that they truly are better than the others, which perpetuates the tension. Some parents will go further and encourage their children to rise above and be 'the better person' or 'the bigger person'. This language isn't helpful either; in fact, it could make the problem even worse.

When our children learn to walk with confidence in humility, they will make themselves available to be used by God in significant ways. As we read through the Bible, we see over and over again that humility was a key character trait in those who were strong in the faith – Moses, Joseph, Job, Deborah, David, Paul, Barnabas and, ultimately, the greatest of them all, Jesus. We have excellent examples before us.

33

Failure

Key question: My child gets really upset when he loses or fails at something. It really knocks his confidence, and I have a hard time getting him to want to try again. How can I help him be confident even through failure?

Failure is the true test of our children's core of confidence. If their confidence is centred on themselves, then, when they are excelling or succeeding, it will be flying high. But when they fail or don't achieve what they set out to achieve, their confidence crumbles, and building it back up again can be a long process. Failure can feel like a real threat to children, and often they treat it as something to be fearfully avoided at all costs.

A deeper look at the issue

In order to help our children engage effectively with failure instead of fearing it, we ourselves need a healthy view of failure. Let's take a look at a few pointers.

First, failure is natural. Children will have been dealing with failure since they were born, whether reaching for toys, crawling, walking, or tying their shoelaces. Their lives have been full of things they wanted to do but couldn't do yet. Failure is a natural part of the growing process, familiar in everyday life. At some point in their lives, though, our children begin to become self-conscious about failing. This change happens not naturally but culturally, as a result of being in a world that values success and perfection.

Second, failure is strategic. We often become frustrated when we're confronted with the possibility of failure, and with failure itself when it happens, but this is a refining process through which God is able to work in our lives and develop us in specific areas. Remember when the disciples were caught in a storm and Jesus calmed the sea (Mark 4:35– 41). If we look back to the beginning of the story, we find that it was Jesus who suggested to the disciples that they should all cross over to the other side of the sea: he deliberately led them out to the place where the storm would

264 PARENTING CHILDREN FOR A LIFE OF CONFIDENCE

develop. He created a situation in which the disciples could succeed or fail, and, in their moment of failure, he taught them valuable truths that laid the foundation for their future ministry.

Remember when the Israelites were brought to the edge of the promised land (Numbers 14). God gave them the opportunity to move into their new land, but they failed to choose bravely to follow him. God then led the Israelites into the desert for 40 years in order to build a generation that would trust in him, and, as a result, when he brought the people back to the edge of the promised land, they were ready to battle with boldness and confidence.

The apostle Paul writes:

> We also glory in our sufferings, because we know that suffering produces perseverance; perseverance, character; and character, hope. And hope does not put us to shame, because God's love has been poured out into our hearts through the Holy Spirit, who has been given to us.
> ROMANS 5:3–5

Sometimes God leads us into places of difficulty to stretch us, teach us and empower us. It is here that we develop character and hope, which ultimately bring us back to God's love. To our eyes the situation can look like a complete failure, but God uses every failure as a wonderful training opportunity to equip us for the future he has called us to.

Third, failure is necessary. If we are going to enable our children to learn and grow, we must acknowledge that failure will be a key part of the learning process. After all, we can't learn something well without making some errors along the way. If our children are afraid of failure, they may hide from growing, learning or taking the risks that lead to great reward and greater maturity. If we truly want our children to have a core of confidence that says, 'God is awesome and holy, and he loves me totally and unreasonably. He is daily shaping me to be like him, and I am not finished yet. I am invited to be a small part of his wonderful plans,' they will have to accept that they are not finished yet. They are imperfect people who will make mistakes and will need to learn, often through trial and error.

When we, as parents, can see failure as a natural, strategic, necessary part of our imperfect children's everyday journey with God, then we can proactively build in them a framework through which they rightly experience current and future failure. We can help to shape failure as a process of life instead of as a crushing blow.

Putting the hearts and minds tools into action

Here are a few suggestions to get you started in building a core of confidence.

Value effort, learning and progress over perfection

Minds: Direct children's attention and values

Make effort, learning and progress key parts of what you praise and reward in your family. Acknowledge and celebrate how hard your children work, the determination and perseverance they show, and how wonderful their efforts are. Encourage them to see that it isn't about being the best; it's just about doing their best in a particular situation or set of circumstances. Help your children to see how far they have come and how much they have improved. Celebrate the improvement with much joy. Encourage them to teach you what they are learning, and be genuinely interested in the information. If you give rewards, consider rewards for concentration, positive attitude, perseverance and giving their best.

Celebrate character within the failure or success

Heart: All tools
Minds: Direct children's attention and values; verbally frame what children are seeing

When you talk with your children after their opportunities or events, celebrate the character they showed in the journey as much as, or even more than, you celebrate the success of the opportunity or event. Say, 'When you forgot your line, you could have let it distract you, but you handled it with such peace and grace, and you totally recovered and kept going. I wanted to cheer! That was well done, son. You fixed it so fast, I don't think anyone noticed,' or, 'I loved watching you from the sidelines. You were so encouraging to every player when they went on or off the field. I could tell that you are a key part of that team. You really made a difference to your teammates.'

Debrief them about the event and praise all the little successes that happened in the midst of it – goals they achieved midgame, improvements they saw in their own performance, things they tried but that didn't work (or did). Rejoice in the fact that they tried something bold, no matter how it ended. Allow your children the space to process their emotions about the day. Ask questions so that you understand better how they feel and why: 'When that happened, what were you thinking? How did it make you feel? What made you choose this over that?' Affirm their feelings and help them find the truth in their moment of vulnerability.

Make experimentation a pattern of play and investigation

Minds: Direct children's attention and values; equip children to be powerful in shaping their own minds

Experimentation is a learning tool, and too often we relegate it to the classroom. It's a great way to train our children to see failure as a strategic opportunity. When we remove experimentation from our homes and lives, our children see failure as only bad, as opposed to seeing it as a potentially helpful tool.

The easiest way to introduce experimentation is to create safe opportunities for our children to explore new ideas in parallel to what you are already doing. For instance, one day when I was making bread with my son, I deliberately made a double batch and asked him, 'What would happen if we put more yeast in?' His mischievous eyes widened and he said, 'Or *juice*?' So we split the dough into three mounds and experimented with two of them. We tried juice in one and quadrupled the yeast in another. The results were not good, of course, but we learned a lot and had fun in the process.

Try asking 'What would happen if...?' questions, and then go about conducting the experiments. You might play games backwards or shrink old clothes that you were going to throw away, just to see if the process really works. Some of your experiments will have positive results, and some will be failures. After the experiments, review what happened and discuss what the children learned through the experience. Children can even strengthen their experimenting muscles by playing games that require perseverance and constant failure, like puzzles or Cluedo. By experimenting and learning from those experiences, children will grow in being able to handle failure better. When our children truly face difficult times in which they try something and fail, they will have a wealth of experiences to help them see their failures as learning points along a journey of growth.

Value growing in competence

Hearts: Understand through curiosity; help children to be powerful for the next time

The second statement in the core of confidence is this: 'He is daily shaping me to be like him, and I am not finished yet.' This implies that today I am more shaped and capable than I was yesterday, and that the growth comes from acquiring competence. Competence is the ability to do something successfully. As we give our children opportunities to persevere and acquire competence, they will grow in the knowledge that if they can't conquer a task today, they can conquer it the next time. They can learn a new skill today and feel prepared to continue to the next challenge.

Caleb's brow was furrowed in frustration as he clutched the yogurt pot to his chest, one hand scraping across the top. 'How's it going, bud?' I asked. With a grunt he replied, 'Hard. I can't do it.' 'Yes, you can. Try a new way!' I called out. He had been trying to get this lid off for about three minutes. Then I saw him start to squeeze the pot as hard as he could to pop the lid off. A part of my brain started screaming about the mess it would make, and everything in me just wanted to walk over, take the pot out of his hands, open it for him and hand it back. But I didn't. 'Interesting approach,' I murmured. I decided I would choose to let it happen. 'If it explodes everywhere,' I thought, 'well, then he'll never try that again. Plus, we'll get to talk about pressure and why things explode, and he'll learn about the clean-up required. All positive things.'

After five minutes of struggling, he finally discovered the right angle at which to hold the pot. As he opened it, he cried out in triumph, 'I did it! I kept trying and I did it!' I leaped off my chair and hooted with pride as well: 'Great persevering, Caleb! You didn't give up and you learned! Go you!' He did a little dance and then proceeded to lick the lid. Once he'd settled down to eating, he debriefed me on what he'd learned and how he felt. He was so proud of himself. He was so chuffed with the result. His eyes gleamed with confidence.

Five minutes before, everything in me had wanted to rob my son of this moment of learning, just for a little personal convenience. I'm not saying we should never speed things along or offer help to our children, but a byproduct of enabling our children to be 'not finished yet' is that we empower them to trust in their ability to learn, persevere, improve, solve their own problems and, ultimately, grow in competence.

A family I know empowers all three of their children, aged five, seven and ten, to get themselves ready in the morning. The children wake themselves up at 7.00 am, and then they have an hour to eat, get dressed and be ready at the door by 8.00 am. At exactly 8.00 am, they walk out of the door in whatever state of readiness they have reached. If one decides to sleep in and miss breakfast, well, that's his choice. If another forgets to make sure she has clean socks ready to wear, it's her job to decide what to do. I chatted with the seven-year-old about it, and he told me, 'I'm using Post-it notes to remind myself of what to pack and bring to school in the morning, but it's not working very well. It only works some of the time. I'm going to try something new this week. I'm going to try to pack my bag the night before and see if that works better.' His occasional failures have resulted in many mishaps in the morning, but he laughed at them and sparkled with his plans to do better in the future. His ability to grow in competency at his own rate means that his failures are just learning tools instead of frustrations.

268 PARENTING CHILDREN FOR A LIFE OF CONFIDENCE

Clean up your mess and see God's redemption

Minds: **Direct children's attention and values; encounter God and his truth; equip children to be powerful in shaping their own minds**

Often our children feel powerless when they fail or make a mistake, because they don't know what to do next. It can be helpful for them to know that they can clean up their messes, physically and emotionally. When we equip them to respond to their own mistakes, instead of swooping in to nag them and fix things for them, we can coach them to deal with failures in a proactive instead of a paralysing way. Whether they have spilt a drink or hurt a friend, we can expect them to clean up their messes, practically as well as relationally, and we can volunteer to help them think through their options.

Failure is not an end point. It isn't a full stop. It's one moment in the midst of a whole story, and what happens next is more important than the failure itself. When your child makes a mistake or fails, try asking them, 'What are you going to do? Do you need any ideas?' instead of rushing in to sort it out for them. Coach them in how to take the next steps toward fixing their failure. We can also encourage our children that 'in all things God works for the good of those who love him, who have been called according to his purpose' (Romans 8:28). As they are fixing whatever they can in the face of their mistake or failure, God is also working to pour his grace into the situation and will be working to bring good out of it as well.

Use stories of failure from your own life and from the Bible

Hearts: Connect children to yourself and God
Minds: Encounter God and his truth

As we have noted before, stories are powerful. Share some of your own everyday stories of failure. Tell your children how you think about those situations, how you felt and how you responded. Talk about what God did in response. Read Bible stories that focus on people's failures. So often, children only hear the stories of how our favourite biblical characters succeeded, but the very same people experienced massive failures as well. Share the stories of Peter denying Jesus, Paul failing to understand who Jesus was until he met him on the road to Damascus, Miriam grumbling against her brother Moses, Abraham lying about his wife, and David murdering Uzziah. They all failed miserably, but what did God do? How did they clean up their messes? How did God work things out for good?

You can even watch secular movies and talk about failure. I find *Meet the Robinsons* a wonderful film for this topic. Why not have a movie night and discuss it as you watch?

Deal with self-criticism

Hearts: All tools
Minds: All tools

One major concern for parents arises when some of our children find themselves in a self-criticism loop. They can't forgive themselves for making a mistake, and we can feel powerless to help. Here are a few suggestions that might help when you feel that your children are beating themselves up about a situation.

Shame

Sometimes, children feel the burden of sin when they fail, and they don't know what to do with it. It is helpful to highlight the difference between a mistake and a sin. Many children carry shame about a mistake they have made, and we can give them the freedom to let it go.

Understand through curiosity: have a deep conversation to understand the root of their shame. To get you started, you might say, 'Sometimes when things happen, they sit on our heart, and we find it hard to stop thinking about them or thinking about our part in them. Have you ever felt that way?' or 'What do you wish was different about this situation right now?' Maybe they think they should be better or that people won't like them any more. They could be afraid or angry. Once you discover the root of their shame, you will be able to respond with empathy and bring truth, and you can help them create some next steps.

Connect them to God and others: God is the one who can deal with sin; he is the one who can restore lightness to our children. Sometimes they need to be reminded that when Jesus died on the cross and came back to life, he took upon himself all our sins and the punishment for all the things we have done wrong. It can be helpful to tell them that sometimes we want to punish ourselves for things we've done wrong, because we know they were wrong and we feel so bad about them, but Jesus died and rose again so that we don't have to carry those things with us.

If your child is up for it, pray with her. Tell God that she is holding on to things in her heart and that you are grateful to Jesus because he can take them away. Suggest to her that, in her mind, she can show God a picture of her heart and how it's feeling. Wait in silence as she does this. Then, suggest that whenever she is ready, she can ask Jesus to take away all the heaviness on her heart. Wait for a little bit more, and then thank God for his love and check in with your daughter about how she is feeling.

Self-labels

Children can come out with some scathing self-labelling. This is when we are most tempted to try the opposite labelling game. A child says, 'I'm rubbish,' and we want to rush in with 'No, you're not. You are amazing and perfect!' Instead of getting trapped into a label competition, try one of these strategies, depending on your child and the situation.

If you don't know where the label is coming from or what the situation was that kicked up that feeling, pursue understanding through curiosity, in conversation, until you understand what is going on. Then deal with it.

If your child is labelling himself out of frustration or anger, or he's unconsciously repeating things he's heard, try taking the direct approach of disciplining the lie. We normally don't allow blatant lies about other people to exist in our home. We wouldn't allow our child to bully his friend or sibling consistently with a label like 'rubbish', 'bad at everything' or 'useless', but we often allow children to believe lies about themselves. I tend to take each of these lies just as seriously, saying, 'You are not rubbish. That isn't the truth. We speak the truth in this family. What is the truth?' If your child struggles to find the truth, you can always help: 'The truth is that you are my son whom I love, who works hard and isn't finished growing in Maths yet, but you are getting better all the time', or, 'The truth is that God has a great purpose for you, regardless of what you think you are good at.'

Sometimes a more light-hearted approach can help. You can try playing a game using a lie jar. When one child catches another lying about himself (such as 'I have no friends'), the first one can call it out and tell the truth: 'That's not true. You have three friends who like you a lot, and all of us love you – ha!' The one who brings truth can get a reward from the jar, or the one voicing the lie needs to put something in: you decide. Also, you could write all the truths on Post-it notes and cover your child's door with them to remind him of the truth and to make him feel loved.

Failure is a wonderful and precious opportunity for growth, and we have the chance to walk our children through it. We can train them to cope with failure positively, so that they can live well in a world that sees failure as catastrophic and fear-filled. Our children can embrace failure as a regular part of their journey, because 'God is daily shaping them to be like him, and they aren't finished yet'.

34

Friendships and peer pressure

Key questions: How do I help my child not to worry about fitting in at school? His friends have such an influence on him, and I think it's because he doesn't want to stand out. How do I help him have the confidence to be himself when peer pressure is telling him to fit in? How can I encourage my child to be confident in meeting new friends and being a Christian where he is?

We want our children to have flourishing friendships within their schools and clubs. As they grow, though, they are increasingly exposed to other people's influence, and we feel as if we have less and less time to combat the world's voice in their lives. How can we equip our children to be confident within their friendship groups? How can we equip them to be confident within the wider context of a non-Christian community that pressurises them to change to its standards?

A deeper look at the issue

Children can often feel powerless when it comes to friendships and interacting with the world confidently. From making friendships to coping with conflicts of values and behaviour, it is a tricky journey for our children to navigate.

When it comes to this issue, I'm reminded of whitewater rafting. When I was a child, my parents took me on a short, one-hour whitewater rafting trip in America. I was nine years old, and I was sure that this was the most dangerous thing I would ever do in my life. After we had waited in a short queue, the guides strapped a lifejacket on to me for the inevitable moment when I would be ejected from the raft into the churning water. They then handed me a paddle, crammed me and my parents into the raft with eight other people and set off with us, down the river. The guide called out which side of the raft we should paddle on and how hard, and we all tried our best. I'm fairly sure my paddle didn't even reach the water half of the time, but I remember watching the guides work incredibly hard at steering and paddling while we did our part. Our job was simply to listen to the men calling out instructions and to follow them well. If we all did that, we would emerge victorious and alive.

Many years later, on a trip with my husband, we too decided to go whitewater kayaking, but this time there would be only one person per kayak. My life was in my own hands. I was nervous. On the previous rafting trip, I had felt safe because the experts had been in my boat, directing the journey, doing most of the hard work and telling me what to do and when. How in the world was I going to handle it on my own?

My husband is an experienced kayaker, so, as soon as we got in the queue, he began to explain all the equipment – why the paddles are shaped the way they are, how to stroke smoothly and turn well, and where to position myself to be the most comfortable. After we had put on our waterproof gear, he showed me how kayaks are balanced and shaped, so that I could understand how to turn them. Once we were in the water, he encouraged me to paddle around while he coached me in the strokes. At first, we paddled in silence while I found my path in the river and tried to find the current. Before we came to the first set of rapids, Mark pulled up beside me and showed me the path he was going to take, the potentially tricky spots ahead, and how to face my kayak into the waves. Then he zoomed off and I was on my own to try. I faced down the waves and dug hard into the turns. I spun once, got stuck once, panicked slightly and figured how to get out. By the time I emerged on the other side of those first rapids, I felt triumphant.

Mark encouraged me as I chattered about my experience, and we went down the river again. For every new tricky bit, he would check to make sure I felt comfortable to navigate it well. He adjusted his briefings to include new information only just before I needed it, and so I continued, comfortably making mistakes and trying to apply all I was learning.

When our children are small, they are in our boat on the journey of life. We do most of the heavy lifting and we navigate the rapids for them. As they grow older, they can't stay in our boat any longer. They must grow in independence and must face the whitewaters of friendships and choices and opposition by themselves. They have to navigate on their own, making their mistakes and learning their lessons, but we can still coach them through the process beforehand. We can give them the skills they need to respond to the next section, to find the wisest path ahead, and to engage with life's rapids proactively, with confidence, handling mistakes and successes with joy and determination.

Helping our children to live confidently when we are not there is a large part of our calling. I feel it is essential that we are proactive in equipping our children's hearts and minds to be ready to respond to issues before they come up. If we wait until a crisis emerges, we will be forever chasing our children as they toss aimlessly in the rapids; but if we can get ahead of potential problems and train our children to handle them well, they will feel ready to engage confidently with problems when they arise.

Above all, we encourage our children to 'throw off everything that hinders and the sin that so easily entangles. And… run with perseverance the race marked out for us, fixing our eyes on Jesus, the pioneer and perfecter of faith' (Hebrews 12:1–2). As our children navigate their race, we must remember that Jesus has gone on this path before us, and, as we coach our children, so will he, shaping them to be more and more like him.

Putting the hearts and minds tools into action

Here are a few suggestions to get you started in building a core of confidence.

Building good friendships

Hearts: **Connect children to yourself and God; help children to be powerful for the next time**
Minds: **Direct children's attention and values; use foundational phrases; equip children to be powerful in shaping their own minds**

When training our children to chart the course ahead of them, we need to teach them how to look for the safe paths, the beneficial places in which to journey. In the flow of relationships and opposition, they need to learn how to establish good friendships and how to operate in a healthy way with their friends.

A key pressure for many children is in finding new friends. Sometimes this is necessary because they are entering a new situation; other times it's because their existing friendship group isn't working for them any more and they need to branch out. Depending on our children's personalities, they may instinctively operate in a powerless or passive way. They can become stressed, hoping that someone will be their friend or just be nice to them and invite them to play. Making friends becomes a combination of chance and of being appealing enough to be chosen. Let's look again at our core of confidence:

**God is awesome and holy,
and he loves me totally and unreasonably.**

**God is daily shaping me to be more like him,
and I am not finished yet.**

I am invited to be a small part of God's wonderful plans.

Who our children become in any situation doesn't depend on waiting to be chosen; it's about being a small part of God's plans, as imperfect and loved as they are.

Have a chat with your child, preparing her for a new situation. Describe how easy it is for all of us to think about ourselves when we are meeting new people, but help her to understand that God has brought her to this place and he has made her to be powerful in this situation with him. When she goes to school tomorrow, perhaps she could wonder with God, 'How are other people feeling? Who needs a friend? Who needs someone to sit with, laugh with and be encouraged by? Who needs to be defended or helped?'

Do some roleplay games about meeting new people. Help your child to think of questions to ask someone in order to start a conversation or invite them to participate in an activity. Pose scenarios for your child to solve: 'What would you do if a new child came into your class who didn't speak English? That's a tricky one! What do you think?' By doing this, children can think through possibilities in advance and have something to remember when the situation arises.

As you read books together, highlight the qualities of good and encouraging friendships within the stories. Look at the friendships and sibling relationships in the Bible, between Jonathan and David, Paul and Barnabas, Mary and Martha, Aaron and Moses, and so on. Give praise when your child is functioning as a good and faithful friend, and praise your children's friends when you hear stories of health in their relationship. Once, our son was punched at school. When we were debriefing him about the situation, he told us how his best friend had tried to stop the aggressive child from hurting him. As this friend had dived in the way to protect my son, he'd received a violent shove and a punch in the head for his efforts. But by doing that, he'd created the space for them both to escape.

Instead of choosing to focus on the altercation straight away, we ended up talking for a long time about how wonderful it was to have such a faithful friend, and what it means to be faithful to someone in friendship. We talked about sacrifice, and how Jesus said that true friendship means being willing to sacrifice ourselves for others (John 15:13), just as his friend did. When we finally went in to chat with his teacher, the incident itself was minor in his mind, but the joy of his friendship had increased.

Encourage your children to love their friends well. Facilitate their love languages. If they show love through making gifts, spending time, writing notes, giving hugs or doing nice things, create space for them to do so. The more powerful your children feel to invest in life-giving friendships, the more their core of confidence will grow.

Navigating the rapids

Hearts: All tools
Minds: All tools

Our children will often be among friends who do not know God. It is essential that we help them explore scenarios about what could happen out in the world, so that they will have a mental framework from which they can make decisions.

Talk to your children about control and manipulation and how some people like to be in charge of others. Explain that it happens a lot. Some people say, 'Do this or I won't be your friend,' or, 'If you were my friend, you would do this with me,' or even, 'You are stupid if you think that.' Some people think they can coerce others into doing things, but tell your children that you know that they are in charge of their own choices. Let them know that you will hold them accountable for their choices with their friends, both good and bad.

When you watch television programmes with them, pause and notice when a friend is behaving in a manipulative way, and give alternatives for the way healthy friendships should work or what the character in the programme could have done about it. Spot it when it happens at home and ask, for example, 'Wait a minute, are you trying to manipulate your dad? Are you trying to control him?' The more we identify different types of manipulation and control, the more able our children will be to spot them and choose not to respond to them.

As your children get older, the kinds of manipulation may vary, but they still reflect the same process. I remember that, when I was eight, my mum told me about note passing in class and how students would try to get others to deliver notes for them so that they wouldn't risk getting in trouble themselves. She told me that I could just say 'no' and that my job at school wasn't to be someone else's postman. If they wanted to do something wrong and risky, they needed to take the risk themselves.

Whereas before I'd felt conflicted when asked to pass notes, the next time it happened I confidently said 'no'. Eight years later, my mum told me that sometimes certain guys might try to manipulate girls by saying, 'If you won't have sex with me, then we can't continue our relationship.' It was awkward coming from my mum, but important to hear. Sure enough, the first time a guy tried that with me, I actually laughed in his face. I couldn't believe he'd said it.

Whatever our children's ages or stages, by preparing them for the idea that people may try to manipulate them, we help them gain wisdom and confidence in choosing to walk in their own path and not in others'.

Empower your children to ask themselves, 'What are God's purposes here and how can I follow him?' As you go about your days together, pray quickly, asking God to give you opportunities to bring his love into the places where you'll be going. Respond with compassion to the needs you see with friends and strangers. Live generously and kindly. As we model this sort of behaviour with our children, we equip them to enter different scenarios in the world, whether they are with their friends or not. They will see that God is doing things all around and is inviting us to make a difference with him. Through their experiences with you, they will be making opportunities for God's love to be powerful and will become aware of how they can sense God's presence and purposes in the everyday world.

Equip your children to know when to stay and when to leave. Sometimes people will be living without love at the centre of their lives. People's words hurt each other or their bodies hurt each other. People make unwise choices because they want others to like them, or they try to manipulate others to do what they want. Sometimes love means stepping in and not letting people hurt each other. Sometimes it means we protect people who have no voice or are being treated unfairly, and sometimes it means that we need to leave a situation. We need to be wise and leave when other people's choices could hurt or damage us, because that isn't right.

Create some tools for your children, so they know how to leave well. This might involve helping them work out how to walk away and play with someone else. As they get older, it might involve working with them on exit strategies for parties or equipping them to choose wisely when to leave an activity, knowing that you are willing to come and fetch them. When our children feel equipped to walk away from a situation, it turns a scary moment of feeling cornered into a moment of freedom and choice.

We need to teach our children how to stick to God's values without forcing their values on others. Children often feel persecuted for their faith, not because they actually are, but because they haven't figured out how to live with their values among people who don't share the same ones. So they make mistakes, which cause other people to get angry. Children can end up defending their own values by attacking and judging their friends and arguing about what everyone 'should do'. Helping them to know how to explain their choices to others, and how to put love at the centre of their interaction with other people, means that they will hold firm to God's values without hurting others.

Have conversations with your child about how God wants every person to know that he loves them, and wants everyone to connect with him. We are all not finished yet, and we are on a journey of life with God as he loves us and transforms us. Other people don't have that wonderful relationship with God yet. It's not our job to judge other people and say, 'Hey, you aren't perfect yet!' Our job is just to be on our journey of love with God and to help people experience his love and see him well. It's okay if people don't understand our choices, just as it's okay if we don't understand theirs. What's most important is that love is at the centre of all our relationships, so that people can know God more and more.

Facing the opposition

Hearts: All tools
Minds: All tools

There will always be children and adults who are cruel in this world. We will never be able to protect our children from all the words and actions of every person at their school or in clubs, so equipping them to deal with criticism, rumours and bullying is an essential part of helping them be effective and peaceful in the world. Remember, parenting for confidence is not about creating perfect children who are able to resist all the temptations and effects of the world upon their lives. We aren't world-proofing our children. We are building a core within them that empowers them to meet the world head on, grapple with any fears and confidently, gracefully, wisely and powerfully engage with it.

It is always helpful to raise opposition as a possibility, not to scare them but to ensure that it isn't a surprise when it happens. When people get hurt, they get angry, and when they get angry they often try to hurt others. Sometimes we are in the path of that anger. It hurts. One day we'll live in a world with no hurt, but today is not that day.

When it happens to your child, ask questions to understand better how he or she is responding. In my experience, a child's hurt can be in response either to the words used or to the encounter in which someone deliberately sought to hurt him with words or actions. Ask questions to uncover your child's hurt and understand the root better. If we focus on the words, when his pain is really about the insecurity of having an angry person in his life, we won't be ministering the right truth, and vice versa. Words are strange things: the most ridiculous ones can hurt deeply. Remember to respond with empathy, as these are the moments in which your child needs to be understood and heard, even if he was called 'boogie face' and you think it's the silliest name in the world.

Coach your children in how to deal with the words that are designed to hurt them. Since my dad is a police officer, he naturally has to deal with a lot of verbal abuse from the people he serves. When I was very young, he taught me simply to ask the question 'Is that true?' Often, children are so busy being offended by someone who tries to hurt them with words that the words themselves stick in and begin to infect the way they think about themselves. Just like in the 'spot the lie' game that I described before, when a word or phrase is in our children's brains, we can train them to ask questions. 'Is that true? Am I really a bogey face? Of course not! That is ridiculous!' We can train them to picture the word being crumpled up and thrown into a bin in their head, never to be seen again. Nothing that isn't good and right and pure and true gets to stay in our brains.

There are circumstances when insults have a grain of truth in them, but they are equally easy to dismiss. When I was a child, a few people tried calling me 'four eyes' because I wore glasses. I remember telling them that I only had two eyes, obviously. My glasses were there to help me see and play sports better and get through school without headaches. But I'm not perfect and neither is my body. Get into the habit of asking questions for yourself and empowering your children to hold up insults and ask, 'Is that true? Is that true, based on what I see or on what you see as a parent?' Help your children to find the core of confidence that removes labels and simply empowers them to be loved by an awesome and wonderful God.

Investigate with your children how to handle conflict when it happens. Often, children are hurt and run directly to an adult for help or justice when they need assistance in achieving proper resolution. I encourage children to look at Matthew 18:15–17:

> 'If your brother or sister sins, go and point out their fault, just between the two of you. If they listen to you, you have won them over. But if they will not listen, take one or two others along, so that "every matter may be established by the testimony of two or three witnesses." If they still refuse to listen, tell it to the

church; and if they refuse to listen even to the church, treat them as you would a pagan or a tax collector.'

Children often run to adults because they feel ill-equipped to deal with conflict directly. Assist your children in learning how to say, 'No, that hurts me' when it happens, or 'I don't like you saying that to me. It's not nice. No, thank you.' The more they feel released in the moment to confront what they don't like in relationships, the better able they will be to deal with situations as they arise, instead of bottling them up. If the aggressive person doesn't adjust his behaviour, then by all means the child can bring someone else in – an adult, if they wish. If the offender still doesn't change, scripture says that we are to deal with them as if they were 'a Gentile or tax collector', which generally means someone who is set apart from you, no longer a close friend but an outsider. Essentially, if a friend is not safe to be around and is not willing to change his behaviour, we need to adjust the level of trust we have with that person and move a bit further away.

Hurt will almost always lead to an issue of forgiveness. For children, forgiveness can be confusing, as they will often equate forgiveness with a lack of justice or a need to put themselves back into an unsafe place. As we discuss forgiveness with them, we will need to explain it well. Jesus doesn't give us an option on forgiveness: we have been forgiven and so we are to forgive others. Often, this topic is best approached as part of a heart conversation, after you have really understood what your children are feeling and you have affirmed their emotions.

I often tell children that hanging on to our anger and hurt makes us want to punish the other person ourselves, to see them punished so that we feel better. But that's God's job, not ours. He is in charge of justice; my job is to love. Forgiving means deciding that I'm going to let God be in charge of the other person. I choose not to spend time thinking about that other person with an angry heart. Instead I tell God how I feel and ask him to heal my heart, and I put the other person in God's hands to deal with as he wants. We can talk with our children about beginning these conversations with God, if they want to, or we can lay the foundation by describing forgiveness so that they can do it on their own later.

Friendships are one of our greatest gifts from God, and, as we see our children grow in healthy relationships and deal with difficult complications, we can rejoice that they know how to face challenges with the peace that comes from a core of confidence in God.

Conclusion

Parenting is a long and arduous journey. It is also one of the greatest privileges of our lives. Please take this book as a set of tools in your parenting box. Do not feel that you now need to use all of them in every moment. Trust that God will direct you to use different tools at different times.

Remember that you are not alone on this great journey. As you partner with God to parent your children, I believe that you will joyfully see the fruit of God in their lives. I pray that you will daily feel confident that the God who made you, who called you to parent these children, will fill you with his wisdom, his strength and his voice.

If you want any free resources or encouragements, please go to **parentingforfaith. org.uk** and sign up for regular communications, tips, videos and ideas to support you in parenting your children for faith, purpose and confidence.

May the God who makes all things possible bless you with terrific sleep, hope and dreams for your children's tomorrows, and with a peaceful heart, that you may walk through this season of your life with deep joy and a greater sense of his closeness.

FAQs

Are 'thank you', 'sorry' and 'please' still good things to pray?
In any relationship, these things are important to say! The key is that they need to be embedded in a relationship, instead of working as the basis for one. As your children grow closer to God, these words will begin to appear naturally in their prayers. I would suggest that you take the lead in modelling a heart-connected way of expressing your thanks, your feelings about sins and your requests through chatting informally with God. It may be helpful to use only one of these in the midst of a wider chat about life so that your children can see it as a part of communication with God, but not the only part.

My child is a very kinaesthetic learner. What about creative prayer?
I have found that people often use creative prayer as a desperate way of making prayer and God 'fun'. The problem is that it can encourage children to make a connection to the activity and not to God. I would suggest working on heart-to-heart connection with God through chatting and catching first. I'm sure you can find creative, active ways of showing children how to chat and catch, but it is important that they know how to access God personally. Your child can connect with you through listening to you and chatting with you, and he or she will be able to do the same with God. Too often, we try to insert an activity to help our children, but the activity ends up getting in the way of their relationship with God.

This doesn't mean that chatting and catching need to be done while sitting down in a quiet place. I know children who go on bike rides to chat with God and hear his voice. Other children perform 'chat dances' for God to show him how they feel, and some listen to music to hear his voice. Some prefer to sculpt the pictures God gives them instead of writing them down. These ideas have come out of the children's desire to spend time with God, and they have decided on their initiative to use these methods.

Once the relationship is established, there are many ways to enhance it by adding creativity to the two-way communication. I would suggest, though, that the connection is established first so that creativity is an individual, natural development instead of the way of praying.

I have a daughter who is very anti-God, encouraged by my unbelieving partner. What do I do?

Many families are in your situation, and it is never easy. My main suggestion is to model the reality of your relationship with God. Your child needs to see that God is real and is powerful in your life, and that she can have the same relationship with him that you have. You can pray for her and invite her to tell you things that she would especially like you to bring to God. She may brush you aside, but at least she will know that you are consistently bringing her to the real God, whom you know personally. It may be hard to see an immediate way forward, but these are long-term goals.

Perhaps a further step would be to look at her experience with God and see if she has formed some wrong views of God that need to be realigned. Many children who are anti-God are rooted in a particular (incorrect) belief about who he is and are rejecting that belief. Most children I know don't want to be controlled or forced to do things, but, if you are modelling and asking questions about her views, there is very little for her to object to. Also, remember that God is longing to connect with her. He is speaking to her and is faithful to wait for her response, so you have a partner in your desires.

What about our family times when we study the Bible and pray together? Are all corporate experiences bad?

Family times are brilliant! This is an expression of what God wanted for all believers – to live and encourage each other in community and praise him together. Family times can be especially powerful when you chat to God together about life and catch from him what he wants to say to your family as a whole. Discussion and learning in the home are part of the way God designed us to learn to love him. It is all about balance: both corporate and individual times create a healthy, growing relationship with God.

What do I do when my child becomes a teenager?

Your approach may begin to need some adjustment, as will all your parenting, as you allow your child to be more independent and to make mistakes. You will then become more of a mentor, ready to help, equip and challenge when and where it is appropriate.

Remember that teenagers are more developed emotionally than younger children, so you can begin to expand the complexity of what you are trying to develop in them. They will be able to see the Bible and their relationship with God differently, and they will have a more mature view of both. Take some time to go back over the Bible stories that they knew in their childhood, and show them new insights about them. The stories of Noah and the flood (Genesis 6—7) and Peter's denial of Jesus (Matthew 26:69–75; Mark 14:66–72; Luke 22:54–62; John 18:15–18, 25–27) are really helpful studies in peer pressure. It is important that we train our children to draw new and relevant truths out of well-known stories. Teenagers are also ready to understand more about how their life choices reflect their relationship with God. They are ready to begin learning from the Bible about wisdom and character, holiness and struggle, persecution and faithfulness in their walk with him.

I have grown-up children, and I feel bad that I didn't do this with them when they were children. Is it too late?
I firmly believe that it is never too late. Your children know you and watch you, so you still have plenty of opportunities to model the reality of your relationship with God in front of them.

I'm not very confident in catching from God myself. Will I be able to help my child?
Yes, you will. We are all on individual journeys with God, and perhaps God wants you to work with him on this aspect of your relationship with him now. There is a great book called *Can You Hear Me?* by Brad Jersak,[13] which is very helpful for adults who want to grow in their ability to hear God. I would suggest that you read it; then, as you grow, you can help your children grow.

My son isn't a very good reader, and all this 'discernment' and 'truth-reinforcing' sounds as if it needs a lot of Bible reading. How can I help my son access the Bible when he hates reading?
Many children struggle with reading, and often it seems impossible that they would ever enjoy reading the Bible. I think we need to expand our ideas of how to empower our children to access the Bible. Many of us feel that the main access route is to read our Bibles consistently every day. For children who struggle to read, this may not be an option. There are plenty of Bibles on CD, and you can partner your child in developing a way to remember the things he has heard. One family I know has a box of index cards on the table, so if anyone reads or hears anything from the Bible that they like, they can write it down and save it for the family. To write down a verse in this way, a child may have to listen to it on the CD a couple of times, which gets it even more strongly into their heads. The cards can then be used whenever the family wants to refer to something.

The goal is for your children to learn how to access the Bible when they want the answer to a question, encouragement or confirmation of God's promises. This doesn't require vast amounts of reading; it requires that you equip them to find the information they need quickly. Concordances are exceedingly helpful. There is a variety of types, including alphabetical (where you look up the word you want), topical, and everything in between. Take your children to a bookshop and find what is right for them.

When is it right for my child to become a Christian? What am I supposed to do to help it happen? How do I explain it?
There is no right answer to this question, as children will be ready when they are ready. Our job is to surround them with the truth and teach them how to access God and his new life for them when they are ready. In the normal course of your parenting, you will be teaching them about sin and what Jesus did for us on the cross. You can tell your testimony, and help them understand what it means for their lives and their relationship with God that Jesus has provided a way for us to get clean.

You can tell your children that if they want help in asking God to give them a new clean life, you would love to do so at any time. After that, you can be available when your children decide that it is important to them. Instead of leading them in a prayer, you can facilitate their communication with God, helping them to express their feelings about their sin and current life and what they want from God. You may be surprised at what emerges. Remember, becoming a Christian isn't about praying a prayer. It's about responding to what Jesus did and to the call of God on our hearts, and wanting to change the way we live in relationship with him. We are all constantly in the process of responding to the gospel and committing and recommitting ourselves to the faith journey, and this is an exciting first step.

What about children who struggle to connect with God? What happens if we pray and they don't catch anything?
These experiences do happen, and we can often feel powerless in the face of them. Sometimes, children feel as if there is a blockage between them and God, and, no matter what they do, it won't go away. They can feel as if there is an abrupt and disappointing ending to prayer. However, there are some tools we can use to help them find a way forward and connect with God, so, if ever our children get into these difficulties, we can be proactive in helping them get out. We need to remember that there are no dead ends for God.

First of all, it helps to enable our children to describe how the blockage feels. On page 36, we talked about having our children draw a picture of what they feel like is between them and God. That can be a helpful first step. We can then ask God to take down the wall, or pop the bubble, or remove whatever the image is.

Another thing we can do is to encourage our children to tell God how they feel about the barrier. Rather than let it push them away from God, encourage them to share their feelings about it with God.

Lastly, after reminding them about all the different ways they can catch, if they are still finding it hard, then help them find a different way of connecting with God. Sometimes children can become so fixated on connecting with God one way, that they need a bit of a release to find a different way that suits them better. Help them try drawing with God, or going on nature walks, or listening to worship music, or even serving and helping people. Connecting with God is an individual journey, not something to succeed or fail at. Some children may need encouragement on their individual journey to explore a bit wider to identify how they and God connect best.

I'm a bit concerned that all of this 'love' stuff is going to make my child unwise about strangers. I don't want her just approaching random people on the street, or trusting casual acquaintances she meets at church. How do I keep my child safe while still teaching her how to love others?
Keeping our children safe is of utmost importance, and we need to be clear about this with our children as we disciple them. This is why 'establishing boundaries' is an important part of the six-stage circle. Here are a few thoughts about how to describe this to children:

- We always need to love wisely. Sometimes hurt people don't know how to receive love well or how to give it back safely. That's why it's important to chat with your parents about how to love people safely and wisely.
- If you see an adult that you don't know who might need help, then go and chat to your parents or a safe adult whom you know well if your parents aren't around. Then you can decide together how to help.
- God is constantly talking to us, and if you ever feel uncomfortable around someone or in a situation, then that could be God encouraging you to go and find someone you know to be safe. It is not rude or unloving to take care of yourself and leave when you feel uncomfortable.
- Because we are powerful people, we are in charge of how we show our love. No one gets to demand love from us, or try to make us feel bad or as if we 'should' do something for them.

You will know your children's sensitivities and how to keep them safe. Establishing boundaries is an important skill in living a life of love. As children grow, you can lay down foundations of how to help people who are hurting, as well as how to have healthy friendships, relationships and marriages.

What about the gifts of the Spirit – the supernatural ones like tongues and healing? Shouldn't we equip our children to learn how to use these?

Those of us within the charismatic church often so desire that our children have all that the adults have, in terms of the things of the Spirit, that we can skew the emphasis too much towards the performance of the gifts of the Spirit, instead of focusing on the purpose of the gifts: for building up and encouraging others. We can become very focused on seeing these gifts in our children instead of cultivating their characters to be desperate to see God's love poured out on people. We should pray for healing when we are moved to out of compassion and from a desire to see people reconnect with God and experience his love, not because we want to see a miracle. We should speak words of knowledge to bring freedom and release to someone, not to impress others by how godly we are or to see how accurate we can be. Love is the purpose of these gifts. As the apostle Paul wrote in his letter to the Christians of Corinth:

> If I speak in the tongues of men or of angels, but do not have love, I am only a resounding gong or a clanging cymbal. If I have the gift of prophecy and can fathom all mysteries and all knowledge, and if I have a faith that can move mountains, but do not have love, I am nothing. If I give all I possess to the poor and give over my body to hardship that I may boast, but do not have love, I gain nothing.
>
> 1 CORINTHIANS 13:1–3

The process of discipling children in using these gifts is the same as for training them how to use the gifts of mercy, faith or administration. They are all gifts of the Spirit – supernatural gifts. We train them to love. We equip them to understand their purpose. We cultivate their character so that when they use the power of God they are humble and not proud. We practically equip them with skills to use the gifts well. This goes for all gifts, from discerning between spirits to giving. When we teach adults about these things, we tend to take it around the six-stage circle. I would encourage you to do the same with children.

So do I equip children to use all the gifts of the Spirit? Yes, I do. If you would like to know more about how to talk to your children about these gifts, how to equip them practically to use them, and what that looks like in the life of a child, head to **parentingforfaith.org.uk**.

Notes

1   Rachel Turner, *Comfort in the Darkness: Helping children draw close to God through biblical stories of night-time and sleep* (BRF, 2016).
2   Often the toilet is a good place for children to have some time out. You can't send a seven-year-old on a walk, and not everybody has their own room at home. It also means that they can keep up the habit outside the home – at school, church or clubs – learning to exercise self-control through sharing with God and seeking his help and understanding.
3   Another aspect to look at is how we, as parents, respond to our child's failures and sins. Often, our responses can contribute to the way our children see God. If this interests you, Danny Silk's excellent book *Loving Our Kids on Purpose: Making a heart-to-heart connection* (Destiny Image, 2009) helps us to model in our parenting the freedom and consequences that God allows in his parenting of us.
4   *The Jesus Storybook Bible: Every story whispers his name* (Zondervan, 2012).
5   Max Lucado, *You Are Special* (Crossway, 1997).
6   lifewayresearch.com/2007/08/07/reasons-18-to-22-year-olds-drop-out-of-church
7   See, for example, Hebrews 10:19–24; 1 Corinthians 12:12—13:13; Acts 2:42–47; Mark 16:15–20.
8   See Kenneth Bailey, *Jesus through Middle Eastern Eyes: Cultural studies in the gospels* (SPCK, 2008).
9   See BBC Lab UK's 'Big Personality Test', with five components (openness, conscientiousness, extraversion, agreeableness and neuroticism).
10 See merriam-webster.com/dictionary/envy.
11 'Girls become self conscious and stop playing sport as young as seven, report finds', *The Huffington Post*, 26 March 2015, huffingtonpost.co.uk/2015/03/26/girls-stop-sport-age-seven-self-conscious_n_6945570.html.
12 For example, search online for Nick Vujicic and Joni Eareckson Tada.
13 Brad Jersak, *Can You Hear Me? Tuning in to the God who speaks* (Fresh Wind Press, 2006).

parenting for faith

Would you like to help your children and teens discover faith on their own terms?

To come alongside them easily and naturally, spotting opportunities to talk about God right where you are: on the school run... in the queue at the supermarket... playing football...?

To encourage them to grow in a two-way relationship with God that lasts a lifetime?

Join our growing network of parents, family members, church workers and others on this journey.

- Access the free Parenting for Faith video course at **parentingforfaith.org/ parenting-faith-course**
- Explore the wealth of tips, suggestions and shared experiences on **parentingforfaith.org** – covering topics from prayer to how to discuss difficult issues such as bullying or Hallowe'en
- Find Parenting for Faith meetings and training sessions near you at **parentingforfaith.org/events-and-training**
- Keep up with useful videos and articles on Facebook (**@parentingforfaithBRF**) and Twitter (**@godconnected**)

The Parenting for Faith course
'Amazing!'   *'Brilliant... life-changing!'*

Stream or download our free video-based course at home or on the move... with your partner or on your own. Or watch the eight videos with your church group as these parents did:

'I've learned to show my children the relationship I have with God. As I was driving the children to school the other day my youngest started talking to God.'

'I've had more relaxed conversations with our teenager and their responses are more relaxed and thoughtful.'

'My wife and I came into the course open and willing to learn new methods to help our children find Jesus on their own terms. This course really delivered on that level.'